SURFACE CITY

SYDNEY AT THE MILLENNIUM

Peter Murphy & Sophie Watson

PLUTO PRESS AUSTRALIA

First published in 1997 by Pluto Press Australia Limited
Locked Bag 199, Annandale, NSW 2038

Cover design: Peta Nugent
Text typeset by Chapter 8 Pty Ltd.
Printed and bound by Southwood Press, 80 Chapel Street, Marrickville, NSW 2204

Australian National Library Cataloguing-in-Publication data
Murphy, Peter, 1949–
Surface city: Sydney at the millennium.

Bibliography.
Includes index.
ISBN 1 86403 033 X.

1. Sydney (N.S.W.). 2. Sydney (N.S.W.) – Social conditions.
3. Sydney (N.S.W.). – Economic conditions. I. Watson,
Sophie. II. Title.

994.41

SEVEN DAY LOAN

This book is to be returned on
or before the date stamped below

−8 MAR 2001 **RETURNED**	15 MAY 2003
RETURNED	−3 MAR 2004
24 APR 2001	10 MAR 2004 17 MAR 2004
25 NOV 2002	22 MAR 2004
14 FEB 2003	
29 APR 2003	

SURFACE CITY

CONTENTS

LIST OF ILLUSTRATIONS & MAPS

Illustrations

Sydney Opera House, August 1995.

Piccolo Bar, Kings Cross, August 1995.

'The Humperdinks go visiting', (Source: *Wireless Weekly*, 4 May 1934, p. 16).

1940s Bondi beach belles, (Source: Frank Hurley, 1948, *Sydney: A Camera Study*, Angus & Robertson, Sydney).

A masculine moment, Bondi, August 1995.

The John Newman murder, (Source: *Sydney Morning Herald*, 1994).

Multicultural Sydney, (Source: *Sydney Morning Herald*, 1993).

Freedom Gate, Cabramatta, August 1995.

Many different cultures, one community; Cabramatta graffiti, August 1995.

Mosque, Auburn, western Sydney, August 1995.

Italian house, Fairfield, western Sydney, August 1995.

Selling Sydney to business, (Source: New South Wales Department of State and Regional Development, 1994).

Selling Sydney to tourists, (Source: Australian Tourist Commission, 1991)

Darling Harbour at work, (Source: Frank Hurley, 1948, *Sydney: A Camera Study*, Angus & Robertson, Sydney).

Darling Harbour at play, August 1995.

Early spring, Bondi Beach, August 1995.

Sydney central business district and Circular Quay in the 1940s (Source: Frank Hurley, 1948, *Sydney: A Camera Study*, Angus & Robertson, Sydney).

Sydney central business district and Circular Quay in the 1990s, August 1995.

Selling Sydney in South-East Asia, (Source: *Sing Tao Newspaper*, 12 April, 1996).

Mardi Gras, Michelle Mika, 1995.

Flamboyance, outrage, spectacle, February 1984.

Pre-gentrification, Blair Street, Bondi Beach, August 1995.

Post-gentrification, Brighton Boulevard, Bondi Beach, August 1995.

Discourses of fragmentation (Source: *Sydney Morning Herald*, 1993–95).

Kings Cross 'home', August 1995.

Point Piper waterfront, August 1995.

Old and new (foreground) styles of inner city public housing, Waterloo, August 1995.

Homes and hazards, Port Botany, August 1995.

Olympic Games site, Homebush Bay, August 1995.

Maps

Sydney at a glance, 1996.

Sydney Statistical Local Areas, 1991.

Percentage of the population born overseas and resident for less than 5 years, 1991.

Percentage of resident workforce unemployed, 1991.

Percentage of resident workforce working in manufacturing, 1991.

Percentage of resident workforce working in finance, property and business services, 1991.

Median household incomes, $ per annum 1991.

Single parent families as a percentage of all families, 1991.

Public housing as a percentage of all housing, 1991.

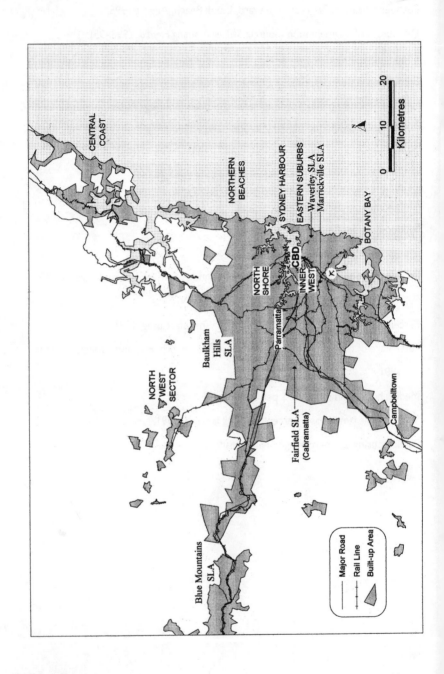

Sydney at a glance, 1996.

ACKNOWLEDGMENTS

An Australian Research Council Large Grant enabled the research on which the book is based. We gratefully acknowledge its support. The book itself would not have been possible without the enthusiasm, organising skills and commitment of Bronwyn Hanna who worked with us for two years. Iain Bruce's insightful and scholarly research was the foundation for chapter 4 and we are most grateful to have had access to his skills for four months. Michael Campbell's photographs enliven the text and he was a delight to be with on the field trips when they were taken. Others we would like to thank are Barbara Mobbs, Robin Connell, Rob Freestone, Jen Craig, Emily Purser, Neil Pfister, Kate Tribe, Penny O'Donnell and Rosemary Pringle for her critical comments and support.

NOTE ON SOURCES

Apart from citations in the endnotes to chapters, we have drawn on the following three sets of information which were assembled in 1993–94:

1. data from the Population and Housing censuses conducted by the Australian Bureau of Statistics in 1971, 1976, 1986 and 1991;
2. focus groups held with five to six groups in each of the Waverley, Marrickville, Fairfield, Baulkham Hills and Blue Mountains Local Government Areas of Sydney. The results of these focus groups were reported in B. Hanna, P. Murphy & S. Watson 1995, *Snapshots of Sydney: Marrickville, Waverley, Fairfield, Baulkham Hills, Blue Mountains Locality Studies,* Department of Urban and Regional Planning, University of Sydney.
3. Fairfax press media articles assembled for us by Infoline for the late 1960s – early 1970s, late 1970s – early 1980s and late 1980s – early 1990s. Unless otherwise indicated, all quotations and statistics used in the text are from these sources.

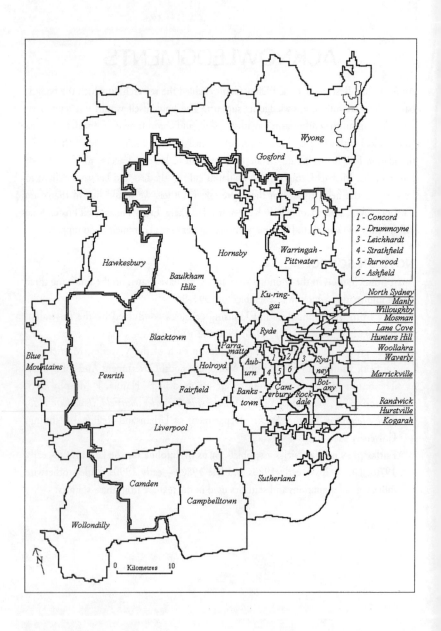

Sydney Statistical Local Areas, 1991.

Legend:

1 - Concord
2 - Drummoyne
3 - Leichhardt
4 - Strathfield
5 - Burwood
6 - Ashfield

1 SYDNEY — CITY OF SURFACES

Sydney — city of surfaces. Superficial Sydney, glitzy Sydney, shiny Sydney. The Opera House sails glisten in the sun, elegant yachts skim the bright harbour waters, cafes spill people onto the scorched city streets while chatter clatters off the hard brittle walls of Sydney restaurants, bouncing from polished parquetry floors to chrome chairs and tiled ceilings. Surfers ride the waves at Bondi while showy young boys on the boardwalk slide from side to side on precipitous metal slopes in silent ritual. At Double Bay new fashions from Paris and Rome are paraded through the streets before jealous eyes and seamless voices. 'That mansion there is worth $5 million and that one $10 million', booms the tour operator from the Captain Cook Cruise as it skirts past the inlets of Point Piper. Sydney — city of surfaces.

What constructs these shifting surfaces of Sydney, its excitement and allure? How has Sydney moved from its recent provincialism to a global city which represents one of American Express's top destinations and the site of the 2000 Olympics in less than half a century? As late as the early 1970s curious young Australians with enough money in their pockets fled the country to settle in London and Paris, New York and Rome and returned reluctantly to recreate ambience in the Piccolo Bar of Kings Cross or the Bar Gelato at Bondi Beach. Writing of her childhood in Mosman, Glenda Adams tells how 'the wider world was almost palpable in that we could watch from the back windows the ocean liners arriving and departing'.[1] Now it is the Australian embassies that are overwhelmed by visa applications and which turn away prospective immigrants. Sydney represents the exotic, joy, fun, sex, pleasure, fantasy, difference and otherness. This is a place to escape to, a place in which to flourish.

One way Sydney is constructed is in relation to Melbourne, its denigrated 'other': Melbourne is dull, Melbourne is serious, Melbourne is full of wowsers, in Melbourne it rains all the time. The two construct each other. David Williamson captures this relationship in his play *Emerald City*. Kate and Colin move from Melbourne to Sydney. At first Colin is rapturous about the city. His enthusiasm for the place is countered by the cynicism of his agent, Elaine, and the frank dislike of his wife Kate, who contrasts Sydney glitter to a superior and more caring image of Melbourne. In the first scene Elaine explains to Colin that 'No one in Sydney ever wastes time debating the meaning of life — it's getting yourself a water frontage'. Kate exhorts a friend: 'You must come up and have a look. On a sunny day when the eighteen footers are out, the combination of striped spinnaker, sparkling blue water and sky is absolutely overwhelming. I don't know how I'm ever going to get any work done'.

The play concerns Colin's and Kate's struggle with wanting and not wanting material success and what this does to their perceptions of Sydney. When Colin declares his determination to make money as a producer rather than continuing to write scripts, Kate chides him: 'You came to Sydney an artist, and you're turning into a businessman'. But when Kate gets her promotion and the view that comes with it, her cynicism is transformed and, simultaneously, she is reconciled to Sydney.

Just as success and views of 18-foot racing skiffs on the harbour are linked, so too is disillusionment and notions of 'the corrupt'. This is another prevalent discourse of Sydney. Echoes of the city's convict past resound in images of ruthless entrepreneurs, fallen heroes and evil which in turn are linked to the city's physicality. Here the rich have got richer through crooked deals, through property development and land rackets.

Philip Noyce's 1983 film *Heatwave* also throbs with the violence of a hot Sydney summer of rabid urban development at any cost. The story concerns the alleged murder of a community housing activist called Juanita Nielsen who mysteriously disappears while trying to fight the demolition of the low-income earners' terraced houses in Victoria Street, Kings Cross.

There are many narratives of Sydney and many stories to tell. Sydney as the frivolous counterpoint to Melbourne is one, but there are countless others. Like other Australian cities, and perhaps most dramatically so, Sydney is constructed in relation to the bush. Here its 'other' is rough, wild, mysterious, untameable, vast and unknowable. In part the bush constructs a certain notion of Australian masculinity. Men are challenged to brave its terrors and tame its passions. The rugged explorer, shearer or swagman is depicted with his long unkempt beard, dirty clothes and tough gaze looking out over the landscape. This is the image that constructs the stereotypical view of Australian men overseas played out by Paul Hogan in the film *Crocodile Dundee*. Les Murray's poem *Sydney and the Bush* is another account of the relation between the city and the bush:

> When Sydney rules without the Bush
> she is a warder's shop
> with heavy dancing overhead
> the music will not stop
>
> and when the drummers want a laugh
> Australians are sent up.
> When Sydney and the Bush meet now
> there is no common ground.[2]

Depending on the lens or the frame of the viewer, a different Sydney emerges. The gaze which constructs the city produces different effects. A rich businessman on the North Shore lives in a different Sydney from the single parent in Liverpool, or the gay

Sydney Opera House, August 1995.

Piccolo Bar, Kings Cross, August 1995.

man in Darlinghurst or the homeless young person in Kings Cross. There is no one Sydney, just many surfaces reflecting different lives, different images and different lenses. It is this notion that underpins this book and the different voices in which it is written.

Cities are heterogeneous and fragmented spaces and *Surface City* sets out to show how this is the case. In constructing a patchwork quilt of Sydney made up from interviews, newspaper articles, statistical material and other sources, different facets of Sydney are explored. We take the reader on a ride through a complex landscape inhabited by people from different cultures, with different incomes and jobs, different genders and sexualities and from different localities. Just as there is more than one voice in the text, so also is there more than one way of thinking and analysing cities. The book ranges from cultural to geographic analysis. Its reader is imagined as the friend who has visited and said 'tell me then about Sydney' or the friend who grew up in Paddington and has never visited Cabramatta. It is therefore not an intervention into contemporary debates in geography or cultural studies as such, though much of the text is underpinned by these literatures. It can be read in bits, from back to front or from the middle, since there is no linearity to its narrative. It is a book intended to enlighten and to amuse and to introduce the reader to this much-loved city of the Southern oceans. One of the striking aspects of the city is how differentiated the various parts of the city are either imaginatively, topographically or materially. This is not simply a west–east divide, though that is the dominant line of fracture; it also operates at the miscro-spatial level of the very local. Thus Bondi is the beach of the immigrant families. Or in Peter Corris's book, *The Empty Beach*, we find these delineations: 'Bondi is flat country. The place is crowded by the impassioned desire of Australians to live by the sea as if they are reluctant to desert the fount of life, a mixture of smart and shabby' and 'Bronte is a notch or two further down the socio-economic scale than Bondi. The flats are smaller and less flash and there are weather board cottages that look as if they haven't changed since the 1920s', while 'Clovelly is a headland tucked in south of Bronte and east of Randwick. It's a bit like those two suburbs but down market of both of them'[3].

Surface City is also a book about change. As soon as you grasp one sense of a city it is already in the process of moving on. Sydney was once a city of predominantly British immigrants; now people come from all over the world. For most of its first two hundred years of white settlement Sydney looked to Europe and the United States, while now its orientation is shifting to East and South-East Asia. For many years there was a dominance of Liberal governments in power whereas for much of the 1970s to 1990s there were Labor governments at state and federal levels. In many ways Sydney has become a more attractive and diverse city to live in, particularly in comparison with many other large cities in the world, which perhaps accounts for the fewer numbers of people leaving for elsewhere. Yet even its much-vaunted attractions mask an underbelly of poverty, pollution and prejudice which this book also sets out to explore.

SYDNEY RETROSPECTIVELY: A BRIEF HISTORICAL NARRATIVE

Since early European settlement, representations of Sydney have sought to resist designations of the city as provincial or as the poor relation to the metropolitan 'others' of London, New York, Rome and Paris. As early as 1848 Joseph Fowles was asserting that few strangers arriving in Sydney for the first time would not experience unexpected delight:

> In place of a paltry town, which many of them are led to expect, they find shops and warehouses that would do credit to an European capital, offering for their convenience every article of comfort and luxury; while, in every direction, are to be seen unequivocal indications of progress and improvement. The handsome equipages that dash past, the elegantly clad females, and the stylish groups of gentlemen, point out the seat of amusement and gaiety.[4]

The sentiment is reflected in Beverley Clifford and Barbara Richards' text *Sydney More than a Harbour: A Photographic Glance at a Surging City*, written in 1969:

> The image of Sydney is one of giant change, of glossy adulthood superimposed on countless infant characteristics. A city tough, bright, sprawling ... new-brilliant, shabby-old, exotic, dreary, spiky, tenacious ... a city of big trade deals and big business and big growth; whose stock market reports continually hit London and Wall Street headlines.[5]

The book ends with a flamboyant declaration: 'today, shaking the dust from its feet, Sydney is moulding itself into the future role of a leading world city'.[6] In these earlier discourses Sydney is the assertive adolescent struggling for independent status from the dominant and complacent parent. There are similar echoes in the Republican debate of the 1990s.

If the early 1970s mark the beginning of the shift from provincial to world city status, how did Sydney look in its earlier years? In one sense Sydney has always been its harbour. The Surgeon General of Governor Arthur Phillip's First Fleet of eleven sailing ships with about 1000 people aboard, arriving in 1788 after nine months at sea, had this to say: 'Port Jackson, I believe to be, without exception, the finest and most extensive harbour in the universe, and at the same time the most secure, being safe from all the winds that blow'.[7] Sydney's topography has to a large extent determined its development and influenced its patterns of wealth and access to resources. Initially, European settlement was at Sydney Cove, now Circular Quay. Rough huts of cabbage-tree stems and wattle and daub were hastily constructed by the convicts, soldiers and sailors of the

First Fleet. But by 1820 order had been imposed and Sydney was described as 'a clean town of cottages and cottage gardens, with hedges of geraniums and orchards of fruit trees. A compact friendly town of 12,079 inhabitants' [8] largely based around the harbour and the Rocks. In the process, the estimated 1500 Aboriginal people living in the area were displaced and killed by violence and disease. Of the original inhabitants of the area few remained by the mid-1800s. For the early owners of the land it was a story of betrayal and decimation at the hands of the white invaders.

By the time Governor Macquarie left in 1820 there were 1084 buildings in Sydney, sixty-eight of which were of stone and the rest brick. Known as the road-building governor, Macquarie made his spatial mark on the city, erecting in 1818 the Obelisk in Macquarie Place as the starting point from which distance on the roads of the colony would be calculated. By 1848 the white population had grown to 49 212, spreading into the suburbs of Woolloomooloo, Paddington, Surry Hills, Redfern, Camperdown, Newtown, Balmain, and across the harbour into St Leonards and Hunters Hill. Over 32 kilometres to the west, and well beyond the city's boundaries, lay the early agricultural settlement of Rose Hill — renamed by its Aboriginal name, Parramatta, in the early part of the twentieth century.

With the creation of an imperial government, Sydney's growth became tied to national and international markets in imports, exports, investment and immigration. The economy was borne on the back of sheep, raw commodities and minerals. Unlike in its European equivalents, industrialisation in Sydney followed its growth, rather than being the motor for urbanisation. Immigrants from England and Ireland were attracted by the prospect of earning a fortune in the gold rushes and were keen to leave the poor conditions from which they came. Over the following century immigration remained an important source of population growth in Sydney, with one-fifth of the population born overseas at the 1921 Census, three-quarters of whom came from Britain and Ireland.[9] With urban infrastructure financed by the colonial government, Sydney's primacy in New South Wales was never really challenged. Not so with respect to 'marvellous' Melbourne, whose prominence industrially, economically and politically in the colony was a constant source of irritation and competition from the early days of white settlement.

Skimming through time to Sydney after the Second World War there emerges a city of many surfaces. A statistical narrative produces a population of under 2 million people in 1946 and an estimated housing shortage of 90 000 homes.[10] In 1947 only 13 per cent of Sydney residents were foreign-born — a figure which almost doubled in the next two decades — with British migrants as the largest group. Immigrants from other parts of the world, mainly southern Europe, were subjected to considerable racism and designated 'wogs' by the earlier immigrants. Nicko, a Greek–Australian growing up in the 1950s, tries to deny his origins by caricaturing others: 'Jimbo's shakin' up a tin of Pepsi. The local Iti's [Italians] are on the prowl in a black Fiat 850. Typical wog act. He's gonna give 'em a spray job next time around he reckons'.[11]

'*The Humperdinks go visiting*' (*Source:*Wireless Weekly, *4 May 1934, p. 16*).

In 1950 Sydney covered an area less than half of its size in the late 1990s and much of the built landscape of today's city was covered with bush and sandstone outcrops. Parramatta was a small town on the edge of Sydney rather than the approximate demographic centre of the city it has now become. In response to the housing shortage, governments and developers set to clearing the inner city slum areas, developing suburbs further and further afield, and building blocks of flats in the inner areas of the city and eastern suburbs. At the same time employment in manufacturing and services began to decentralise away from the rail and tram lines to capture the demand for goods and services and to access the work force.

The suburban dream was rampant. Women were exhorted to return to the home after their wartime employment and active service to create the domestic haven for their men and children. The dream was reflected in the proliferation of single dwellings on the quarter-acre block stretching in every direction. Home ownership rose to 60 per cent by 1954 and was to reach 71 per cent seven years later. Development was at such a pace that in many cases the provision of services and infrastructure was unable to be kept up. Roads were un-guttered and many areas were without basic services. By 1976 only 67 per cent of Sydney was sewered.[12] The dunny man clanking down the back lanes emptying the dunny can in the early morning remained a Sydney icon well into the 1970s.

Consuming memories? The postwar period was the era of the department store. Suburban dwellers and country people made monthly or annual trips to the city centre to feast their gaze on the latest fashions and commodities of Grace Brothers at Broadway, David Jones in the city, Mark Foys on the corner of Elizabeth and Liverpool streets and Anthony Horderns on the World Square site. Tea was taken in the cafeteria or on the roof garden. Shopping constituted a major outing, and for those from the country it was often combined with the annual visit to the Easter Show or a holiday in Bondi or Manly. These were the days before shopping centres had hit the suburbs with huge flashy malls and windswept car parks. Groceries and vegetables were delivered weekly, bread and ice came by in a van and the ring of the ice-cream seller's arrival echoed through the suburbs.

And what of other pleasures and fantasies? The cinemas were going strong in the local town centres like Manly and Bondi Junction, while suburban dwellers occasionally took a night out in the theatres and music halls of the central city. More common, though, were visits to the local leagues clubs, the take-away Chinese restaurants, the tennis clubs, cricket and backyard barbecues. At the end of the decade the government launched the competition for the new Opera House to be built on Bennelong Point. By the early 1960s a Danish architect, Joern Utzon, and his engineer, Ove Arup, were embroiled in their designs for the shell-shaped Opera House using new geometrical designs that were to thrill residents and visitors alike over ensuing decades.

Corporeal pleasures were key markers of Australian identity in the postwar period and organised sport on a Saturday afternoon was a standard pastime. Half a century after W. H. Gocher of Manly, incensed at the prohibition on public sunbathing and swimming, in 1902 defied the law and entered the surf during the noonday sun, the beach had emerged as the central site of pleasure in the city. From Palm Beach to Cronulla boys surfed while girls lay on the beach frying in the midday sun with little heed to sunburn or skin cancers. By 1948 there were more than one hundred clubs in the NSW Surf Life Saving Association, with a membership of approximately 6000, and shining muscular male bodies paraded the beaches on weekends competing with adjacent beaches in expert manoeuvres in the towering waves. Masculinity was constructed and affirmed with a vengeance on the beaches of the city.

And where were the thrills away from bland suburbia? Kings Cross had for many years been constituted as a bohemian space as well as a den of iniquity and forbidden

1940s Bondi beach belles, (Source: Frank Hurley, 1948, Sydney: A Camera Study, *Angus & Robertson, Sydney).*

A masculine moment, Bondi, August 1995.

pleasures. Originally called Queen's Cross in honour of Queen Victoria's Jubilee, it was renamed on her death. Many writers and artists lived in the locality, along with immigrants from Europe and other parts of the world. This was the place that Australians, nostalgic for their overseas trips, stopped by for coffee at Coluzzi's or the Piccolo Bar where photographs of celebrities adorned the walls. Kings Cross was cosmopolitan, glamorous, risqué, exciting and sexy. Here was the Greenwich Village and Bloomsbury of Sydney — an imaginary and real space of otherness for the suburban dwellers of further afield: 'Here', wrote Australian poet Kenneth Slessor, 'the lion lies down with the lamb, the serpent with the dove, the wolf with the chicken, layer over layer of human life in every manifestation of good and evil, riches and poverty … Fashionable hotels, home unit blocks and shops stand flank to flank with Bohemia'.[13]

By the late 1960s key shifts had begun to occur in the fabric of the city. The trams which had once carried passengers from the Quay to Bondi, Mosman and other localities were phased out in 1961; at the same time as the motorcar came to dominate the city. From 1946–47 to 1971 the number of private cars increased from 178 695 to over a million.[14] The old terraces of Paddington, Glebe and Balmain began to discover a new cachet as gentrification took hold and the waterside industries dependent on shipping declined, releasing salubrious sites with waterside views. The long economic boom from the 1950s to the 1970s had reached its peak and was shortly to tumble.

In 1966 the racist White Australia Policy was brought to an end, opening the city to immigrants from a wider cultural spectrum. The Aboriginal population in the city had also increased as people from country areas moved into La Perouse, Redfern and outer suburban localities in search of jobs and housing and a less antagonist environment than the country areas.

These are some of Sydney's surfaces in the years preceding its rise onto the global city stage. Sydney, like other cities, is a mosaic of stories, images and representations, of facts and figures, of maps and texts, of the real and the imaginary, and of words and experiences. There is no one representation that can make sense of the complex whole named Sydney.

Notes

1 Glenda Adams 1989, 'Beyond the turkey gobblers', in D. Modjeska, *Inner Cities*, Allen & Unwin, Melbourne.

2 P. Tranter & P. Mead 1991, *The Penguin Book of Modern Australian Poetry*, Penguin, Melbourne.

3 Peter Corris 1983, *The Empty Beach*, Allen & Unwin, Sydney, pp. 15, 30.

4 Joseph Fowles 1984, *Sydney in 1848*, National Trust of Australia, Sydney, p. 26.

5 B. Clifford & B. Richards 1969, *Sydney More Than a Harbour*, Murray, Sydney, p. 7.

6 ibid., p. 57.

7 ibid., quoted p. 8.

8   ibid.
9   Peter Spearrit 1978, *Sydney Since the Twenties*, Hale & Iremonger, Sydney, p. 1.
10 ibid., p. 2.
11 Angelo Loukakis 1981, *For the Patriarch*, University of Queensland Press, St. Lucia, p. 30.
12 Spearrit, op. cit., p. 40.
13 Quoted in Clifford & Richards, op. cit., p. 27.
14 Spearrit, op. cit., p. 168.

2 MULTICULTURAL MYTHS

He sits alone and contemplates … the dense tangle of leaf that reflects each wave of immigrants to the city: fig tree, lemon, grapevine, blue gum, banana palm, white frangipani and there, in a fraught clump by the fence, a climbing red rose entwined with a scarlet hibiscus, while at their base wild tomato plants run riot. The English, the Mediterranean, the tropical and the native bush entwined in a ceaseless tangle, and above them the sweet heady smell of frangipani floating on an acrid wave of gasoline.[1]

PREAMBLE

This account was written in the early part of 1995. It was written in the climate of the then Labor government led by Prime Minister Paul Keating who vociferously argued for reconciliation with the Aboriginal population. This meant not only attempting to establish a framework for Aboriginal claims for justice in the future, but also admitting the wrongs of the past. Here also was a prime minister who advocated a republic and greater ties with Asia and who espoused multiculturalism as the underpinning of Australian society at the end of the twentieth century.

Having myself emigrated from an apparently more troubled and divided part of the world, I was both delighted to encounter such idealism but also somewhat sceptical. Was there a less receptive world lying behind the political commitment to, and celebration of, reconciliation and multiculturalism? Were there sections of the Anglo–Australian population who were publicly silenced in this climate of anti-discrimination? Were there those who harboured private prejudices and fears behind the closed doors of city suburbs and rural Australia?

The optimist in me hoped not. I returned some 15 months later to find a Liberal government in power and a new prime minister. John Howard's rhetoric of free speech provided the frame for racist discourse to erupt and be heard. In dismay I found my fears confirmed. Rather than adjust the text of this chapter, since it is embedded in its time, a postscript has been appended to mark these deplorable shifts in the sociopolitical climate.

One final note: this is an account of multicultural, not Aboriginal, Sydney, since these are different. Aboriginal Sydney appears later in the text.

THE END OF INNOCENCE?

On Monday, 5 September 1994, Labor politician John Newman was shot dead outside his home in the Sydney western suburb of Fairfield. Australia's first political assassina-

The John Newman murder, (Source: Sydney Morning Herald, *1994).*

tion rocked the complacency and sense of security of Australian politicians and citizens. Australians had previously thought themselves protected from what was seen as growing violence in other parts of the world. The local Liberal MP, Dr Liz Kernohan, said at the time, 'If this meant Australia has become a member of the world community I don't want to be a part of the world. I want to be Australian where people can speak out for what they believe'.[2] Or as *Sydney Morning Herald* journalist Tony Stephens wrote of the funeral: 'Most of the mourners knew that the more humanity advances, the more it can be downgraded, and that they were witnessing the last rites of a degradation not seen in Australia before'.[3] Perhaps Bishop David Cremin most accurately reflected the mood of the occasion with his words: 'All of us here are utterly ashamed that this has happened in our country, our city, in this beautiful multicultural part of the world'.[4]

Notwithstanding the sadness or horror associated with the murder of any individual, and a public figure in particular, this murder had more specific meaning. The interesting questions are whether the murder at gunpoint marked significant shifts in Australian social and cultural life, whether it allowed new discourses to erupt which by their very articulation marked a shift in the multicultural success story of Australia, or whether it was simply one of those newsworthy events, which, though tragic, represented nothing very different from what had gone before. In other words, would multicultural Australia and multicultural Sydney, with all the complexities such a notion implies, continue down its inevitably winding and intricate path with nothing much having changed? There are no easy answers. What is interesting are the discourses which came into play in the media immediately following the event and how these relate to questions of multicultural Sydney more broadly. We will return to the Newman murder later in the narrative. First, let us look at the wider historical picture.

Multicultural Australia and Multicultural Sydney are relatively recent phenomena, particularly in their Asian and non-European manifestations. Australia's initial invasion and settlement by white people from 1788 onwards remained a largely British phenomenon until after the Second World War. There were obviously some exceptions — such as the arrival of Chinese to work in the goldfields. But as the Second World War began most Australians were of Anglo-Celtic origin. The main racial conflicts had been those between white settlers and Aboriginal Australians, with marked shifts in discourses throughout this period. Initially it was assumed that those not killed by guns would die out from disease and displacement. Once it was realised that Aboriginal people, though decimated in numbers and displaced from their lands, were here to stay, there was a shift in the mid-twentieth century to discourses of assimilation. These have been forcefully challenged over three decades by arguments for self-determination, land rights and, more recently self-government.

At the end of the Second World War, as part of the strategy to strengthen Australia's economic, industrial and skill base, immigration policies changed to admit people from Northern and then Southern European countries. Dutch, German and other professional and managerial skilled immigrants were welcomed into Australia. At the same time, immigrants from poorer parts of Europe, especially Greece and Southern Italy, were brought in to work in the coal and steel industries in towns like Wollongong, Newcastle and on the massive Snowy Mountains hydro-electric scheme. Overall though, immigrants with fair complexions were favoured as they were easier to assimilate. On the long passage to Australia, immigrants were taught some English-language skills to equip them to assimilate more quickly on arrival.

It was not until the mid-1960s that the White Australia Policy was abolished. Changes in immigration policy brought Lebanese and Turkish immigrants, followed in the 1970s and 1980s by large numbers of political refugees from Asia and Latin America in particular, and immigrants entering under the family reunion program. There were thus a growing number of immigrants from countries of greater cultural and religious difference than in the already settled population, and who were more visibly 'different'. This pattern of immigration has continued into the 1990s, with people from Asia now forming a large proportion of the immigrants to Australia. In the three months to June 1991, 19 960 out of a total of 49 000 permanent and long-term settlers, gave their country of birth in Asia (this includes South-east, North-east and Southern Asia). The change in the immigrant intake has seen an increase in the preference for settlement in Sydney. By 1991 nearly half of Sydney's population was of first- or second-generation non-English-speaking background, and one in four of the total Australian population in 1991 was born overseas.

Multicultural Sydney, (Source: Sydney Morning Herald, *1993).*

This same period has seen a shift from the discourses and policies of assimilation to those of multiculturalism. Multiculturalism was designed under the Whitlam Labor government in the 1970s to mark a complete withdrawal from the racist White Australia Policy and the official immigration policy of assimilation. As Sneja Gunew put it: 'Belatedly it was felt national identity would benefit from acknowledging the realities of cultural diversity — but only within strict limits … Australia was colourfully reconstructed as a liberal and pluralist nation and became the haven for victims from other repressive regimes'.[5] Gunew herself suggests that the notion of multiculturalism was useful, first because it incorporated notions of European cosmopolitanism which helped break the cultural nexus between Britain and Australia, whose paternalism has always irked Australian republicans and, second, because it obscured the battle for land rights waged by Australian Aborigines.

Newspaper articles across the period give some flavour of the shifts in the discursive terrain. As today, in the 1960s and early 1970s each wave of new arrivals was open to critical scrutiny — first the Italians and Greeks, shortly followed by the Lebanese and Turks. Asians were mentioned less, since the large wave of South-East Asian immigration had not yet begun, that is, with the exception of the Chinese whose presence in Australia by this time had already had a long history. Forty thousand Chinese arrived to work as miners in the gold rushes of the 1850s and 1870s, a population which was expanded by the immigration of students and long term residents to 34 000 by 1971, with well-established patterns of residence and employment in parts of the city. In newspapers of the time,[6] what is first striking is that there was a great ambivalence of response to the new arrivals by already settled Australians. On the one hand immigrants were constructed as exotic — a night out in a Greek taverna dancing and drinking retsina, not unlike turpentine it was said — allows you to unleash emotions. While in Leichhardt, we are told you could almost be convinced that you had been transported from Sydney to an Italian village: there are macellarias, not butcher shops; Italian music and driving schools, delicatessens, pizza parlours. But the cappuccino revolution had not yet hit, and reverence for the cosmopolitan lifestyle was not yet public discourse. The story is tinged with uncertainty: 'suddenly you are a stranger in your own city'; the known is destabilised; the ground is beginning to shift and shudder.

There were a number of concerns, the most important of which was successful assimilation into what was defined as the Australian way of life. This was a normative framework where sociospatial practices which did not conform were derided, 'othered', constituted as outside, marginal and threatening. In countless articles judgments were made as to which immigrants had succeeded best at the task, with different groups being placed at different points in the assimilation league table according to latent prejudices or contemporary events. Just as Asian gang wars are the concern of the 1990s, so then the 'honorata' were 'stalking the Sydney streets' bringing criminal activity from the Calabrian South to Fairfield; this was not the highly suburbanised built environment of Fairfield of the 1990s, this was a 'war being fought in the shadows, in the suburbs, in the orchards, in the vineyards, the markets, the backyards'[7] — this is rural suburban life which is under threat.

In 1971 it was suggested that the Greeks were least likely to assimilate since 92.3 per cent married within the community compared with the 67 per cent of Italian men who married women born in Italy. Intermarriage was seen as the crucial issue.[8] The reluctance of new immigrants to blend with the existing population would, it was argued, threaten to produce ghetto-like developments, a theme echoed once again more than two decades later in Professor Helen Hughes's comments to the Bureau of Immigration, Population and Multicultural Research Third National Outlook conference in Adelaide that high jobless rates and lack of English were creating crime-ridden residential concentrations.[9] This theme was taken up the following day by the National Party leader, Tim Fischer, who stated that if non-English-speaking ghettos emerged across the cities of Australia it was quite reasonable for Australians to be uneasy about current immigration policies.

Yet reflected also in the newspapers were positive, although often patronising, perceptions. Italians were said to have a great capacity for hard work and to contribute to economic growth. The Turks were a primitive people who were anxious to adapt themselves to Australian ways — 'excellent migrants' — while Muslims were 'very clean people'. Egyptians on the other hand were portrayed as an unobtrusive and contented ethnic group who cost the country nothing since they paid their own way here, were qualified as engineers, doctors, teachers and accountants, found their own flats, assimilated with a minimum of fuss and were quick to adapt to an alien way of life.[10]

There was also the problem of the return migrant — 'four-year slog, then goodbye' — the migrant who could not adapt to Australia, who felt dislocated and bereft. Here the social and cultural space encountered was seen as alien, and even economic security and apparent success were not enough to constitute a viable sense of identity or belonging. According to the *Daily Mirror*, in 1971 the greatest ambition of many of the 6000 Turkish immigrants of the previous two years was to return home as soon as possible. For one Oehmeh Duijaci the rupture and sense of dissonance derived from religious difference. For a Muslim like himself there was no mosque nor Imam with whom he and his family could worship. This is a picture which changes dramatically in the following two decades, although not without controversy. These are the immigrants who were 'unable to master the problems of the new land — can never suppress their duality, that part from overseas which drives them in to the mental ghettos which mar the immigration scheme'.[11] A stark contrast here was offered in the media portrayal of the 50 000 Lebanese settled in Canterbury, Parramatta, Marrickville, Bankstown and twelve other suburbs, who were said rarely to get into trouble or riot at a soccer match, nor to adopt 'the ghetto outlook', and on the few occasions that they did 'extraordinary forces of discipline within their community usually restore a detergent cleanliness'![12]

An analysis of the 1976 Census data showed growing numbers of non-Anglo immigrants. In Sydney alone there were 44 935 Greeks of whom 12 per cent were in Marrickville, with further concentrations in Canterbury (6206), Randwick (3455) Rockdale (2655) and Botany (2287) The 63 146 Italians remained concentrated in the near city municipalities of Drummoyne (10.5 per cent), Ashfield (9 per cent) and Leichhardt (6.3 per cent). While the numbers of Asians had started to increase to 55 014, at this stage they were rather more widely dispersed throughout the city than many of the other ethnic groupings, a pattern which changed as the 1980s progressed. Thus the highest concentrations of Asian-born were in Waverley and Randwick (7.3 per cent) reflecting the student population at the University of New South Wales, 6.3 per cent in Ashfield and Burwood, the traditional home of Sydney's middle-class Chinese; while Sydney's Japanese community mainly lived in Northbridge. The impact of the South-East Asians on Fairfield, where Asians constituted only 2.1 per cent of the population in 1976, had barely begun to be felt.

By the early 1980s the concerns had changed. So too the existing population had become more used to a diversity of cultures and ethnicities living in the city and were less crude or stereotypical in their perceptions and how these were represented. Of increasing concern at the time were higher levels of unemployment and poverty among non-Anglo immigrants: 'Italian workers destitute: survey finds struggling Snowy Mountains veterans' runs one headline.[13] Of the 18 000 Lebanese, over half of whom were living in Canterbury, 18.8 per cent were out of work compared with 5.3 per cent of the Australian born. The narrative of success had taken a dive. According to the NSW Ethnic Affairs Commission, employers in the western suburbs expressed reservations about Lebanese people because they were seen as violent and inclined to complain about work conditions and to demand workers compensation too often. Asians, whose unemployment rate was only 9.2 per cent, were favoured instead.[14] Alongside stories of unemployment and poverty, tales were told of a vicious war among Lebanese political factions, with reports of savage beatings and stabbings spreading shock waves through the city.[15]

So who had replaced the Lebanese in the narrative of success? In 1981 the *Sydney Morning Herald* ran a lead story on 'How the Hungarians conquered Sydney'. This is the immigrant group that radiates confidence and wealth. Far from the poverty or lack of employment and services of the western suburbs, the Hungarians had claimed Double Bay, a 'better class of ghetto, where they sit separated by a street choked by double parked Jaguars and Valiant Regals. Coffee cools on tables at the Cosmopolitan ... the women are elegant, the men immaculate'.[16] This is the Paris or Vienna of Sydney. Yet new discourses had erupted creating new winners and losers in the migrant game.

At the same time, by the early 1980s there was a clear shift in assumptions about what constituted perfect assimilation. No longer was it necessarily the erasure of difference. Quite the opposite. Governments, particularly federal and state Labor governments throughout the decade were keen to espouse multiculturalism as opposed to assimilation in their social and cultural policies. This ran in tandem with an immigration policy of the Hawke and Keating Labor governments from 1983 to 1996 which encouraged large numbers of immigrants under the humanitarian and family reunion categories, from South-East Asian countries in particular. In terms of the urban environment this was reflected in changing built forms. Cultural facilities — the Nineveh Club for the Assyrians in Sydney's west, the Casa D'Italia in Surry Hills, the Cabramatta Migrant Centre — began to be recognised as legitimate separate cultural spaces.

As a result of these major shifts in the immigrant intake over the decade the cultural demography of the early 1990s was markedly different from that of the early 1980s, with corresponding shifts in public attitudes and discourses regarding new immigrants and multiculturalism. Yet there are the same marked tensions between a positive celebration of what migrants have to offer versus discourses of fear and hostility to what is constituted as 'other' and threatening and disruptive to Anglo–Australian identity.

THE MULTICULTURAL SUCCESS STORY? SYDNEY IN THE 1990s

To pose the question of whether Sydney and other Australian cities represent a multicultural success story is already to create a discursive framework which contains certain assumptions. Certainly there is a dominant public discourse of successful multiculturalism in Australia which is deployed strategically in many contexts to encourage investment or tourism. The promotional packages of the Australian Olympic Committee were not slow to see the advantages of multiculturalism in attracting the Olympics to Sydney. A *Sydney Morning Herald* 'Spectrum' article on 4 February 1995, entitled

'Orient Express' tells us that Sydney has reinvented itself as Australia's first truly Eurasian metropolis.[17] The United Nations conference on global diversity which has since been hosted in Sydney, would, it was said, be an opportunity to show off multiculturalism as practised peacefully in Sydney.

However multicultural discourse is used, and even when the term is replaced by 'cross-cultural' or 'people of diverse cultures', non-Anglo Celtic cultures are still constructed as 'other' to Australian: it is 'them' and it is 'us'. And if 'they' fit in with 'our' way of life they are welcome. Such a formulation is clearly under fire from a number of quarters and in the process of change. New discourses are being deployed with different strategic intentions and effects. On the one hand Aboriginal claims for the land and assertion of prior ownership and settlement have finally been acknowledged in the High Court Mabo decision of 1993. On the other the Republican push, also loudly espoused by the Australian Labor Prime Minister Paul Keating, is challenging the old British ties and attempting to forge a new kind of Australian identity. Amanda Lohrey calls this the 'interregnum, that is that period in the nineties when we move from being the old Commonwealth of Australia, presided over by the Crown, to the new republic of Australia, presided over by God knows whom; when we rewrite our constitution and rethink the symbols of nationhood, including the flag'.[18] But let us turn to the terrains and spaces of multicultural Sydney in the early 1990s.

It would be hard, and probably foolish to argue that large numbers of people from many countries and cultures have not settled successfully into Australian cities, and been accepted in many respects by those who arrived before them. And, like other countries which have experienced similar migration patterns, each wave of new immigrants are the ones to suffer the greatest levels of prejudice and hostility until they too are superseded by the new arrivals. The majority of immigrants have jobs and dwellings and have established social and cultural networks and sites which meet many of their needs. But it is not a homogenous picture. Not all immigrants are employed or housed, neither have all localities been as receptive as others to change. So too the lives of immigrants are fragmented, multiple and differentiated.

In Sydney the picture of migrant settlement is illustrated in the map below showing where recent immigrants have settled. In 1991 Ashfield had the largest percentage (17 per cent) of immigrants who had been resident for less than five years, followed by Marrickville (14.3 per cent), Canterbury (14.2 per cent) and Fairfield (12.9 per cent), reflecting the concentration of migrant hostels and facilities in that area over a long period. Wollondilly, Hawkesbury, Camden and the Blue Mountains had the smallest percentages: 1.1 per cent, 1.7 per cent, 1.8 per cent and 1.5 per cent respectively. In Fairfield 40 500 of the 71 379 residents were born overseas. Sydney as a whole took 36.2 per cent of the recent overseas immigrants compared with Melbourne 23.5 per cent, Perth 11.56 per cent, and Brisbane 6.8 per cent. If all immigrants are added into the picture they account for 30 per cent of the Sydney population .

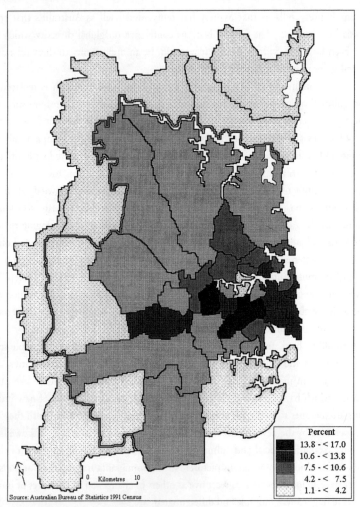

Percentage of the population born overseas and resident for less than 5 years, 1991.

The impacts of immigration on Sydney localities have been complex and differentiated. Following the patterns of settlement in many cities of the world, immigrants to Sydney have tended to move to areas where other people from their own country have concentrated. Sites of cultural significance, such as mosques and synagogues, shops meeting different culinary and other needs, employment contacts and relevant services, combined with friends and relatives in close proximity, make such concentration inevitable. What establishes a group initially in an area is a more complex question, but it is largely an amalgam of access to housing, the location of migrant hostels and employment opportunities at the time of initial settlement. It is also a question of accident.

Areas of Sydney have been affected differently by the arrival of people from a particular country or region: Vietnamese-born people are concentrated in Fairfield; Turkish in Auburn and Lidcombe, people from Hong Kong, Malaysia and Singapore are in North Ryde and Chatswood; South Africans in St Ives; Japanese-born in Northbridge; East Europeans in Vaucluse and Double Bay; Greeks in Marrickville; Koreans in Campsie; Lebanese in Lakemba, Bankstown and Punchbowl; Italians in Leichhardt, Ashfield and Burwood; and New Zealanders in Bondi. Although it is clear that immigrants usually choose to live in areas with familiar faces and community support, it is not always clear how the process of selection began.

For every logical choice of an area — such as proximity to factories or religious or educational facilities — there are as many accidental areas of settlement. Cabramatta was the first area that the Vietnamese got to know from their hostels. Campsie was once declared the place for Koreans by a persuasive local business entrepreneur. When an early Lebanese migrant, Adib Marabani, arrived in 1951 he chose Lakemba to be near to the only other person he knew in Sydney. Joining the twenty-odd other Lebanese families there, an association was formed to build Sydney's first mosque in 1975, which fast became the social centre for about 6000 Lebanese. For most ethnic groups there is a similar foundation stone. In St Ives the Masada College has been significant as a community centre, synagogue and hall which is used for bar mitzvahs and weddings.[19]

But obviously economic factors are a major determinant of where an immigrant lives. Often where an immigrant household settles is only the first port of call while money is accumulated. Thus there was a steady flow of Greeks out of Marrickville into the more wealthy surrounding suburbs such as Earlwood and Bexley, while the home units of Chatswood are the first stop for many Hong Kong Chinese en route to Cherrybrook once they can afford to buy dwellings there. Immigrants of refugee status and from countries riven by poverty, unemployment or conflict have considerably less choice than those who come under the business migration programs from countries enjoying economic prosperity. More often than not their first experience in Sydney will be in a migrant hostel at Fairfield. The South African Jews came too late and with not enough wealth to join the European Jewish community in the eastern suburbs and chose St Ives instead where houses are modern and spacious, with large gardens that resonate with those left behind in Johannesburg. Yet despite the shifts over time, the early distinctive ethnic settlements remain strong, with visible effects on the cityscape.

Not only do different immigrant groups inhabit different parts of the city, they also experience different levels of employment, make different housing choices and inhabit the spaces of the streets in different ways. So also the reactions of local residents to new immigrants in their locality vary. There are quite striking variations in the employment rates of immigrants across the city which obviously affects the levels of income and wealth that people have and where they can live. At one end of the scale are the immigrants who enter as part of the business migration program, which means bringing a

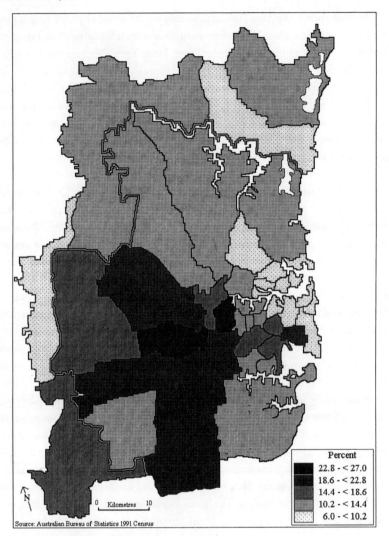

Percentage of resident workforce working in manufacturing, 1991.

substantial sum of money to establish an industry or business or having skills that are currently designated to be in short supply in the Australian economy. Many of the business migrants are Chinese — from Hong Kong in particular — Koreans and Singaporeans who live in the wealthier suburbs on the North Shore or in the Hills districts. For these groups the high house prices there (as much as $500 000 in West Pennant Hills) are not prohibitive. The houses are remarkable in their size, often taking up most of the block of land on which they stand. Gardens are not usually desired.

At the other end of the scale are the political refugees from Vietnam and Cambodia who have far greater difficulties in finding employment. For the Vietnamese and Cambodians, language problems, low levels of education and limited skills frequently militate against getting jobs, especially where young men are concerned. In Fairfield the 1991 Census indicated that 30 000 of the 185 000 residents were unable to speak English well. Only three out of ninety school leavers applying for a position of library assistant in the area were considered appointable. The unemployment rate among recent Vietnamese was around 41 per cent in 1991, with young men again particularly affected. Where there are jobs they are often in new technological, computing or informational sectors for which the local residents are not qualified. Cambodians in the locality, especially women, do a lot of piecework at home, such as sewing, in order to supplement the dole or low incomes of their husbands, and in some cases without this money families simply could not survive. These meagre opportunities are so sought after that it is easy for employers to exploit workers and keep wages low. This is not to ignore the fact that other South-East Asians have successfully set up their own businesses, particularly in Cabramatta, and employ friends and relatives to work for them.

For many Asian families who are larger than the average and who have low incomes, public housing is the main option. But the waiting lists are long, and small flats, which are deemed unsuitable for larger groups by the state housing authority, are the norm. Another cultural clash occurs when Chinese and Vietnamese go to the banks with considerable assets and low incomes, confusing the banks with their rules that a banking history and deposits are necessary for home loans to be approved. What is happening here is the 'tontine' system similar to the old stavorca system practised by the Russians. Here a group of say thirty people join an informal lottery where each puts in $300 a month and turns are taken in drawing the money for their own use until all the group have set up their own business or bought a property. When the winner of the draw arrives at a bank with a sum of money and no explanation as to where it came from the application is denied. Other concerns unique to different cultures may be the site of the dwelling: the *feng shui*, the direction it faces, or the potential it has for offering space for worship or gardens for fresh vegetables. In *Camille's Bread*, Amanda Lohrey describes Marita's house in Leichhardt:

> The charm of these houses is their small, subtropical courtyards which exist in defiance of the smog. The immigrants bring little packets of seeds from the homeland. Next door the elderly Donna Maria sings wailing songs in Portuguese while she weeds her vegetable gardens full of strange plants. One evening she gave Marita a green leafy vegetable called grelos. They cooked the grelos and it was bitter.[20]

Yet the lack of flexibility in housing options and structures can delimit the practices and customs of different cultures.

For older, more established residents there are less clear trends and employment and housing patterns look more like those of the longer established residents. Italians in the suburbs are known for building big flamboyant houses right up to the corner of the block and adorning the exterior with elaborate columns and wrought iron balconies, while the Eastern Europeans of Double Bay retain a taste for elegant dwellings more evocative of the cities from which they came. But stereotypes and fictions are hard to disentangle and potentially dangerous.

So how is this growing cultural diversity across the city now viewed on the cusp of the twenty-first century after over forty years of immigration, including a non-Anglo component? 'Moral panic' is a sociological discourse deployed for the eruption of a generalised fear or anxiety in a community. A series of newspaper reports on the rise of home invasions in Asian communities could well be said to constitute a moral panic. On 27 April 1993 a *Sydney Morning Herald* headline read: 'Wake in fright: The growing terror of home invasion'. This was a story about 'raids by armed strangers in which families are bound and gagged' by gangs armed with machetes, shortened rifles and other such weapons in search of money. According to the article this was a crime which had struck more than thirty Asian families in Sydney in the previous year. These crimes, it was reported, are characteristic of a community — the Vietnamese — whose youth have been traumatised by war and who come from broken homes.[21] There is a connection here with the media's other dominant concern: the relationship between drugs, gangs and crime. As Vietnamese households have become more settled over the last decade ever more media reports highlight Cabramatta as the site of growing crime and violence. Comparative statistics are difficult to come by. Whether the levels of crime are dramatically higher in Cabramatta than other places is hard to establish and hotly disputed. One report suggested that while Fairfield housed 5 per cent of Sydney's population, it figured in 14 per cent of robberies.[22] The stories are colourful and dramatic and designed to frighten: 'There's a switchblade knife scar on the right lung of … Andrew Nguyen … He is no stranger to terror. When the blade slid between his ribs he was sitting in the lounge room of his suburban home' — the family were early victims of house invasion'.[23] Cabramatta has taken over from Kings Cross as the distribution point for heroin.[24] Locals will tend to argue that the accounts are exaggerated. Crimes in other places may be less visible or of a different kind.

In direct contrast, other reports from Cabramatta paint a picture of thriving success. In a *Business Review Weekly* cover story in early 1995 Tony Thomas describes how the driving commitment of Australia's 130 000 Vietnamese has revitalised many shopping strips and given rise to a thriving and competitive plethora of small businesses. The positive impacts, we are told, are immense: every Vietnamese enclave 'creates an urban renewal where estate values improve and customer traffic escalates.' By 1981 shop rentals in Cabramatta had reached levels only slightly under those in exclusive Double Bay. Yet business success is only one side of the economic narrative. The Vietnamese have been beset by high levels of unemployment of between 20 and 30 per cent since

Freedom Gate, Cabramatta, August 1995.

Many different cultures, one community; Cabramatta graffiti, August 1995.

1980. It is this high level of unemployment, particularly among youth, stemming from low levels of education and qualifications, which generates the alienation into which the gangs tap. There are sharp resonances here with the stories of the Italian immigrants of the early 1970s and the Lebanese of the early 1980s, with one clear difference being the growing drug culture and connections with the drug magnates and organised gangs of South-East Asia. Perhaps it is simply a repetitive cycle of hostilities and fears being replaced by acceptance and celebration as one group of immigrants becomes more firmly established and is superseded in media and popular demonising by another. As the *Sydney Morning Herald* article in September 1994 put it: 'The British had complained about the Italians when they arrived, who complained about the Yugoslavs, who complained about the Vietnamese, who complained about the Cambodians'.[25]

MULTICULTURAL SPACE

Edward Said claims that if 'culture is a system of discriminations and evaluations ... it also means that culture is a system of exclusions'.[26]

Sydney's built environment bears some marks of cultural difference in its housing forms and public spaces, although the overriding visible impact, particularly in the outer suburban areas, is one of homogeneity of urban form. Planning discourses and practices have so far been little affected by multicultural debates, although changes to planning regulations have occurred in some localities such as Fairfield to accommodate cultural differences. For example, there is a trend in many immigrant groups, particularly those from South-East Asia, to establish home-based industries. These tend to be perceived as a nuisance by neighbours and treated with hostility. Fairfield has confronted the issue by setting standards for such activities to combat their negative impacts without disallowing the practice. Similarly, the preference among some immigrants to live in extended households has been accommodated by allowing dual occupancy on a single site.

Almost all immigrants, particularly more recent ones, share a history of some displacement or dissatisfaction with their places of origin, at the least, and in many cases share more turbulent or violent histories of exclusion, terror or poverty which has precipitated migration and diaspora. They also share a desire to represent and locate themselves in their new place of residence. In the context of Australia, and Sydney in particular, this is a question of finding a space in what is already defined as Australian society or urban life with its preconceived notions of what constitutes 'Australian'. Yet 'Australian' is an identity which is continually contested, rearticulated and reproduced. As Homi Bhaba puts it: 'it is in the emergence of the interstices — the overlap and displacement of domains of difference — that the intersubjective and collective experiences of *nationness*, community interest, or cultural values are negotiated'. He asks the question:

> How do strategies of representation or empowerment come to be formulated in the competing claims of communities where, despite shared histories of deprivation and discrimination, the exchange of values, meanings and priorities may not always be collaborative and dialogical, but may be profoundly antagonistic, conflictual and even incommensurable?[27]

That this is a complex and contested process is well illustrated in the built environment. Cultural difference can be perceived as a threat or as emblematic of the exotic 'other'. In Sydney it seems that where cultural differences in the built form or use of space have been perceived as exotic by local residents and planners there has been less resistance to the non-traditional uses of public space, and even their encouragement as tourist sites. Where different uses have been constructed as threats to local dominant styles, norms or patterns of social interaction and cultural life, discourses of resistance and racism are more often deployed. The boundary between the two perceptions can shift and change over time and space, as has happened in the Cabramatta shopping centre.

By far the most contentious cultural practices involving public spaces in Sydney suburbs have been in the religious arena. So much so that in New South Wales the state government set up an interdepartmental committee chaired by the Ethnic Affairs Commission to examine planning for religious developments. Its report concluded that:

> *Over the past ten years, minority religions, especially ethnic minority religions have found themselves at the centre of major legal battles as well as community conflicts over their right to pursue developments of places of worship and religious instruction as is required by their various doctrines.*[28]

One pattern in the 1980s was for Muslim or Hindu communities to acquire a site on which a residential dwelling, and possibly an outbuilding or warehouse, was situated and use it for a mosque or temple with no application for change of use submitted. A second pattern was for a group to submit a development application for a new site. In the first scenario, once the local Muslim or Hindu community used the building(s) as a place of worship, complaints from local residents began to be lodged. Tension rose on festival days when very large numbers of people arrived, causing traffic and noise problems for the local residents who then alerted the council. Typically, planning officers visited the site and informed the group that it could no longer be used as a mosque or temple unless certain regulations were complied with. The lack of adequate space for parking legitimated their insistence that the group apply for another site.

In several cases a great deal of conflict arose during site selection processes, with council officers suggesting sites on open space land away from residential areas. These sites are contentious for several reasons. The architectural forms are distinct and the patterns of usage are different from those of the Christian norm. Parking becomes an issue because of regional drawing power, and poor public transport exacerbates the need for cars. It was also argued that the noise impact of mosques was greater than churches since mosques and temples are social meeting places as well as sites of worship. Controversial cases arose where groups were unaware of what was and was not permitted. As recently as the late 1980s local politicians were not embarrassed to express racist attitudes: 'the temple will not be an asset. There are no Vietnamese people living there. You are hoping to put in a complete foreign body in anticipation of people coming to use it'.[29] (The body metaphor is interesting here: Anglo-Australia is the 'pure' body in danger of contamination.)

On some occasions buildings were refused simply because they were different or 'other'. An increase in the height of the mosque spire at Smithfield in the Fairfield locality was refused by council 'on the grounds that it was likely to spoil the amenity of the area'. The council report stated that 'the visual privacy of adjoining properties would be reduced. It is out of character with the surrounding areas and the height is considered to be excessive'.[30] There were no similar instances where a church tower had not been permitted. More often than not refusal was legitimated on the grounds of inadequate parking provision.

In 1991 a Greek bishop submitted an application for a private chapel on his property in Penrith. The local council objected on the grounds that it was too close to the house and that its 'design was not in keeping with the area'. New plans were submitted and fifty-nine objections were received — mostly concerning crowds, noise and traffic. Some residents also complained that 'the fence is not in keeping with the area and that trees have been cleared and a track cut through the land'. This was followed by claims that the bishop was not an authentic bishop of the Greek Orthodox Church. The council then deferred its decision until they received a statutory declaration that the chapel would only be for private use. Opponents of the site said the aldermen were 'fence sitting to avoid being labelled racist.' Eventually permission for the private chapel was granted, but on condition that the bishop furnish a letter of intent. It was recognised that a refusal would constitute an infringement of his freedom of religion, which could be taken to the Anti-Discrimination Board. One alderman shouted during the debate 'I'll stand here and say Germans are better than bloody Greeks'. Another, who was speaking on behalf of the majority of residents, pointed out that it would be difficult to provide evidence should the bishop break the ruling at weekends.[31] In cases such as these, planning norms and regulations are invoked to neutralise objections which derive from a different source.

Despite sporadic conflicts over some sites there is no doubt that by the mid-1990s a far greater tolerance towards different architectural and cultural sites had developed. By 1991 there were 147 507 Muslims in Australia, estimated to have risen to 180 000 by 1996. Half of these live in Sydney, with the highest concentrations in Auburn (15.9 per cent of population), Canterbury (7.7 per cent), Bankstown (6.0 per cent) Rockdale (5.5 per cent), Botany (5.1 per cent) and Marrickville (4.0 per cent). This contrasts markedly with affluent suburbs like Ku-ring-gai, Mosman, Hunters Hill and Hornsby where the respective percentages were 0.3 per cent, 0.4 per cent, 0.4 per cent, 0.4 per cent and 0.5 per cent. In total, sixty-seven countries are represented in Sydney's Muslim population. As time goes on more and more mosques are being built to accommodate the desire to worship — by 1995 there were fifteen mosques in Sydney — at the same time as private Islamic schools, like the Malak Fad Islamic School at Chullora, have been built for Muslim children. Such has been the recent growth of Islamic facilities that the newspapers have suggested a Muslim-based building boom.[32]

Mosque, Auburn, western Sydney, August 1995.

Other contested sites have been social clubs, particularly senior citizens' clubs, where long use is seen to denote ownership. In one case in Fairfield a group of Anglo–Australian senior citizens considered that it was legitimate to keep a local club for their exclusive use. According to the president of the club the rooms had been used by this group exclusively for fifteen years: 'Last year the Spanish senior citizens began using our rooms, and wished to use the inside toilets. This is not possible without allowing access to our private lounge room, the heart of our organisation, which contains all our records, private furniture and other material'.[33] Again a metaphor of the body as sacred is evoked. This is an interesting illustration of how seemingly public space is re-constituted as private.

In Penrith some Assyrians wanted to develop a house into a community centre and community hall to provide a link 'between the two cultures the migrants straddle'. According to the local newspaper, it was 'causing some heartburn among neighbouring residents worried about their rural ambience'. Twenty attended the council's Planning and Works Committee. One neighbour, a poultry farmer, said his chickens had been literally scared to death by the noise from a (fundraising) disco and cars and that this would threaten his livelihood. Another resident said that it did not fit into a rural area, even though the zoning allowed it, and a third said it was out of character with the area.[34] In this same locality there are clubs, such as the Returned Services Leagues (RSL) Clubs, which serve the mainly white community but do not evoke an equivalent hostile response. The largest of these is the Penrith Leagues Club, the Panthers, which contains thousands of poker machines, a cable water-ski park, bars, restaurants, a video store and aqua-golf. Here public space has been privatised to produce the largest site of recreational facilities in western Sydney.

Where migrant use of public space can be construed as exotic there appears to have been much less resistance from the Anglo–Australian community and from town planners. Newtown, in the Marrickville Local Government Area, is one such place. Here King Street is marked by Thai restaurant after Thai restaurant (imaginatively called the Bow Thai or the Thaitanic), filled to the brim on every night of the week with locals and visitors. The Vietnamese shopping centre of Cabramatta in Fairfield is another. Here Chinese dragons guard a walking street where signs and symbols of ancient China are interspersed with Asian shops and restaurants, and people come and go, sit around, play music and pass the time of day. As one migrant resource worker commented: 'a few years ago when there was nothing there no-one came. Now they come just to do a bit of shopping and, particularly older people, to have a social life there'. This has also become constructed as a tourist site where inner Sydneysiders come to experience a slice of the 'exotic' and an Asian yum cha Sunday breakfast. In 1992 more than a million visitors made the trip to Cabramatta which bills itself as a place 'where the East meets West'.[35]

Cabramatta is the exception rather than the norm and its tourist status was not achieved without controversy even over the choice of name for the plaza — Freedom Plaza. The symbols that have been used to construct Chinese identity, to evoke China, are those of ancient Chinese culture ossified in time. Chinese culture is being reinvented and reconstituted by myths and symbols which have been superseded and changed in the very places from which they originate. Such is the mapping of past memories and spaces in new terrains. Writing on post colonial immigrants from India to the United States of America, Ganguly suggests 'the past acquires a more marked salience with subjects for whom the categories of the present have been made unusually unstable or unpredictable, as a consequence of the displacement enforced by post-colonial and migrant circumstances'.[36] As time has passed Cabramatta has shifted from being perceived as a threat (its earlier derisive epithet was Vietnamatta), as a cultural invasion, as alien, to representing an exotic place and a tourist attraction where income can be generated. There are some parallels here with migrant writing. As Sneja Gunew puts it: 'Multiculturalism becomes too often an effective process of recuperation whereby diverse cultures are returned homogenised as folkloric spectacle … In this formulation, multiculturalism functions to amalgamate and spuriously to unify nationalism and culture into a depoliticized multimedia event'.[37]

Most of the formal recreation areas in the western suburbs of Sydney are given over to traditional sporting fields: football, soccer, cricket, baseball and any organised team

Italian house, Fairfield, western Sydney, August 1995.

sport. Not only are these spaces gendered and caged, but they are mostly used by young men. They are not conducive to more informal practices such as walking, sitting around, bowls, volleyball and other games. The landscape is often barren, with few areas that are shaded and pleasant to sit in. In many of the countries of origin of the immigrants, recreational pursuits such as badminton and chess take place in the town square and are less formalised. Yet few spaces exist for these here. It is rare to find a landscaped piazza, places to sit or tables to sit by. It was fascinating to discover, travelling north once, that a spring-sourced hot public bath in Lightning Ridge, an opal town in the far northwest of the New South Wales, is seen as a desirable holiday place for eastern European refugees from Liverpool, western Sydney, seeking to re-find the everyday corporeal pleasures of the land they left.

The homogeneity of the Australian outer suburbs constrains the expression of difference. David Sibley makes a related argument about gypsies:

> *Spaces which are homogeneous or uniform, from which non-conforming groups or activities have been expelled or have been kept out through the maintenance of strong boundaries, can be termed pure in the sense that they are free from polluting elements and the purification of space is a process by which power is exercised over space and social groups. The significance of such purified spaces in the construction of the 'other' is basically that difference is more visible than it would be in an area of mixed land use and social diversity.*[38]

This tale of contested sites in western Sydney illustrates the tensions and conflicts inherent in immigrants representing themselves symbolically and literally in Australian suburban spaces. It is a story with which Aboriginal Australians are only too familiar.

THE NEWMAN CASE

The assassination of John Newman reflected similar ambivalences and tensions bubbling beneath the surfaces of allegedly successful multicultural Sydney. It is a story like those in the narrative so far where there is no simple reading of multicultural Sydney. The media discourses following the event reflect the ambivalences that permeate the skin of the multicultural success story. As one journalist wrote: 'Cabramatta is the fulfilment of our migration dream and its nightmarish conclusion. An amalgam of poverty and prosperity, marked by high rise flats with laundry-draped balconies, it is a dazzling collision between Australian suburban ugliness and South East Asian big-city garishness'[39] and 'Cabramatta knows its days of innocence have died'.[40] A headline two days later: 'Australia — "paying the price" for lax migration laws'[41] showed how contentious Asian immigration has been. Negative images were reinforced by headlines reporting comments by Asians in broken English: 'We no go back'.[42] A survey conducted on the perception of different immigrant groups confirms the picture, with 70 per cent saying that they did not favour Asian immigration.

In the days following the Newman murder the newspapers were full of heartfelt dismay. Newman had set himself up as the politician who would successfully combat the Asian gangs who allegedly were destroying suburban family life. These are the gangs, like the 5T gang, who are modelled on gangs in Hong Kong and other cities, particularly American cities, across the world. There is one unique characteristic among Indochinese gangs, which is the trend towards scarring or mutilation of skin, as opposed to tattooing, to create the desired marks. Some of this apparently refers to Indochinese culture and traditions where in order to atone for guilt a person is expected to undergo pain or even death.[43] Photographs of menacing looking young men appeared in the newspapers with descriptions of the tattoos of king cobra snakes, a flying eagle with outstretched wings and claws, a black panther, a full-masted sailing ship, a dragon, a swastika, a coffin with candles and, among females, a pair of open scissors.[44]

Insinuated in the articles and public debate was a clear presumption that the Asian gangs were to blame for the assassination, giving ample ammunition to the anti-Asian immigration lobby. Newman had gone so far as to suggest the deportation of Asians found guilty of participating in home invasions. His view was that the success of the Australian experiment in co-existence in Cabramatta would ensure its success throughout the nation. Local Vietnamese politicians responded to the attacks. One community leader, Councillor Ngo, complained that if Vietnamese people did not become part of the political process they were accused of living in ghettos and not being part of the broader community. Yet when they did enter the party political arena they were tainted as branch stackers.

What the Newman case showed was that despite the large number of immigrants who now live and work in Sydney, there remains an uneasy accommodation of cultural difference which can be threatened when adversity strikes or when people experience lack or thwarted desires. The same can be said of responses to the Aboriginal population. The shops where Aboriginal art is sold are welcomed, as also are the interesting cultural events. But in inner city Redfern, where the majority of urban Aborigines live, there are no restraints on the building of an Advanced Technology Park bringing few advantages to Aborigines in the area. The neighbourhood itself, with its the pockets of poverty and lack of amenity so close to the inner city, is vulnerable to incursions by gentrifiers but little respected. What Sydneysiders celebrate are the cultural differences that enrich their daily lives — restaurants, exotic foods, colour, music, festivals and the like. As Salman Rushdie put it: 'food passes across any boundary you care to mention'.[45] But where immigrants have been unsuccessful in employment and their communities are up against problems of poverty, displacement and difficulties like drug use, there is less sympathy. Despite former Labor Prime Minister Keating's enthusiasm for entering Asia and integrating Australia into the Asia–Pacific region, there are complexities and contradictions in multicultural Sydney, particularly with respect to newer Asian immigrants, which cannot simply be talked away. There is no one narrative of multiculturalism.

POSTSCRIPT

On re-reading the text, I imagine saying to a friend: 'I told you so'! Previously, I had watered down my concerns, not wanting to give discursive power to other voices and resistances to multicultural Sydney. My optimism was misplaced.

To turn to events. In March 1996 John Howard's federal government was elected. The Liberal–National Party coalition had gone to the polls committed to cutting the Aboriginal and Torres Strait Islanders Commission budget by $100 million. During the election campaign, John Howard made a number of gratuitous references to the 'Aboriginal industry' and supposed mismanagement of funds in Aboriginal programs. Unlike his predecessors since Malcolm Fraser, he also expressed antipathy to the moderate Aboriginal leadership who had facilitated the reconciliation process.

In September 1996 Pauline Hanson, the new independent member for the Queensland seat of Oxley, made her maiden speech to the Australian Parliament. It attracted immediate and wide media coverage. In summary, Hanson said excessive public money was allocated to Aboriginal people, who brought disadvantage on themselves; recent Australian immigration policy was too pro-Asian and the country was in danger of becoming a mini-Asia and, thirdly, that multiculturalism was promoting ghettos in the cities and destroying traditional Australian values. In Hanson's view, Asians were responsible for many social problems including unemployment and heroin addiction.

More interesting than the parochial and ignorant views of Pauline Hanson were the responses they did — or did not — provoke. John Howard initially refused to comment on the speech. By using a discourse of free speech to legitimate his silence, the Prime Minister allowed a space for the expression of prejudice and opinions which had been absent from public debate for more than a decade. Under the Keating government, public expression of hostility to Aboriginal and Asian people was discouraged. This was sometimes dismissed as 'political correctness'. Aboriginal author Sally Morgan sees it differently: 'If you were redneck under Labor you thought twice before you came out of the closet. But the Howard government has given people permission to be racist, to say extreme right wing things. I think that what he'd ultimately like to do is to mainstream Aboriginal people out of existence'.[46]

Politicians who did respond to Hanson's speech seemed little more than instrumentally driven. For example, although Trade Minister Tim Fischer was one early voice of dissent, his main concern was the potential threat posed by Hanson's views to trade and investment with Asian partners.

Out on the streets, opinion polls reported that 53 per cent of respondents agreed with Hanson's sentiments on immigration and Aboriginal funding, 38 per cent were opposed to her views and the balance were undecided.[47] At schools, and in private and public spaces, these opinions were articulated verbally and physically and reports circulated of Asian children being spat at, and told to 'go home'. At one stage there were media reports blaming immigrants for the spread of tuberculosis and many Aboriginal leaders and organisations received hate mail.

Two other parallel events are worth mentioning. The first is the unfortunate response of Senator John Herron, the Minister for Aboriginal Affairs, to the 'stolen generation' inquiry. In 1996, the Human Rights and Equal Opportunity Commission investigated the cases of some of the estimated 100 000 Aboriginal children who, during a period of over sixty years, were taken from their families and fostered into white families or placed in institutions. Despite the testimonies of physical and mental distress, health and social problems and even suicide caused by this government policy, Senator Herron asserted that it had improved the material circumstances of some Aborigines. He likened the forced removable of Aboriginal children to white children been taken off to boarding schools.

At the same time, Australians Against Further Immigration (AAFI) gained unexpected prominence in national politics after standing a candidate in an important by-election in the western Sydney electorate of Lindsay. AAFI made headlines when it decided to give its electoral preferences to the Labor Party candidate, Ross Free on the basis that he had expressed concern in Parliament about his party's immigration policy — a depressing alliance in troubled times.

What are we to make of these disturbing events and political shifts? It seems that the fears and anxieties of Anglo-Australians are being tapped. Gone is the cosy, white, suburban, familiar Australia they once knew. This is an effective resistance, a cry of the frightened child. There is nostalgia and yearning for an Australia that is now gone. Peter Robinson puts it this way:

> It is true … the old Australia of simplistic values, loyalties to the 'mother country', naïve white Australian immigration policies and happy Anglo-Saxon families living soberly and untouched by foreign influences in neat houses behind white picket fences has disappeared forever.[48]

Or as Peter Cochrane argues: 'Hanson is a primal scream. She represents the greed that goes with the loss of cultural centrality and the loss of identity that happens when a cosmopolitan (mostly Anglo) elite lines up with the new social forces on the block.'[49]

The story ends as the book goes to press. It ends with the Prime Minister and the leader of the Opposition moving together to establish a bipartisan framework for a 'decent, civilised, non-racial immigration debate'.[50] Prime Minister John Howard has now re-focused his stand on Asian engagement, while Opposition leader Kim Beazley has criticised Pauline Hanson directly and championed multiculturalism.

However, despite these alarming shifts in the terrain, there is still no one narrative of multiculturalism. And despite the new climate of political cowardice and spoken hostilities to Asian immigration and Aboriginal self-determination, new allegiances will be struck, new strategies will be deployed and new diversities will be celebrated. Multicultural Sydney is simply here to stay.

Notes

1   A. Lohrey 1996, *Camille's Bread*, HarperCollins, Sydney, p. 91.
2   *Sun Herald*, 11 September 1994, p. 14.
3   *Sydney Morning Herald*, 10 September 1994, p. 6.
4   ibid.
5   S. Gunew 1994, *Framing Marginality: Multicultural Literary Studies*, Melbourne University Press, Melbourne, p. 103.
6   *Daily Mirror*, 23 May 1969, p. 7.
7   *Sunday Telegraph*, 9 June 1969.
8   *Sun Herald*, 17 January 1971.
9   *Sydney Morning Herald*, 24 February 1995.
10   *Woman's Day*, 21 June 1971.
11   *Daily Mirror*, 6 May 1971.
12   *Sun Herald*, 20 July 1971.
13   *Sydney Morning Herald*, 3 September 1981.
14   ibid., 19 September 1981.
15   For comparison, here are some 1991 unemployment rates for selected birthplace groups at the 1991 Census: Australia-born (7.5 per cent); total overseas-born (9.9 per cent); Vietnam-born (26.8 per cent); Lebanon-born (25.1 per cent).

16   *Sydney Morning Herald*, 13 June 1981.

17   ibid., 4 February 1995.

18   Amanda Lohrey 1994, 'Australia Day', in G. Papaellinas (ed.), *Republica*, Angus & Robertson, Sydney, p. 65.

19   *Sydney Morning Herald*, 4 May 1993, p. 37.

20   Lohrey, op. cit., p. 65.

21   *Sydney Morning Herald*, 27 April 1993.

22   *Sun Herald*, 11 September 1994, p. 2.

23   ibid., p. 15.

24   *Sydney Morning Herald*, 7 September 1994, p. 1.

25   ibid.

26   E. Said 1984, *The World, the Text and the Critic*, Faber, London, p. 11.

27   H. Bhaba 1994, *The Location of Culture*, Routledge, London, p. 2.

28   NSW Ethnic Affairs Commission 1990, *Annual Report*, Sydney, p. 17.

29   *Fairfield Advance*, 3 March 1987, p. 4.

30   ibid., 21 November 1989, p. 11.

31   *Penrith Press*, 16 April 1991–23 July 1991, weekly news articles.

32   *Sydney Morning Herald*, 15 May 1995, p. 15.

33   *Fairfield Advance, 18* August 1987.

34   *Penrith Press*, 2 October 1990, p. 7.

35   *Telegraph Mirror*, 2 March 1993, p. 5.

36   K. Ganguly 1992, 'Migrant identities, personal memories and the construction of selfhood', *Cultural Studies*, vol. 6, p. 29.

37   Gunew, op. cit., p. 112.

38   D. Sibley, 1992, *Geographies of Exclusion: Society and Difference in the West*, Routledge, London, p. 114.

39   *Sydney Morning Herald*, 7 September 1994, p. 8.

40   ibid.

41   ibid., 9 September 1994, p. 5.

42   *Sun Herald*, 11 September 1994, p. 15.

43   ibid., p. 2.

44   *Sydney Morning Herald*, 8 September 1994.

45   S. Rushdie 1988, *The Satanic Verses*, Viking, New York, p. 246.

46   *Sydney Morning Herald*, 'Good Weekend', 12 October 1996.

47   ibid., 8 October, p. 1.

48   *Sun Herald*, 6 October 1996, p. 38.

49   *Australian*, 10 October 1996, p. 11.

50   ibid., p. 1.

3 SELLING SYDNEY

Two headlines in the *Sydney Morning Herald* in 1994 signalled Sydney's changing relations with the global economy. The first, 'Australia is as cheap as chips: just ask IBM', led Peter Smark's article about 'Big Blue's' decision to set up a $30 million regional computer services centre.[1] The second, Sydney's pink pot of gold, headlined a story highlighting economic benefits flowing from the annual Gay and Lesbian Mardi Gras.[2] Both events typify the dominant contemporary discourse that assumes Sydney's economic future will be driven by transnational corporations and international tourists. Sydney competes with other Australian and foreign cities for international businesses and tourists and, recognising this trend, government strategies to market the city have exploded.

Sydney is represented as a bright, shiny magnet for all that is vibrant and dynamic in the modern world. A glossy brochure used by the New South Wales government to market Sydney as an international financial centre for the Asia–Pacific region reflects this portrayal. The clichéd icons — Harbour Bridge and Opera House — are juxtaposed with a cluster of office blocks and the futuristic Centrepoint Tower. Sydney is nothing but a central business district (CBD). The vast, messy, socially heterogeneous mass of the metropolis does not feature. As all roads once led to Rome, now telecommunications, air planes and ships converge on Sydney from all points of the globe. The city's arrogantly assumed economic dominance is signified on the brochure by its covering much of the Australian land mass and by the railway line converging on the city from its national hinterland.

The New South Wales government's mission to lure nationally and internationally mobile flows of investment funds and tourist dollars has produced a sharp-edged commercial appreciation of Sydney's selling points. The potential of these economic flows to confer benefits on the city's population is argued to justify marked changes to the built environment. As well as advantages though, the supposed trickle-down benefits which international tourism and business investment have on the city's population are offset by a darker story excluded from the glossy marketing. The problem has its origins in an earlier political discourse of the 1970s and 1980s when Australians were exhorted to shake off the shackles of state welfarism, and protection from import competition, and to stride bravely into the world to make great fortunes. While major structural changes to the Australian economy over the past couple of decades were difficult to avoid, it is only the greatest beneficiaries of change whose interests are represented in the glossy brochures and frenetic globe-speak.

Peter Smark's article on the IBM decision asked why the corporation was spending

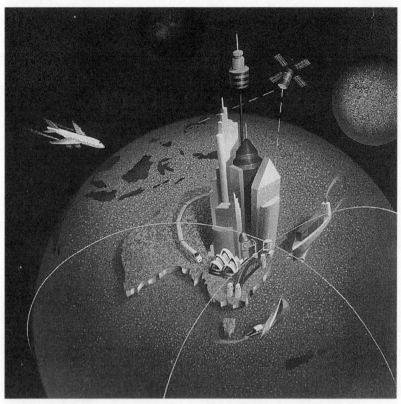

Selling Sydney to business, (Source: New South Wales Department of State and Regional Development, 1994).

$30 million to set up its regional computer services centre in Australia. The answer is that Sydney is cheaper than Hong Kong and Singapore:

> *Cathay Pacific recently announced the move of its computerised passenger bookings to Sydney. Now IBM has joined in to remind us that places like Singapore are increasingly pricing themselves out of the regional headquarter business. Rents and the costs of servicing the housing and recreational needs of expatriate executives, as well as the salaries of locally hired executives and skilled staff, have soared out of sight. In Hong Kong they are horrendous, in Singapore merely sky-high.*[3]

But it is not cost alone. Sydney has a cheap but highly skilled and highly educated labour force, expatriate executives are attracted to the city for its schools, up-to-date communications systems, spacious golf courses, beaches, hedonistic pleasures and manageable costs of living. Bruce Beaver captures some of Sydney's charm:

Watching Rushcutter's bright bayful of masts and coloured keels,
Half-sensing Dufy's muse walking on that gull, sail
And cobalt sky reflecting surface,
I open my senses to the gift of it and hear
The yacht club telecommunication paging
A Mr Fairweather over the water.[4]

The attraction of IBM for the NSW government is the 189 skilled jobs that the operation was expected to create initially, with more expected to follow, together with downstream jobs in businesses servicing the corporation. Most of these are likely to be long term, and to generate export income from computer software. Significantly, IBM — playing the good corporate citizen — decided to split its investment between Sydney and Melbourne so as to soften the perception of dependence on foreign capital and to maintain access to possible state government contracts. Sydney–Melbourne rivalry, at a time when Sydney has been gaining the upper hand, is assuaged simultaneously. Although the location split is political, as Smark put it, 'the underlying sums [in favour of Australia] are not political at all'.

Sydney's annual Gay and Lesbian Mardi Gras is a key signifier of this subculture's flamboyant presence in the city. The event symbolises the much vaunted (and highly contestable) tolerance of Australian society to social difference. The Mardi Gras ranks with Armistead Maupin's widely read tales of San Francisco as an internationally acclaimed marker of gay political activism and liberation. As the *Sydney Morning Herald* put it: 'what started in 1978 as a protest street march for gay rights to mark the anniversary of the Stonewall protests in New York the year before has become a major celebration of gay and lesbian culture'.

The commodification of gay culture, as a sales pitch for Sydney to attract domestic and international tourists, extends the significance of Mardi Gras well beyond a celebration of marginalised sexualities or a voyeuristic curiosity for Sydneysiders. The Mardi Gras is now deployed as an event to be embraced and encouraged as it has direct and indirect economic benefits to many outside the gay and lesbian scene. Surveys conducted during the 1993 Mardi Gras estimated that the event generated $38 million of expenditure.[5] Of this, $26 million was spent within the boundaries of south Sydney and Sydney City local government areas. The Mardi Gras attracted more international and interstate visitors than any of the major cultural festivals in Sydney, Melbourne, Perth and Adelaide, earning QANTAS something like $1.5 million. And while both the Grand Prix — the motor cycle race then at Eastern Creek in Sydney, and the Formula One car race in Adelaide — may have attracted more international visitors, they spent less than those attending the Mardi Gras.[6] International visitors spent close to $6 million, and of all these events the 1993 Mardi Gras had the greatest impact on the Australian economy, despite almost no public subsidy ($50 000 from Sydney City

Council in 1993). Other major festivals and special events are typically subsidised by up to 30 per cent of total expenditure by organisers. It brings an ironic twist to the current climate of self-help entrepreneurialism when the stigmatised 'other' has become financially holier than the mainstream.

The IBM and Mardi Gras cases illustrate the two main targets of contemporary city marketing.[7] Integral to official discourses on place marketing is the notion that the competitive advantages of cities have shifted markedly. Sirens which attracted tourists and investors in the past have now lost their power or sing less sweetly. Like an ageing Thespian seeking to arrest a career on the slide, facelifts, new make-up, anatomical reconstructions, and a new agent, are the order of the day. The verbal and visual texts which frame representations of Sydney as an ideal site for international business headquarters, and as a must-visit destination on the international tourist trail, warrant close inspection.

SELLING SYDNEY TO TOURISTS

The number of tourists visiting Australia increased by over a million, to 2.2 million, between 1980 and 1990, at an annual growth rate of 9.4 per cent and is expected to hit 7 million by 2003. Massive world growth in international travel derives from business trips associated with globalisation of the production of goods and services and the resulting expansion of international trade. Growth also stems from burgeoning affluence in high growth economies including, increasingly, those of East and South-East Asia. Asian countries have become a major source of tourism to Australia and governments are bending over backwards to encourage and capitalise on it. Including Japan, Asian nations accounted for 37 per cent of the tourists in 1990, compared with 15 per cent in 1980. Of all visitors, 56 per cent were on holiday in Australia, 21 per cent were visiting friends and relatives and 10 per cent were travelling on business.

Australia sells itself to tourists through images of nature, the 'raw', the untouched 'other' — the Great Barrier Reef, Kakadu in Arnhem Land, Uluru in the Red Centre, and the dramatic outback vastness. Though these quintessential elements of the country's stock of tourist attractions are, especially in Queensland and the Northern Territory, significant sources of job creation and business opportunity, it is the larger cities — primarily Sydney — that are the key sites. Business travellers descend on the cities, and immigrants receive friends and relatives on visits from their old countries, particularly in Sydney and Melbourne where 60 per cent of Australia's overseas-born population lives, while to Asian visitors cities offer the culture of shopping and consumption not found in the Australian outback.

Of all Australian cities, Sydney is by far the top tourist destination, with about one-third of international tourist nights being spent there. Melbourne, in contrast, attracts about 15 per cent, while Brisbane and Perth are but a pale reflection. The reasons for Sydney's dominance are simple enough. As the national hub of international air traffic, and as the site of the fabled Harbour Bridge and Opera House, Sydney is unquestionably the best known Australian city internationally. The scale of business travel marks Sydney's emergence as an international commercial hub and its relative and strengthening dominance over other Australian cities. Sydney has attracted a high proportion of immigrants to Australia which has multiplier effects when friends and relatives come to visit. While Melbourne and Sydney attracted roughly equal shares of immigrants in the 1950s and 1960s, the trend with recent immigrants has favoured Sydney,[8] and this again means more tourists. Sydney's dominance also derives from the strength of its education system, since foreign students studying in Australia are visited by friends and relatives. Unlike tourists and immigrants, foreign students, of whom there now some 60 000 in Australia, are distributed more in proportion to the populations of the capital cities. Indeed Brisbane, Perth and Adelaide each have shares of foreign students somewhat larger than their respective shares of national population.

These various forms of linkage, with the high growth Asian economies in particular, are mutually reinforcing and work to Sydney's advantage. Take, for example, the case of an ethnic-Chinese Malaysian citizen who comes to Australia for her tertiary education. After returning to Malaysia she works in a company investing in the Sydney property market. She sends her children to Australia for their education. Perhaps the family then emigrates. When the children complete university studies their relatives may visit Australia for the graduation. These linkages have a synergistic effect in diffusing the perceptual knowledge of Sydney, which in turn encourages more immigrants, investors, students and tourists. An official in the Australian Education Centre in Hong Kong noted that among potential students: 'Sydney is the sort of place of golden opportunity. I would say that most people here, particularly more mature students, particularly postgraduates, about 70 per cent of them want Sydney before anything else … Sydney is probably the only place they have heard of'.[9]

On top of, and reinforcing, the dramatic increase in international tourist arrivals are 'hallmark' events, most obviously the 2000 Olympics and, on a lesser scale, the Gay and Lesbian Mardi Gras and the Motor Cycle Grand Prix. These events not only bring in tourist dollars, and the jobs and business opportunities that those dollars create, they also provide international media opportunities to sell Sydney's charms in the global marketplace. Holidaying tourists are obviously more susceptible than other travellers to images of places when they choose their destinations. Travel is about fantasy, the imaginary, the promise of new experience and possibilities. The representation of places through advertising thus assumes major significance in economic development strategies. The Australian Tourism Commission and the tourism bureaucracies of state governments expend substantial resources to sell Australia as a tourist destination. But what is being sold? To what extent does the sales imagery match what people desire and what is actually on offer?

The stereotypical view of Australia from the outside excludes cities in favour of exotic wildlife, surf, tropical forests and the dramatic outback. Playing on this imagery, an Australian Tourism Commission brochure distributed in Asian cities presents Sydney as a gateway to what is represented as the real Australia:

Tourists come to see Sydney and travellers go beyond — into the experiences that are Australia. Sydney is surrounded by National Parks — not the sort that allow farming or settlements, but true wilderness areas where our native plants and animals thrive ... Beyond Sydney's ring of greenery the expansive outback stretches westwards ... Come and experience the Australia you have come to love through TV and films! *The Man from Snowy River*, Coca-Cola's sky surfer and XXXX's Outback advertisements ... 'The Flying Doctors', 'Neighbours'.[10]

The 'real' traveller will clearly not linger in Sydney but will merely use the city as a staging point from which to explore the 'authentic' Australia. The problem, of course, is that the construction of Australia as a vast outback, populated by self-sufficient, down to earth people and exotic native fauna, not phoney, degenerate city dwellers, denies the fact that most of the nation's population lives in large cities. At the 1991 census, 61 per cent lived in the state capitals, Canberra and Darwin, with one-fifth in Sydney alone. Yet 'travellers', those who despise commodified culture, are more likely to be influenced by the *Lonely Planet Guide* than by Australian Tourism Commission brochures.

The marketeers, especially in the Asian growth economies, now acknowledge that the cities themselves are important destinations rather than mere stopovers on the way to the 'real' Australia. Yet, where Sydney is projected as a tourist destination in its own right, the sales rhetoric still contains every cliché imaginable:

> *Sydney is all you would expect it to be and more. There are a million more diamonds sparkling on Sydney Harbour than you could ever imagine, the sails on the Opera House really do seem to hover between the water and the city skyline, and the Harbour Bridge is even more dramatic than it looks in pictures. But the most stunning thing about Sydney is what lies behind the picture-postcard images ... genuine hospitality, English that is not quite English, an ancient history steeped in the Dreamtime, a modern history steeped in struggle and a contemporary lifestyle based on the finer things in life.*[11]

The final issue of *Share the Spirit*, one of the Sydney Olympic Bid Committee's products, deployed similar hyperbole but was rather more upbeat and geared to an audience of well-travelled International Olympic Committee members and business travellers: 'Sydney voted top city to do business in: Asian businessmen reckon Sydney is the easiest city in the world to do business in'.[12] A striking feature of this document is its focus on Sydney's multicultural character: 'Sydney says "welcome!" in many languages'. Two pages are devoted to ethnic Australia, including a whole page showing numbers of people by birthplace. Multiculturalism is deployed as a marketing strategy. As an Australian immigration officer based in Hong Kong said: 'We push the line of multiculturalism at a million miles an hour'. The sophisticated young couple on the

Australia Now

VOLUME 14 NUMBER 2 1991

Selling Sydney to tourists, (Source: Australian Tourist Commission, 1991).

cover of another Australian Tourism Commission brochure make this point in another way. The man is unambiguously Asian but dressed with casual (western) elegance, topped by an Akubra-style hat. The woman is ambiguously exotic, probably southern European, possibly Eurasian, elegance vying with sex in an off-the-shoulder simulated lizard-skin sheath.

But what is the perspective from Asia as opposed to that represented in local texts? Although booming, the Asian tourist market is still relatively new. As a consequence, most people travel in tour groups rather than independently as free and independent travellers or, in tourist industry discourse, FITS. What tourists see is thus to some extent determined by tours. It is now clearly recognised by marketeers of tourism that the stereotyped images of Australia as a tourist destination need to be modified so as to attract continued growth: 'The Australian Tourism Commission is ... working very hard to let Asian markets understand that Australia is a hell of a lot more than wide open spaces, kangaroos, koalas, Qantas and Ayers Rock'.[13]

There are three 1990s themes emerging in Australian Tourism Commission advertising in Asia: 'Fun in the sun' primarily signifies the Queensland coast and resorts; 'Cultural discovery' involves the promotion of more Asian-oriented sites in Australia, such as Chinatowns in Sydney and Melbourne and dragon-boat races; the third theme, 'City glamour', highlights sophisticated night life, shopping and entertainment. Since shopping in Singapore and Hong Kong has become so expensive with the reversal of the economic balance, Australian shopping is a considerable attraction.

What marketeers call 'bragging rights' are important in the Asian tourism market. As one tourist official based in Hong Kong put it: 'If you've got a picture of yourself in front of an internationally recognisable building, or structure, or monument, or whatever, you can show that to somebody and say, see, I've done that. And that is a very important thing. It's a thread which runs through all Asian markets'.

Although Australia is still relatively unfamiliar to South-East Asian tourists, Sydney has the image of the fastest and most sophisticated of Australian cities. But what is sophisticated and exciting? The answer according to the Australian Tourism Commission officer in Hong Kong is: 'Shiny buildings, bright neon lights, traffic jams, the sort of tension of the fast pace, shopping available 'til late at night, nightclubs, karaoke, etc. ... everything that is glitzy, shiny, sparkly'.[14] Paradoxically, 'Western tourists have stopped visiting Singapore in large numbers because they say that "local culture is being destroyed and is being replaced by all these skyscrapers and it looks like any other city in the world". Yet this is precisely what Asian visitors want to see'. Sites such as Uluru (Ayers Rock) are well known internationally, and hence notionally desirable, but the whole concept of the wide open spaces is alien to many tourists, and big city dwellers in particular. A new travellers guide produced by the Australian Tourism Commission has no pictures of empty beaches, beautiful blue skies and palm trees. People, it is argued, would be anxious because nobody is there.

'AND THE WINNER IS SYDNEY!'

The importance of 'hallmark events' to the short and longer term economic benefit of a city is illustrated by the Gay and Lesbian Mardi Gras. But the biggest of all global spectacles is the Olympic Games which Sydney captured to mark the opening of the new millennium. Writing of the 1996 Atlanta games, Stephen Roulac pointed out that:

> *Perhaps no other event in contemporary society equals the impact of the Olympic games on a region's economy, sense of self and perceived role in the world community … By hosting the Summer Olympics in 1996, Atlanta will have the chance to strut its stuff in the global place market.*[15]

Similar arguments were deployed for Sydney — though they are hotly contested — particularly by Greenpeace who submitted an alternative bid for the Olympics. Hard-headed economists outside of state government have also looked anxiously at the losses incurred in other host cities. Such events may not, in themselves, ensure instant prosperity for the city affected. What is relevant are broader issues of sustained long-term economic viability and social harmony, as is vividly demonstrated by the racial tensions and economic divisions characterising Los Angeles in the years following the Olympics there. As Roulac put it:

> *The pageantry of the Olympic celebration is no substitute for the fundamentals of place appeal: as a place to live and work, with an educated and motivated work force, accessible and affordable housing, effective transit systems, responsive government that does not impose undue restrictions and burdensome taxes on business, and overall quality of life.*[16]

Los Angeles is not the only city to see adverse effects. Much of the Barcelona Olympic village remains empty, with facilities under used or abandoned. Though hosting the Olympics means worldwide media exposure and a boost for the city in the public imagination, what remains when the cameras, sports people and spectators are gone is anyone's guess. Though Sydney sold itself on a 'Share the Spirit' slogan, implying community and togetherness, already voices of dissent are ringing loud and clear. Anti-Aboriginal policies of the national Howard government, and its cuts to public expenditure, have precipitated moves to use the Olympics as a stage for resistance. While the rest of the world looks on, plans to expose the hypocrisy of Australia's self-presentation as a multicultural and just society are afoot. One idea circulating is to crowd out public transport, which is already feared inadequate, from the city to the Homebush site. If the current Liberal–National party government in Canberra continues to undermine Aboriginal rights, and to perpetuate income inequalities and social–spatial divisions across the city, Sydney may live to regret its eagerness to win the Games and thereby bear the brunt of widespread dissatisfaction with national government policies.

PLACE MARKETING AND THE BUILT ENVIRONMENT

Growth in tourism to Sydney has produced or been used to justify marked changes to the city's built environment. A large stock of tourist accommodation has been built and the design of tourist hot spots has been improved. While some of these changes may be socially benign, others have a negative aspect which is usually discounted by governments in pursuit of the tourist dollar. The Darling Harbour redevelopment on the western edge of Sydney's CBD, and tourist developments in beach-side suburbs, are cases in point.

The redevelopment in the 1980s of the disused railway goods yards at Darling Harbour into a waterside pleasure gardens with exhibition and conference centres, was based on foreign models and aimed at boosting the city centre's attractiveness to tourists. The redevelopment generated considerable controversy. Planning control was removed from the Sydney City Council and vested in the Darling Harbour Authority so as to prevent what the New South Wales government represented as the parochial and slow-turning wheels of the council from inhibiting redevelopment. Any grassroots democratic involvement in the redevelopment was thus precluded. A lot of public money was spent on the redevelopment and issues of cost effectiveness, not yet settled, were raised. No part of the site was used, as local lobby groups requested, for much-needed inner city public housing. Apart from any questions of financial return, the state government asserted that public housing would detract from an area set up to attract affluent tourists.

Sydney's beaches, especially Bondi, are central to the city's image for tourists. The increasing value of building sites adjacent to the beaches has resulted in changes which are often not popular with residents. At Coogee Beach, to the south of Bondi, in the late 1980s the Oceanic Hotel was demolished to make way for a Holiday Inn. But the new building was higher and bulkier than the New South Wales government's planning guidelines allowed for. In spite of vocal local objections, the state government changed the rules to enable the development to proceed. In the same locality Randwick Council has spent large sums of money refurbishing the beach front. Again it was a mixed blessing for local residents; the closure of Beach Street redirected a lot of traffic onto surrounding streets, causing massive local protests, but these were ignored by the council.

At Bondi the gentrification of what until the 1980s had been a large stock of predominantly 1920s blocks of flats, occupied on a private rental basis by low-income earners, has been a hotbed of local contention.

Until 1983, the Gelato Bar — famous for its strudel, poppyseed cake and chicken soup, rather than its style — was the only café on the beach. The opening of the Lamrock Café, with its glass walls and up-beat brasserie menu, marked the beginning of Bondi café culture. A decade later, all but the most tenacious of stores have been replaced by groovy surf shops and by cafes and restaurants with menus and names revamped overnight to capture the fickle but discerning foodies.

Darling Harbour at work, (Source: Frank Hurley, 1948, Sydney: A Camera Study, *Angus & Robertson, Sydney).*

Darling Harbour at play, August 1995.

There is no doubt that the upgrading of commercial facilities on the Bondi beach front has accelerated the gentrification process. Anne Susskind reported in the *Sydney Morning Herald* that for Bondi's low income renters:

> the news [about the up-grading of Bondi's main street, Campbell Parade] is bad — increased rents are likely to squeeze them out. Already, many low-income households have been under financial pressure, and some specific population groups have moved from the area.[17]

Yet the keepers of boutiques, smart restaurants and tourists hotels are pleased to see the original inhabitants depart because the tone of the area is seen as being more attractive to tourists.

The gentrification of Bondi has been a twin-edged sword in another respect. With drunken youths on the rampage at Christmas 1995, and the senseless killing of an English tourist, Brian Hagland, by two local men in a Bondi street in September 1996, for many this quintessential image of Australia has lost its innocence.

The writer Robert Drewe reminisced about his 1950s childhood Christmas day swim at Bondi in the *Sydney Morning Herald* of 14 September 1996:

> The nature of the day meant the beach would usually be deserted, except for a few kids trying out their Christmas-present boards and flippers. These crystalline days gave us a peculiarly Australian and not inappropriate joy. It was like a pantheists version of going to church ... never, until the gentrification of Bondi began some 10 years ago, did it seem dangerous any time of the day or night. New Years' Eve was as safe as Saturday at midday.

Following the Hagland murder, a moral panic pushed aside such romantic nostalgia. In its place we read of the increase in local assaults from 187 incidents in June–December 1994 to 237 incidents for the same period in the following year.

SELLING SYDNEY TO BUSINESS

Cities sell themselves on existing attributes or on new qualities created by government and private sector investment. These points of competitive advantage may be tangible, like airports or waterfront redevelopments, or they may consist of less definable, but no less important, subjective drawcards, such as an atmosphere of tolerance to difference, or an image of political stability. Over time there are shifts and changes in the importance of both tangible and intangible qualities. City-marketing experts stress 'perceptual knowledge' of a city in the target markets as an essential prerequisite for economic growth. A city's selling points need to be identified and enhanced by governments if city-marketing efforts are to pay off.

The discourse of city marketing, and the new economics of competitive advantage which underpin it, exhort city governments to move with the times or be left behind.

Early spring, Bondi Beach, August 1995.

The Zeitgeist is entrepreneurialism, an anything-is-possible mentality which casts politicians and government workers as dynamic players in the restructuring of their urban economies. They are encouraged to take a 'devil take the hindmost' attitude towards competing cities. This discourse has been fostered and, to a large degree, disseminated by a new industry of place marketing advisers.[18]

Marketing strategy reports for Sydney and promotional material targeted at transnational corporations offer good examples of this discourse. The standard line is that city enterprises need skilled labour, access to advanced technology, venture and investment capital, appropriate physical infrastructure and a desirable quality of life in order to compete in global markets. Apart from venture and investment capital, which are limited, all these requirements are present in Australia.

Knowledge is seen as the key — a far more significant factor in the production of goods and services in the late twentieth century than it used to be.[19] An example from the field of legal services is a small business which deals only with customers in Sydney and needs advice on contracts with its suppliers. Although the advice is professional, it is relatively simple and routine. In contrast, a transnational corporation setting up in a foreign country needs advice on the local legal system. The level of complexity of advice, and its price relative to other factors of production, is likely to be much greater

Sydney central business district and Circular Quay in the 1940s, (Source: Frank Hurley, 1948, Sydney: A Camera Study, *Angus & Robertson, Sydney).*

Sydney central business district and Circular Quay in the 1990s, August 1995.

for a transnational company. A simple example from manufacturing would be wheel-balancing on a motor vehicle. In the past the balance was done subjectively by a mechanic's trained eye. Today a machine, incorporating sophisticated electronics, will do the job. The level and complexity of knowledge embodied in the machine is far greater than that embodied in the training and experience of the mechanic.

Robert Reich gives the label 'symbolic analysts' to workers involved in the production of knowledge for use in the production of goods and other services.[20] They, or the businesses that they run, or that employ them, are prime targets for city marketeers. Many are employed in the transnational corporations (TNCs) which, since the Second World War, have come to dominate the global economy. TNCs have headquarter and regional headquarter operations (HQs and RHQs) in different countries to perform their 'command and control' functions. These themselves need to be 'produced' through the purchase of 'producer services' ranging from advanced services such as legal, accounting, tax, computing and marketing, to lower-order activities like office cleaning and data entry. There thus emerges around HQs and RHQs a cluster of what Saskia Sassen labelled 'producer services complexes'.[21] All these workers spend money in a city's economy and induce further rounds of job creation.

According to marketing hype from the New South Wales government, Sydney is well placed to attract command and control and producer services jobs in competition with other Australian and international cities. It has a substantial work force of business professionals and many Sydney-based accounting, law, management consulting and data management firms have the international experience and expertise needed to service international financial markets. Partly for this reason Sydney has emerged as the preferred Australian — and increasingly regional — base for multinational business services firms operating in the Asia–Pacific region. Compared with that in international cities, Sydney's professional labour force is cheap to hire. An accountant in Sydney might cost $55 000 a year but $75 000 in Hong Kong or Singapore. There are similar differentials in wages for office managers, systems analysts, engineers and plant managers.[22]

Sydney also has five universities and several international schools where students can follow international and Australian curriculums, a consideration for expatriate professionals and business personnel who might only be working in Australia for a few years. The perceived high quality of Australian secondary and tertiary education also attracts educational exports, thus further boosting the city's economy. Sydney is not unique in these respects — other Australian cities have similar facilities — but in terms of variety Sydney is strong.

In this game of attracting business, good quality standard infrastructure — for personal and goods transportation, water and energy supply, and waste disposal — and advanced infrastructure that supports specific industry needs are also stressed. High quality, uninterruptable sources of electricity, effective mass transit and high-speed personal communications are examples. But the buzz phrase today is the information superhighway. Advanced communications systems must be available to link industry clusters to markets and sources of information around the world.

The state government has not been slow to catch on. A marketing brochure points out that Sydney-based companies benefit from direct, reliable access to global facilities and trading systems using the city's modern international telecommunications networks. Telstra, the Commonwealth-owned (but soon to be privatised) domestic and overseas telecommunications carrier, is claimed to offer: 'comprehensive geographical coverage, price stability, operational integration and technical strength, and close to 100 per cent service availability and reliability. While Australia's domestic telecommunications network includes the world's most extensive high-capacity optical-fibre system'. These of course are shared with other Australian cities and international competitors, but without them Sydney's competitive edge would be challenged.

Another selling point for Sydney is argued to be its longitudinal position. Because it is the first international financial centre to open for trading each day it occupies a strategic time zone spanning the closing of the American markets and the opening of those in Europe. In government brochure-speak: 'this strategic position provides the foundation of a financial centre with world class attributes'. Given that Australia is in much the same time zone as East and South-East Asia it makes doing business, especially via telephones, easier than from east to west. Ease of business travel, nationally, and internationally, also matters. While good levels of (especially international) connections are available from several Australian cities, Sydney is the prime hub of international air traffic into and out of Australia. Kingsford Smith Airport is serviced by more than forty international airlines offering 500 flights a week to more than 100 destinations — nonstop to the United States, Japan, Korea, Hong Kong and South-East Asia, and one-stop to the United Kingdom and Europe. Against vociferous opposition, the capacity of Sydney Airport was expanded with the opening of a third runway in mid-1994.

Cultural connections between actual or potential trading partners are another piece of the jigsaw. An example here is the symbiotic and dynamic relationship which is evolving between Hong Kong, a command and control centre and conduit of investment capital, and the explosive growth of manufacturing in the adjacent Pearl River Delta of China. There is a parallel relationship between the United States and Mexico. Less tightly symbiotic and not as strongly based on shared culture is the relationship between Australia and the Asian growth economies. Here discourses of multiculturalism, and the high number of Asian immigrants to Sydney in particular, are deployed by Australian and New South Wales governments to stress cultural continuities, while Australia's closeness to Asia relative to Europe and the United States is argued to give it an advantage in attracting business headquarters and tourists. In a very practical sense Sydney's dominance as the preferred point of settlement for recent immigrants to Australia has produced a great variety in language skills. For example, at the 1991 Census, 126 400 peo-

Selling Sydney in South-East Asia, (Source: Sing Tao Newspaper, *12 April, 1996).*

ple spoke Chinese dialects at home in New South Wales compared with 76 369 in Victoria. There were 16 433 Korean speakers in New South Wales, 81.7 per cent of the Australian total, and 11 372 Japanese speakers, 40.3 per cent of the national total. In Victoria there were 1364 Korean speakers and 4733 Japanese speakers.

A good quality of life is seen as the icing on the cake in attracting international business to a city, and Sydney is represented in marketing hyperbole as a clear winner here. The Harbour, iconographic Bridge and Opera House provide the city's CBD with a spectacular setting for its office accommodation. While expensive compared with other Australian cities, commercial rents are low compared with Asian competitors. Similarly, Sydney's residential accommodation is, in international although not national terms, of reasonable cost. For example, average monthly rentals for executive housing in 1995 were A$2700 in Sydney, compared with A$1500 in Brisbane and A$1300 in Melbourne. In Singapore, however, the figure was A$11 447 and in Hong Kong A$18 355. And it is not just a matter of cost. As Citibank Australia's chairman eulogised in a *Business Review Weekly* article in 1990: 'it is possible to live in green countryside only 20 minutes away from the central city, and be totally relaxed. That's virtually impossible to do in London, New York or Hong Kong'.[23]

Sydney operates on a globally competitive stage where all these things become crucial in the fight for investment and business. The Big Three global cities are generally considered to be London, New York and Tokyo. Because of their established roles as business centres, and their geographical locations, their preeminence seems unlikely to be threatened in the foreseeable future. A notch below these three are many cities vying with each other for rungs near the top of the ladder. In the Asia–Pacific region Sydney's competition comes primarily from Hong Kong and Singapore and, within Australia, from Melbourne and to a lesser extent Perth and Brisbane. Hong Kong and Singapore have the obvious advantage of being at the hub of the Asian growth economies, where relatively low personal and company taxation levels are in place. But these advantages are offset by ever-reducing telecommunications costs, high-quality air links from Australia, and by specific disadvantages compared with Sydney. Office rents, housing prices and costs of professional and managerial labour favour Sydney. As Peter Smark wrote of Singapore: 'As the local currency strengthens, rents soar and local skilled salaries jump, the supermarket with a scent of satay offers few bargains for outsiders'. And, of Bangkok: '[i]n pollution, traffic congestion and availability of top education and medical services, it may not be Hell but it certainly gives Purgatory a nudge'.[24]

While Sydney lags well behind Hong Kong and Singapore as a site for RHQs, in the field of business services Sydney is now the preferred location. Of the regional head offices of the top twenty firms in four sectors — accounting, advertising, management consulting and international real estate — 39 per cent are in Sydney. Ten per cent are in the other Australian states and the remainder are split between Hong Kong (32 per cent), Tokyo (13 per cent) and Singapore (6 per cent).[25] In 1994, of thirty-two RHQs setting up in Australia, twenty-one chose Sydney and seven Melbourne.[26] In the year to July 1996 more than 40 RHQs set up in Sydney, 63 per cent of them from the United States. According to the Minister for State and Regional Development, 'these developments have generated $A1.78 billion in investment and over 4000 jobs for the people of New South Wales'.[27] Both perceptually and literally, Sydney is Australia's international gateway. More than 1.1 million overseas business visitors arrive annually through Sydney's international airport. This is crucial to the city's competitive advantage, as is the range of services which Sydney's size enables its economy to provide to its businesses and residents. These initial advantages are being brazenly capitalised on in the late twentieth century through the transformation of Sydney in market-driven but government accentuated ways.

Over the last two decades Sydney has ousted 'marvellous Melbourne' as the financial capital of Australia and as the nation's corporate headquarters. By the early 1980s, seventy-three of the ninety-four representative offices of overseas banks were headquartered in Sydney and only six in Melbourne. In merchant banking, forty-one of the fifty-five in Australia had headquarters in Sydney as well as sixteen of the twenty-four major finance companies. Of the top 100 companies in Australia fifty-two had their headquarters in Sydney in 1978 compared with thirty-eight in Melbourne, reversing the proportions of 1953. In 1983, 100 of the top 200 companies in Australia were in Sydney and seventy in Melbourne.[28] Sydney is also strong in insurance — headquarters for example, of the AMP Society, Australia's largest insurance company — with a virtual monopoly in the growing futures and options trading business. In the post-deregulation era since the early 1980s, most new foreign banks, particularly the Japanese, moving into Australia chose Sydney as their headquarters with Sydney home to 85 per cent of merchant banks, a dominance underlined by the decision of the Australian Merchant Bankers' Association to move to the city.[29] The reversal of Melbourne's long-established preeminence over Sydney as Australia's business capital has created anxiety in the southern capital, caught in the caption of a *Sydney Morning Herald* article: 'Melbourne loses grip on power'.[30]

One rough measure of jobs associated with business command and control functions and producer services is the number of people employed in finance, property and business services (FPBS). The number of jobs in this sector in Australia has grown massively since the 1970s, but the regional distribution of growth has varied markedly. Of the capital cities, Sydney gained 120 000 jobs between 1971 and 1991 and Melbourne was next with 80 000. The 1991 shares of Australian jobs in this sector for those two cities were much greater than their shares of national population, reflecting their roles as headquarter sites for national and international business and associated producer services. At the same time, the figures reflect Sydney's takeover of Melbourne's traditional role. In Sydney in 1991, FPBS jobs comprised over 15 per cent of the work force, the highest percentage in Australia, while in Melbourne the figure was just below 13 per cent.[31] Although Brisbane and Perth are getting to population levels at which agglomeration economies are substantial, and there is a steady accumulation of some command and control functions, they are likely to remain in Sydney's shadow for a long time.

THE SALES FORCE

Both the federal and state governments are acutely aware of the economic advantages of attracting both Australian-controlled TNCs, and especially RHQs of foreign-owned corporations, and actively seek to lure such operations to Australia and to particular cities. Two recent reports — from the Australian Financial Centre and the Sydney Financial Centre — highlighted public policy measures required to enhance prospects.[32] The attraction of transnational RHQs and offshore banking units (OBUs) was the particular focus of both reports. Although the Sydney Financial Centre report is designed to boost Sydney's prospects, it is interesting that no attempt was made to examine the advantages of Sydney relative to other Australian cities. The presumption seems to be that there is no real competition. If softening of tax imposts by the Australian government were the key to encouraging growth as both reports argued, then market forces, bolstered by enthusiastic state governments, were to determine where such activities located.

In the New South Wales Government, the Department of State and Regional Development has established an International Business Group to increase the participation and success of New South Wales in the international economy. An important part of its role is to attract international investment to the state. The International Business Group identifies international business opportunities and establishes priorities for exports. It works collaboratively with the department's industry groups and across New South Wales regions. It also develops and implements targeted programs to assist Sydney to become internationally competitive and increase exports or decrease imports. The group works closely with Austrade in the promotion of New South Wales overseas. It does a significant amount of information gathering and matching of local investment opportunities with visiting overseas delegations of government officials and business-people. It has offices in Japan and England. In short, the group works to promote New South Wales in key overseas markets and is working with the Australian Government on a major campaign to attract RHQs to Sydney. New South Wales recently introduced a program to provide newly establishing RHQs with a one-off tax rebate of $300 000. This amount can be applied to Financial Institutions Duty, Debits Tax, Loan Security and Conveyancing and Lease Duty. The Australian Government also provides a wider range of concessions.

In the period of Australian economic restructuring since the early 1970s, the discourse of 'boosterism' has firmly established itself in the world of urban planning. Sydney's 1988 metropolitan planning strategy reflected this: 'A major concern of the Metropolitan Strategy is to ensure that all appropriate measures are taken to encourage and promote the economic growth of the Sydney Region and the growth of employment in the Region'.

Flouting its confidence, it continues:

> The Sydney Region will maintain its dominant role in New South Wales both in economic and population terms. Sydney's emergence as the major financial business centre in Australia, its pre-eminence as destination of overseas migrants and its extensive national and international linkages will encourage continued growth.[33]

But what of the social costs which may arise from marketing campaigns and interstate competition? The question is increasingly forgotten. Subsidies are used as carrots to attract business, and the fact that the bidding war can produce locational outcomes which are less beneficial were the Australian government alone negotiating foreign capital, drops out of the picture. Nor is this a new problem since interstate competition has been going on since the nineteenth century when each colony, as they were then, selected different rail gauges to funnel trade into their own and away from the other colonies' ports. In the 1970s, New South Wales and Victoria virtually gave away electric power to entice foreignowned aluminium companies to set up refineries. Recently the Australian Government's Industry Commission conducted an inquiry into bidding wars and concluded the following:

> *States engage in competitive bidding for major investments and events because they perceive a gain for their State in terms of employment and income. Gains from providing assistance at the State level are largely an illusion. Most assistance has little or no positive effect on the welfare of Australians. States find it difficult to abstain because of the perceived economic and political cost of losing out to other States.*[34]

TRANSFORMING SPACE TO ENHANCE MARKETABILITY

The attraction to Sydney of HQs and RHQs and advanced producer services serves a number of interests. Governments gain when they deliver actual or even illusory economic benefits to their constituents. These may be in the form of cleaning jobs in five-star hotels or capital gains accrued by insurance companies with investments in CBD office space. But a city's wins in the marketing game are equivocal; there are negative outcomes from the physical manipulation of the built environment. The third runway at Sydney Airport is a prime example. Commissioned to cater for the rapidly growing demand for airline access to Sydney by enabling a greater number of aircraft movements, and by shifting the pattern of flight paths, many Sydneysiders now face deafening noise every few minutes. Conversation over a cappuccino in Leichhardt is punctuated by deafening roars, as the train of thought is interrupted. Passengers wave from the windows as the planes follow the line of Norton Street. While the very worst affected have been financially compensated to enable them to soundproof their houses, many others have not. The Australian government has decided that such adverse effects are the price that has to be paid (losers can never, realistically, be fully compensated), even arguing that the people affected will, in the longer term, benefit from the stronger economy created by the airport. Despite political resistance in the form of airport blockades and local campaigns the runway's use will continue.

Cathay Pacific Airlines' decision to relocate a major computer facility to Sydney is another such case. The site chosen, Norwest Business Park, in the leafy outer suburbs to the north-west of Sydney, is typical of commercial developments in the outer city, labelled 'edge cities' in the United States. Facilities like Cathay's, while bringing certain benefits, have a negative aspect. Unemployment rates are high in the western and south-western outer suburbs of Sydney. But jobs created in the north-west are inaccessible to the unemployed. Most of the technical and managerial jobs available at sites like Cathay Pacific do not match the skills of the unemployed. And, because cross-city public transport is poor or non-existent, the few lower-level service jobs (secretarial, data entry, security, cleaning — many of which are done by women — are difficult to get to from the areas of higher unemployment.[35] Other negative impacts of space transformation are the broader social outcomes in cities, like declining housing affordability and a growing welfare gap between those who benefit from the new economy and those who are marginal to it. These are considered in chapter 5.

PLACE MARKETING IS NOT NEW

A reader coming to notions of place marketing could easily form the impression from the virtual avalanche of texts on the subject that this is a very new activity for governments. This is hardly the case. Governments have always sought to attract investment and consumption expenditure to their cities. What has changed is the pace of this activity and the proliferation of new discourses of community development, local economic development and regional development planning. Central to this process have been the rapid pace and shifting geographical focuses of global economic restructuring since the 1970s, a process which has benefited some cities and disadvantaged others. Disadvantaged cities, such as those in the advanced capitalist world which built their prosperity on manufacturing industries in the first three-quarters of the twentieth century, have shed many jobs in the past quarter and have looked to their political and business leaders to find ways to resuscitate growth. Cities which have been advantaged by global shifts in economic force fields have actively sought to capitalise on their fortunes rather than wait passively for market forces to bring the new fruits of growth.

The previous monopolies of cities over their rural and small town hinterlands have been massively eroded with incursions by cities in the same country and also internationally. Whereas in the past, for example, far north Queensland was an isolated place for tourists to get to, the international airport at Cairns has made it possible for the region to tap into the booming growth in tourism from Asia, along with many competitors for this trade. What modern communications and transport systems imply is that places can no longer easily ignore competition because of the isolating effects of high transport and communications costs. The converse is that places are increasingly able to attract growth-generating investment and consumption flows which, in the past, would not have been conceivable.

David Harvey suggests that '[t]he task of urban governance is to lure highly mobile and flexible production, financial and consumption flows into its space'.[36] They can do this in three ways: they can use their own capacity to produce goods and services for local use or export, which may involve leaning on local labour forces to keep costs down and eliminate disruptive industrial action, a common strategy in the Asian growth economies; they can invest in infrastructure like airports and telecommunications systems; or they can offer direct state financial support for business in the form of tax holidays, loan guarantees and the like. A second broad strategy is to make cities better places to live and do business by building up-market recreational complexes, such as theatres and opera houses, or by the propagation of 'good' urban design in its many forms. The third strategy is to attract 'command and control functions' and associated producer services complexes and join the global city stage. Sydney has to a certain extent followed all these strategies since the mid-1970s. The city has sold itself to the world and the world has responded. But the question is — has Sydney sold itself short?

THE FUTURE: SYDNEY RULES, OK?

Sydney's capacity to continue attracting geographically, especially globally, mobile investment and consumption flows is a good bet. From a global perspective burgeoning economic growth in Asia, alongside persistent amenity and price (land and labour) differentials, together with further improvements in telecommunications and air travel (eventually supersonic) ought to sustain Sydney's claims against Hong Kong, Singapore and other Asian alternatives for a long time to come. Sydney's strong international image, alongside and integral to the cumulative impact of investment, trade and migration flows attracted so far will power a competitive edge into the foreseeable future. This may, however, be at a decreasing rate with more competition from other Australian cities.

Domestically, several shifts suggest that Sydney's dominance may decline. Well-publicised liveability problems have emerged in Sydney since the mid-1970s: air and water pollution, long journeys to work, traffic congestion, high costs of housing. Over the same period, employment and business opportunities and quality of life have substantially improved in places like Brisbane and Perth. As a result, for many years more people have left Sydney to live in other parts of Australia than have moved to Sydney. Population growth has been sustained by immigration and natural increase. Further deterioration of living conditions and increasing costs in Sydney can only accentuate this trend. While top-end businesses which can afford to may continue to prefer Sydney, as may tourists, increasing shares will go elsewhere. Image building by governments together with more savvy customers will propel places like Perth and Brisbane into greater roles. From a national viewpoint this 're-balancing' of Australia's settlement system is to be strongly encouraged.

Rod McGeogh, the main driver of Sydney's Olympic bid, has sounded this warning note:

> In helping sell Sydney some time ago, I became even more passionate about its beauty and the lifestyle it provides for its people. Yes, we are very lucky, but the city's natural advantages and the way we use them, will not alone always guarantee us pre-eminence in Australia or in our region. The strength of the city will ultimately depend upon a measure of unified support for it, which is evidenced in tangible attempts to create a greater sense of fraternity and understanding of all the stake holders and how we all interrelate … My sense of Sydney at the moment is that, as a result of our natural advantages and our successes such as winning the Olympics, a complacency is afoot which cities such as Melbourne are taking advantage of to reassert their own position and which, beyond 2000, we may have cause to regret.[37]

Notes

1 *Sydney Morning Herald*, 16 June 1994.

2 ibid., 4 June 1994.

3 ibid., 16 June 1994.

4 Bruce Beaver, 'Angel's Weather', in J. Tranter and P. Mead 1991, *The Penguin Book of Modern Australian Poetry*, Penguin, Melbourne, p. 149.

5 I. Marsh & J. Greenfield 1993, *Sydney Gay and Lesbian Mardi Gras: An Evaluation of its Economic Impact*, Australian Graduate School of Management UNSW, Sydney.

6 Melbourne has since recaptured both the Motor Cycle and F1 Grand Prix. The sense of this sort of interstate competition has, however, been sharply questioned by the Industry Commission, 1996, *State, Territory and Local Government Assistance to Industry*, Canberra.

7 It needs to be recognised that while much attention is given to business services and high technology manufacturing in contemporary city growth strategies, other sectors are important. The so-called 'high touch' industries are also important. They include clothing, fashion accessories and the media. *The Sydney Morning Herald* of 20 January 1996 carried an article headlined 'Cities fight it out for fashion capital crown': 'It has been dubbed the war of the frocks. In the Melbourne–Sydney battle for title of Australian fashion capital, key players in each city are boasting that their big event will be the premier date on the fashion calendar.' Rupert Murdoch's Foxtel production facility at Sydney's former Showground site at Moore Park is a major example of this trend and was hard-fought for by the NSW government.

8 In 1991 Sydney had 28.5 per cent and Melbourne 23.7 per cent of total overseas-born persons. The figures for recent overseas born — those who came to Australia between 1986 and 1991 — were 36.2 per cent and 23.5 per cent respectively. More than this, since much of the tourism now comes from Asia, and since Asians are increasingly significant part of the immigrant inflow, Sydney should be increasingly favoured by friends and relatives tourism. See L. Dwyer, I. Burnley, P. Forsyth, & P. Murphy 1993, *Tourism–Immigration Interrelationships*, AGPS, Canberra.

9 Interview by the authors at Australian Education Centre, Hong Kong, 9 December 1993.

10 NSW Tourism in cooperation with Austravel n.d., *Australia: Sydney and Beyond*, p. 3.

11 ibid.

12 *Share the Spirit*, September 1993.

13 Interview by the authors at Australian Tourism Commission, Hong Kong, 10 December 1993.

14 ibid.

15 *The Futurist*, November–December 1993, pp. 18–19.

16 ibid.

17 *Sydney Morning Herald*, 16 September 1996.

18   A book entitled *The Economics of Amenity*, published in 1985 by Robert McNulty, principal of the firm, Partners for Liveable Places, Washington DC, was a landmark of this trend. City marketing has been good global business.

19   See Manuel Castells 1991, *Informational City*, Blackwell, Oxford. Robert Reich's widely read 1991 book, *The Work of Nations*, Simon & Schuster, London, has also dealt, in more intellectually accessible terms, with this process.

20   Reich, op. cit., chs. 14, 15.

21   S. Sassen 1991, *The Global City*, Princeton University Press, New Jersey.

22   NSW Department of State and Regional Development 1996, *New South Wales Competitiveness Report*.

23   Tim Blue 1990, 'Nation's powerhouse leads the recovery', *Business Review Weekly*, 5 June.

24   *Sydney Morning Herald*, 16 June 1994.

25   Blue, op. cit.

26   NSW Department of State Development 1994, 'RHQs Announced/Established Since last Year', in-house list supplied to authors.

27   Letter from the minister accompanying release of *NSW Competitiveness Report* 1996.

28   M. T. Daly 1988, 'Australian cities: the challenge of the 1980s.' *Australian Geographer*, vol. 19, p. 154.

29   Blue, op. cit.

30   *Sydney Morning Herald*, 17 November 1992.

31   FPBS is not a particularly satisfactory measure of the internationalisation of the Australian economy since many of the jobs included in this sector are related to population size and have nothing to do with global activities. Real estate, for example, is both very localised and an international service. The same is true of banking and business services.

32   Sydney Financial Centre May 1992, *Sydney Financial Centre Taskforce Report*: ;Australian Financial Centre Committee 1992, *Developing Australia as an International Financial Centre*.

33   NSW Department of Environment and Planning 1988, *Sydney Into its Third Century: Metropolitan Strategy for the Sydney Region*, Sydney.

34   ibid., note 5, p. xi.

35   P. Murphy, & R. Freestone 1994, 'Towards edge city: business re-centralisation and post-suburban Sydney', ch. 8 in K. Gibson & S. Watson, (eds), *Metropolis Now*, Pluto Press, Sydney.

36   D. Harvey 1989, 'Urban places in the global village: reflections on the urban condition in late twentieth century capitalism', in L. Mazza, (ed.), *World Cities and the Future of Metropoles*, Electa, XVII Triennale, pp. 21–32.

37   *Sydney Morning Herald*, 23 August 1996.

4 GAY SITES AND THE PINK DOLLAR[1]

Gays in Sydney occupy space both publicly and privately. Publicly, they are manifest through community action such as processions of celebration or of protest, and through the thriving commercial provisions for the community. Privately, they occupy space as residents either in concentrations, largely in the inner suburbs, or in an amorphous and diffuse way throughout the rest of Greater Sydney. The major site of community and commercial provision is Oxford Street, Darlinghurst. King Street, Newtown is a significant alternative. The areas of concentrated residence are several: Paddington and Darlinghurst, the original locations; Bondi, on the coast; Glebe, near the University of Sydney and Newtown.[2] In this chapter we look at the gay spaces of Sydney. Lesbians make another appearance in chapter 6, since gender as much as sexuality defines the spaces they inhabit. Though the question is not clear-cut, and certainly contestable, it is income differences between men and women rather than sexuality which appear to have the more profound spatial effects.

MARDI GRAS

The greatest assertion of gay and lesbian territoriality in Sydney is Mardi Gras, held every year at the end of February or the beginning of March. By occupying the streets, the parade asserts the claim of gays and lesbians to organise and be recognised. Mardi Gras is a political statement in disguise. It differs from the tradition of the political protest marches that have characterised the century: the massed marching (or shuffling) group; the display of demands on banners; the rallying point; and the speeches — a more solemn style still to be found in the London Gay Pride March and, indeed, in other gay and lesbian marches in Sydney such as the Stonewall commemoration in June (attended in 1992 by 1500 people)[3] and the march in support of the New South Wales Anti-Discrimination (Homosexual Vilification) Bill held late in 1993. The Mardi Gras is a different sort of event: it is not obviously confronting. It involves the crowds by its flamboyance and outrageousness, by its spectacle and sound, by its boldness and inventiveness. In 1994 it attracted 600 000 spectators out of a Greater Sydney population of 3.5 million. The fact that it happens at all indicates how far the public position of gays and lesbians in Sydney has advanced since the early 1980s.

What that crowd is witnessing, however, is a subversive act, and subversive not simply because of the sexuality on display. Peter Stallybras and Allon White trace the long, strong tradition of carnival in Europe and record its suppression, marginalisation or

Mardi Gras, Michelle Mika, 1995.

Flamboyance, outrage, spectacle, February 1984.

debasing in the nineteenth century: 'its feasting, violence, drinking, processions, fairs, wakes, rowdy spectacle and outrageous clamour were subject to surveillance and repressive control'.[4] They fell victim to a variety of 'normalising' decisions. In 1855 the Bartholomew Fair in London

> succumbed to the determined attack of the London Missionary Society ... The Paris carnival was rapidly being transformed into a trade show cum civic/military parade ... In 1873 the famous Nice carnival was taken over by a comite des Fetes, brought under bureaucratic bourgeois control and reorganised quite self-consciously as a tourist attraction for the increasing numbers who spent time on the Riviera ... In Germany after the Franco-Prussian war, traditional processions and festivities were rapidly militarised and incorporated into the symbolism and 'classical body' of the State."[5]

In banning or in other ways disabling the rituals of their society, the nineteenth century legislators sought to repress the irrational, rebellious and anarchic 'other'. But, as Stallybrass and White point out, the carnival is a resilient form and has a history of mutation and reappearance. In Sydney the state tolerates a violation of bourgeois order and grants space to the otherwise-repressed. Mardi Gras also saw off one of the *ersatz* carnival substitutes. Leo Schofield, a columnist on the *Sydney Morning Herald* recalls:

> There used to be a lethally dull Festival of Sydney Parade called the Waratah[6] Festival Parade. It was breathtakingly parochial and uninspired. Everyone who had something to sell — from a new Toyota Corolla to whatever — put it in the parade and it was alternated with the odd band and marching girls. It was just like some hick town in the mid-West. It was horrible.[7]

The re-emergence of the repressed in the form of participants on their floats and bikes and roller-blades mocks Christian-derived bourgeois values. The Reverend Fred Nile, member of the New South Wales Legislative Council, head of the Call to Australia Party and leading member of the Festival of Light, is right to see it as inimical to traditional values. It is precisely because those traditional values made no space for lesbians and gay men that they have muscled their way onto the streets.

Saturday, 24 June 1978 saw two parades in Sydney by gays and lesbians. The first was to commemorate the raid in 1969 by New York police on the gay Stonewall Bar in Greenwich Village and to celebrate the unexpected and unprecedented resistance by the gay customers which resulted in the riots that mark the birth of the modern gay liberation movement. This first Sydney march took place in the morning, and involved 300 to 500 people, a large number by Australian standards, and had the traditional protest form.[8] On the same day a forum on gay issues was held at Paddington Town Hall. There already existed in Sydney a growing gay confidence fostered by CAMP (Campaign Against Moral Prejudice) NSW founded in 1971 and a more militant gay liberation organisation.[9] The second parade was intended to be 'non-confrontational, a celebration of gay pride. Something that would link up the politics of gay freedom with the people in Oxford Street in the commercial scene' and be 'purely a street party, a walk down Oxford Street where we could be a bit frivolous.' [10] It was held at night to encourage those who feared public exposure to join in. The name 'Mardi Gras' was not on any of the leaflets or posters advertising the event. Ken Davis remembers that it became current in the succeeding days, initially with an indefinite rather than definite article to reflect this mood. Compared with the morning's turn-out, some 1000 people started off, their numbers swollen to 1500 by bystanders and those who responded to the calls of 'out of the bars and into the streets'. Few people were in costume though Davis, who hailed from Tamworth (the country and western capital of New South Wales) was appropriately dressed in a large orange and mission-brown polka-dot dress, 'a little Loretta Lynn number', he said.[11] In a tactical move, he was to shed this shortly when it became wise to be less conspicuous.

Twenty minutes after its start, the parade had reached its licensed destination at Hyde Park where the police turned off the loudspeakers of the truck and tried to arrest the driver.[12] The call went up to move to Kings Cross. There, what had been a celebratory and jubilant affair had, by 11.30: 'become a two-hour spree of screaming, bashing and arrests. In one incident, police took off their identification numbers and waded into a crowd of homosexuals'.[13] Bystanders at Kings Cross joined in to rescue those who had been arrested. The police were deeply hated by anyone who was considered a social deviant, as were many in the red-light district of Kings Cross. The police had a record of corruption and of violence which extended to bashings and rapes within Darlinghurst Police Station cells. An unlikely alliance of straights and gays was formed for the occasion, cemented by a common loathing of the police. In the ensuing melee thirty men and twenty-three women were arrested, not all necessarily gay or lesbian. The *Sydney Morning Herald* published their names, streets and suburbs of residence, ages and occupations.[14] Of those arrested, only three were over 28; over 60 per cent were under 24 years of age. Many were in semi- or unskilled jobs and there were both students and unemployed among them. In the end, only two of those arrested were fined, the others being released without bail and the charges subsequently dropped.

It was as if the gauntlet had been thrown down and seized by the gay community. Activists targeted the New South Wales *Summary Offences Act* under which the police had charged those arrested on 24 June 1978. They argued that this Act allowed the police, in effect, to determine standards of acceptable behaviour. It was used against all minorities against whom the police held a prejudice, be they gays or Aborigines. Nor was there a right to march and demonstrate. Gay activists developed the tactic of responding to arrests at protest marchs by demonstrating again and demanding that the first group arrested be freed. June 1979 saw another Mardi Gras on the theme 'Power in the Darkness' in which an impressive 5000 took part. The repeal in 1979 of the

Summary Offences Act by the Labor government of Neville Wran was entirely the work of the gay movement.

Three new pieces of legislation — the *NSW Offences in Public Places Act 1979*, the *NSW Public Assemblies Act 1979* and the *NSW Prostitution Act 1979* — took its place.[15] The *Public Assemblies Act 1979* laid the onus on the police to prove to a magistrate that a proposed march would cause a public nuisance or danger and so be banned. It removed absolute discretion from the police. No gay march has been banned under this Act. Queensland under the far-right government of Sir Joh Bjelke-Petersen is still held up as an aberrant form of Australian dictatorship maintained by gerrymander. It is sobering to remember how oppressive a regime operated formally and informally against dissent within New South Wales until the 1980s and how significant a part the gay movement had in the process of liberalisation.

In 1981 the parade was held in summer, leaving Stonewall day in June as a more directly political event. With the rescheduling of Mardi Gras came a declaration of its nature. It was decided that it should be: 'a celebration of coming out, with its main political goal being to demonstrate the size of the gay community, its variety of lifestyles and its right to celebrate in the streets of Sydney so as to enable a broadening of support for gay rights'.[16] Decisions taken about the format of the 1981 Mardi Gras, unfortunately, deepened the split between gays and lesbians. Lesbians feared that the inclusion of floats by businesses would result in sexist and racist use of drag. They also felt that the focus would shift away from the political. Having led the attack at the first Mardi Gras, the lesbians increasingly absented themselves from the celebration, returning in significant numbers only towards the end of the decade.

In the years that followed, the Mardi Gras parade and subsequent party grew dramatically in terms of the number of participants and the number of spectators. In 1983, there were 44 floats in the parade which was watched by 20 000 spectators. Some 2000 people attended the post-parade party. By 1994, there were 137 floats in the parade, watched by 600 000 spectators and 19 500 people attented the post-parade party.[17] The Australian Broadcasting Corporation (ABC) created a national audience for Mardi Gras in 1994 after it broadcast an hour of edited highlights of the parade in prime time on the next day. The program achieved top ratings for the ABC, a rare achievement. Relays on ATV International also took the Mardi Gras parade into South-East Asia.

What does it mean for the parade to occupy, so flamboyantly, prime space within the city? At its most basic level, it is to do with self-presentation. The image presented can be described by Fred Nile as 'a promiscuous orgy'[18] and as 'offensive, obscene and blasphemous' or as 'outlandish, vibrant, attractive and innovative' in the words of Chief Inspector Kerry Beggs at Surry Hills Police Station, in whose territory most of the parade takes place.[19]

After centuries of being corked, there is a lot of bubble in the bottle. The images that are made public are the significant, subversive topoi and icons of the gay and lesbian community. Generally forced to conceal its identity, the community bursts out perversely in disguise, fancy dress, travesty and drag. It flaunts gay identity as if to say: 'Haven't you spotted us; we're so obvious'. It parodies its own oppression. Two T-shirts present paradoxes: 'Nobody Knows I'm Gay' and 'I'm not gay but my boyfriend is'. Each offers the norm while wittily undermining it.

Of the entrants in the parade in 1989, two-thirds chose costume or uniform.[20] In the 1993 parade, Batman resumed his liaison with Robin, Spiderwoman found a female Captain America, Noddy and Big Ears drove by with 'Just Married' on the back of their familiar red car. From *The Flintstones*, Wilma and Betty's car bore the sign: 'Drop Dead Fred, Betty's Better in Bed'. Thelma was with Louise.[21] The statements made by these four parade entries are not intended to abuse but to disabuse. Their political claim is the right to form partnerships on the community's terms. They laugh, too, at the horror of the wowser or the straight-laced when the 'innocence' of Enid Blyton and Fred Quimby is violated by reinterpretation. They say 'don't read everything with your either/or spectacles'.

There are more obvious targets presented for mockery — the *bêtes noirs* of the community. The 1989 parade brought Fred Nile's brilliantined head on a platter — a martyred St John the Baptist to the libertine Salome. It may have been the result of this perceived insult that Mr Nile organised a 'Cleansing March' in October 1989 to implore God 'Not to treat Sydney like Sodom and Gomorrah because of drug pedlars, pornographers and homosexual groups'.[22] In seeking to occupy the heartland of queerdom — Taylor Square — he found himself outnumbered 2000 to 5000, having claimed he would have the support of 100 000 Christians.[23] The 1992 parade brought Bruce Ruxton, then president of the Victorian Returned Service League (RSL) and a noted campaigner against homosexuals. He was represented in effigy 'adorned … in a 1940s one-piece swimsuit and looking coquettishly over his shoulder'.[24] This was paraded by a women's battalion in jungle fatigues and glitter and accompanied by former servicemen — one in immaculate naval whites on top and harlequin lycra tights below — giving the lie to the Veterans' leader's claim that homosexuals do not exist in the services. There was no direct pillorying of Aussie Ockerdom, though in 1992 there was one group in the yellow and green national football uniform bearing a placard: 'Yobboes against Bashers'.

In other cases, icons of institutions which have oppressed gays and lesbians are portrayed. The church is one of these. A group of four 'pregnant' transvestites bear the sign 'Proud of their immaculate conception'. Nuns of the Order of Perpetual Indulgence (pre Vatican II) play bagpipes or roller-blade down the street.[25] Institutions that trade on 'wholesome' family images are mocked. Three-metre effigies of Colonel Sanders and the McDonald's clown embrace. In other cases, in a light-hearted vein, the community celebrates its heroes. Elvis Herselvis self-proclaimed 'gender stylist and drag king' sweeps by in a high-finned convertible to the delight of lesbian followers.[26]

The parade displays sexual stereotyping overturned. There is dressing up and dressing down. Bodies are transformed. They are seen as the *opportunities* for display — either the severe (generally leather) or the exuberant (generally drag). The Dykes on Bikes roar by[27] — wearing less in 1993 than in 1992, weaving and roaring, seizing the stereotyped image of the macho-male Harley Davidson bikers, parading in a phalanx, bare-breasted and buttocked, sporting shades, leathers and tattoos.[28] Women sprout dildos and exaggerated nipples. Another group of women strip down to become human versions of the mannequins on which clothes shops hang their wares — divested of display, apparently naked but for the high heels and bouffant hairstyle. A group of men turn against male uniformity, swathing themselves in diaphanous material to become birds of display with costumes that shimmer, that move, that blow, that sparkle, that reveal, that catch the eye, that enlarge and extend and have as their cultural referents the eastern voluptuary and the harem. They embody the essence of camp proposed by Susan Sontag: 'the love of artifice and exaggeration'.[29] She adds: 'The most refined form of sexual attractiveness (as well as the most refined form of sexual pleasure) consists in going against the grain of one's sex'.[30] The displays in Mardi Gras combine the subjective pleasure of the exotic with the desire to shock.

There is, too, an ironising of masculinity through exaggerated worship of the muscled male body. This is a less clear-cut case than the travesties and parodies. The muscles on display are not put on in the hours before the 8.30 p.m. start of the parade. They are sweated for, with or without the help of steroids, in countless hours in the gym. They are the same muscles that serve behind the bar at the Albury or that stand, inviting admiration, at the Midnight Shift. They are real and for real. Nonetheless, in the context of the parade, they become display of another sort. The attempt to become more masculine than the queer-basher who will prey on you is subsumed into the knowing exaggeration that is the essence of this most unrepresentative night.[31] By concentrating on spectacle, a fantasy world is temporarily created which soothes or amuses. What the parade submerges are the dangers faced by gay men and lesbians. The bashers in the crowd look at the queers on the floats: the queers know the bashers are there and know that that is another aspect of the reality of being gay in the golden mile.

The extent to which the parade is 'readable' by the majority of those who watch it is debatable. At a quite literal level, messages and banners are often indecipherable. Acronyms and abbreviations mean little to most of the spectators. There is rarely a relationship between the purpose of the organisation and the image offered. (The Gay and Lesbian Teachers and Students Alliance were an exception, going for academic gowns and school uniforms, but this 'text' may have been too dull to read with interest.) The danger is that the parade becomes pure spectacle leaving its overt political points to be understood by the few. Bombarded with glitter and light, the straights in the crowd may simply read what they see and confirm what they always thought they knew: 'queens will be queens'.

The political demands made in recent years have been around AIDS, vilification and violence but also around the institution that underpins traditional social organisation. In 1994, the International Year of the Family, the lead theme of the parade was '*We* are Family', puzzlingly represented by the opening float depicting a barge of ancient Egypt by Cecil B. De Mille out of *Antony and Cleopatra*. The attempt to extend the definition of 'family' is deeply unsettling to social conservatives and brought protests in newspapers and chat shows. It caused fissures to appear within the federal Opposition. The leader, John Hewson, acknowledged the diversity of Australian culture and sent a letter of support to Mardi Gras; his Coalition partner Tim Fischer, the leader of the National Party, complained of the 'hijacking' of the word 'family'.[32] A prominent Liberal backbencher, Chris Miles, complained that homosexuality was not 'an activity which is beneficial to our society' and regretted Hewson's support of Mardi Gras.[33] The principal argument against broadcasting the 1994 Mardi Gras at 8 30 p.m. was that it was in family viewing time. The ABC countered by pointing out that two commercial channels were showing 'M' [mature] rated movies at that time. The ABC rated their program 'M' too. Mardi Gras, despite its representational shortcomings, can still sting.

The parade also demonstrates that gays and lesbians have formal political clout. In 1992 ten state MPs, mainly Labor and organised by the only openly-gay politician in Australia, Labor's Paul O'Grady, marched under the slogan 'MPs Supporting the Community'; in 1993, twelve joined in. One was Elizabeth Kirkby, leader of the state Democrats. Several were former Labor ministers. (The Liberal premier did not attend, saying that he did not have anything to wear.) The 1993 programme carried messages of support from Sydney's federal,[34] state and local politicians and a full-page message from the Labor Party. The 1994 program upped the ante, containing messages of support from the Prime Minister and the leader of the federal Opposition, from the premier and the leader of the state Opposition as well as from Sydney MPs and municipal politicians. Gays, at least in the eastern Sydney electorate of Bligh and in the inner west electorate of Port Jackson — held by a veteran of the first Mardi Gras, Sandra Nori — count.

Clover Moore, state Independent member for Bligh, which covers the most densely gay areas of Sydney, and a constant champion of gay rights, recognised the power of the pink vote in the state elections of 1991. Between the previous election in 1988 and that of 1991, the electorate boundaries were redrawn. Projections from 1988 gave a predicted outcome on first preferences of Labor 25.8 per cent, Liberal 49.7 per cent and Clover Moore, the sitting MP, 22.1 per cent. After the redistribution of preferences, the predicted result gave the Liberals 54.1 per cent and Clover Moore 45.9 per cent.[35] The actual primary vote results were: Moore 43.9 per cent, Liberal 39.8 per cent, Labor 16.2 per cent. On redistribution of preferences this produced the following results: Moore 56.1 per cent; Liberals 43.9 per cent.[36] Evidence from individual polling booths showed that Moore gained votes across the board — even in Liberal areas — but that her greatest swings were in the predominantly gay areas. The Oxford Street booth recorded an increase in her primary vote from 33.8 per cent to 63.3 per cent. She gained an average increase of 20 per cent on her 1988 performance in Kings Cross and Surry Hills.[37] Non-party paid advertising in the gay press was entirely pro-Moore. The group Gays and Lesbians for Clover took out a page-one box and two full-page advertisements in the issue of the *Sydney Star Observer* immediately preceding the election[38] which, with a half-page paid advertisement by Moore herself, easily outweighed the Liberals' paid full-page advertisement. Labor disconsolately took a meagre corner of one page.

Moore's cause was further strengthened in the week before the New South Wales election by a decision of the federal Liberal Party to oppose the Commonwealth government's regulation to allow foreign partners of Australian gays and lesbians to have right of residence. The *Star Observer*'s front-page headline rang out: 'Libs attack gay couples'.[39] Another positive aspect as far as the pink vote was concerned was that Moore did not 'niche-market' her gay policies. She was the only candidate who spoke up for gay issues in her general campaign literature.[40] The 1991 election returned a Liberal Government but one which had to rely on the support of minor parties or independents in both Houses. In the Legislative Assembly, the Independents held the cards: in the Legislative Council, the Call to Australia Party (CTA) represented by Fred and Elaine Nile held 'the balance of prayer and responsibility'.[41]

The need to rely on minority parties with two diametrically opposed value systems for its majority in each of the two Houses posed the knottiest of problems for the Fahey government — and none more knotty than the gay issue which crystallised out into the Anti-Discrimination (Homosexual Vilification) Bill. For Clover Moore the Bill was her gift to her gay and lesbian supporters; for Fred Nile it represented the latest peak of a growing moral degeneracy. To the Liberal government of John Fahey it was the rock on which his government might shatter. The government introduced its own anti-vilification legislation but withdrew it when the Call to Australia Party threatened to cut off its majority in the Upper House on all government legislation. This left the way open for Clover Moore to push her own Bill, thereby strengthening her position with her gay and lesbian electorate, which was further alienated from the Liberal Party. Being sympathetic (as Premier Fahey was generally supposed to have been) is not enough.

What is true at the state level (and increasingly at the federal) is as true at the local. The relevant council, that of South Sydney, had three 'out' gay councillors at the time of writing. Its mayor, Vic Smith, became embroiled in a controversy in late 1992 in which he as the delegated officer seemed to gays and lesbians to be supporting moves by seven local residents to ban the Mardi Gras Party at the Showground. In a half-page advertisement in the *Sydney Star Observer* he denied any such intention and declared: 'South Sydney City Council supports the Gay and Lesbian community and I am confident … that the party will go ahead'. The council found itself attacked from the other side too. It had agreed to provide 225 square metres of office space to the Gay and Lesbian Rights Group for a rent of $50 per week on second-floor council premises on Oxford Street, stating the council's policy of supporting community organisations and recognising that 'the gay community has a part to play in the life of South Sydney'.[42] Somewhat belatedly, an eastern suburbs property free-sheet, the *Eastern Express*, ran a story: 'How it pays to be gay'.[43] It characterised the mayor, 'the former rugby league playing kid from the mean streets of Redfern', as making a play as the potential Labor candidate for the state seat of Bligh in the next election by touting for the gay vote. 'They [lesbians and gays] are certainly very purposeful and they know what they are about and what their needs are,' it quotes him as saying. He defended the rent to the Rights Group, and to the Anti-Violence Project and the Quilt Project as well as a grant of $50 000 to Mardi Gras as being part of a $500 000 budget to support activities of the various communities in the area.

What the *Eastern Express* was picking up on was a new concentration of services for gays and lesbians in Oxford Street. In the area are the premises of the AIDS Quilt Project, People Living with HIV and AIDS, the Anti-Violence Project, the Gay and Lesbian Teachers and Students Alliance, the Gay and Lesbian Immigration Task Force, the Gay and Lesbian Rights Group, and the Metropolitan Community Church. With these have also come professional services in medicine and counselling. Oxford Street has become more than simply an entertainment centre. Suggestions have been made to give it a special status similar to that of Chinatown. These have been rejected by the lord mayor of Sydney; but the mayor of South Sydney which covers most of the street, has acknowledged its special status and has promised to use such devices as planning permission to preserve its identity.[44]

What is clear is that having established itself as a visible presence (most spectacularly through Mardi Gras) with a claim to generally acknowledged territory (a particular section of Oxford Street) and having consolidated an electoral claim through residential concentration (thereby gaining considerable political influence and securing the return of pro-gay MPs in Bligh and Port Jackson), the gay and lesbian community has gained acceptance on its own terms by different levels of government. The community in Sydney, like its counterparts in the United States of America, is looking increasingly 'to the local state apparatus as a potential ally in its struggle against the more hostile popular culture'.[45] The representatives of that state apparatus now use the gay community's terms and, cynically or not, reject attempts to deny or reject a significant part of their electorate.

To the members of the Gay Liberation movement of the early 1970s, for whom the bourgeois state incorporated and enforced the family values that oppressed them, such co-option would have been anathema. The change in principle vis-a-vis the state parallels another move. The separatism of gays from lesbians that increasingly marked homosexual organisation in the late 1970s and 1980s has been softened into a coalition of gays with lesbians to achieve common goals. The word 'Lesbian' was added to the title of the Gay Mardi Gras in 1989,[46] as it was to other groups such as the Gay Rights Group. The word 'gay' in the early days of the Gay Liberation Movement included both men and women. By the mid-1970s it had been narrowed to cover men only. The alteration of the name 'Gay Mardi Gras' was, therefore, more a return to the celebration's original comprehensiveness. The change was opposed by some gay men ignorant, perhaps, of the role of women in the early days. David McDiarmid, one of those who took part in the 1978, march reports that: 'It was the dykes who were at the forefront of the riot and they were the ones who took the risks initially'.[47] Of the fifty-three charged with various offences at the Central Court of Petty Sessions, twenty-three were women.[48] Although in a number of ways, the two groups have different agendas, their unity on the common agenda has given added strength. Their gains have been significant, as we have seen.

With the lead from Parliament, attitudes have shifted, most surprisingly of all perhaps in the group that was the catalyst for the whole Mardi Gras — the police. Although there are cases of individual police violence and entrapment against gays and lesbians,[49] there is a deliberate move to change the police culture. The 1994 Mardi Gras program carries a message headed 'Towards Safer Streets' and announces that fifty-three police stations have gay or lesbian liaison officers. Although there is only one 'out' constable[50] there are regular training sessions organised bi-monthly at Surry Hills and at other stations for the younger constables.[51] Elsewhere in 1993, thirty-eight patrols received training.[52] If 'poofter bashing' had been part of the police culture in the early 1980s — an opportunity for police to 'bloody their hands' — the leadership is seeking to expunge the memory.[53] The police force is covered by the Anti-Discrimination Act which outlaws discrimination on grounds of, among others, homosexuality. The commissioner has declared that 'A person's sexuality has nothing to do with how well they do their job …'.[54] Although there are occasions where older patterns re-emerge, times do seem to have changed for the better.[55]

Mardi Gras is the noisy demonstration of the power of the gay vote. It is indeed 'Politics On Parade' as the headline in the *Weekend Australian* had it.[56] It is inconceivable that discriminatory legislation such as the British Clause 28 denouncing 'pretended [homosexual] families' could now be passed in New South Wales. Such conservative reactions are things of the past outside Fred Nile's party. The artist Peter Tully put it this way: 'We've come too far in politics and it's been a very long fight. It's been going on for twenty years and we're very strong, committed and very proud. Clause 28 we just wouldn't stand for.' [57] Australia, which had in the 1970s looked enviously for its leads — to the United States, Canada[58] and Britain[59] now has its own norm-setting agenda, seen in the opening of immigration to same-sex partners.[60]

What is demonstrated on the streets in Mardi Gras, then, is more than sculpted bodies and pretty frocks. It is a proud and determined reminder that gays and lesbians are co-tenants of Sydney space. As the chant had it: 'We're here, we're queer and we're not going shopping. Get used to it!'

There is, however, a not so obvious reading that can be made of Mardi Gras: its relationship with the institutions of the state and the way in which those relationships have altered the perceptions the gay and lesbian community has of itself. This is most apparent in the principal thoroughfare of Mardi Gras and of the gay and lesbian community — Oxford Street.

OXFORD STREET

Sydney, like all major cities, has a continuing homosexual tradition. Jan Morris in her book *Sydney* notes the existence of homosexuality from 1788 but submerges it disingenuously in an account of the orgy which greeted the landing of the women convicts a fortnight after the First Fleet's men: 'Sex in Sydney ... began with a bang'.[61] In her present-day world, homosexuals (as she calls them) inhabit the genteel harbourside suburbs such as Neutral Bay where the owner of one 'unassuming small villa ... has turned it into a kind of grotto, its walls painted all over with trompe l'oeil and tomfoolery'. For Morris, homosexuals add something 'raffishly defiant' to the 'potent stratum of the unorthodox, if not the anarchic amongst [the] bourgeoisie'. They are, mysteriously, attended by 'unidentified acolytes'.[62] Few who are acquainted with the generality of gay and lesbian life in Sydney would choose to offer this Firbankian picture as typical. Even fewer would spot anything 'anarchic' in the attitudes of Sydney's bourgeoisie. Morris herself does not mention homosexuality again. It transpired, indeed, that she had not heard of Mardi Gras, if she had, she might have concluded that homosexual defiance was a little more than raffish.[63] For a truer, more comprehensive, history of homosexuality in Sydney, we can turn to authors such as Robert Hughes, Robert French and Garry Wotherspoon.[64]

The development of a distinctive gay area is comparatively recent, although it is still subject to change. Between the wars, bars catering to homosexual males were exclusively in the city;[65] by 1960 they were clustered in Kings Cross[66] and the city, but had begun to spread to the Darlinghurst section of Surry Hills and to Bondi Junction; by 1982 Darlinghurst had the lion's share of forty-two sites of differing types. Space was claimed in Newtown, Leichhardt, Rozelle and Balmain; by 1990, Darlinghurst had forty-eight recorded gay sites, including bars, baths, bookshops, cafes, restaurants and clothes shops.

The development of Oxford Street as a gay area grew accidentally out of two of the staples of New South Wales society: political gerrymandering and corruption. Political gerrymandering was practised by both the Liberal and Labor parties when they gained state power, though Labor had the dirtiest record. The prize was Sydney City Council and the wealth that could be generated from office development both legally and by way of kickbacks to officials. This put Sydney through one of its worst periods of corruption. It was described as 'the crime capital of Australia' and 'the most corrupt city in the Western world after Newark, New Jersey and Brisbane, Queensland'.[67] The Sydney City Council was dismissed and three commissioners were installed to run the city for twenty-two months from September 1967,[68] although the commission was more to do with the Labor Right's determination to keep out the Left as it was to clean up corruption. The details of the shamelessly self-serving manipulations of local government are beyond the scope of this chapter, but the creation of South Sydney Council in 1968, its abolition in 1982 and its recreation as a larger area in 1988 led to planning uncertainty.[69]

The re-creation of an enlarged South Sydney Council in 1988 was, however, the key moment in the consolidation of a gay geography. The City Council elected in 1984 after the commissioners relinquished control was a radical one. In power was a coalition of radical Independents and Left Labor members who developed a social agenda involving ethnic, environmental, gay and other groups. It was not a council sympathetic to the demands of big business, which had its own agenda for the CBD. The Labor state government was controlled by the right-wing 'Machine'. Alarmed both by the complaints of business and by the success of the Left, and fearing that the Liberals would not stand in the upcoming September elections thereby giving the Independents a clearer run and the likelihood of becoming the majority on the Council, the Government accused the City Council of 'a record of maladministration',[70] expelled the Left Labor members from the party and postponed the election while preparing to split the South Sydney Council area from the city.[71] At the split, the city was given to business and South Sydney to its residents.

The policies of the first council continued those that had led to the dismemberment of the old Sydney City Council. Sympathetic to the groups that formed the electorate, it set about maintaining the character of Oxford Street. Fears had persisted into the mid-1980s that Oxford Street would become a second George Street architecturally — full of undistinguished high rises and vacant excavations.[72] It was not until 1986 that Bob Carr, Labor's Minister for planning and the environment, announced a halt to the building of high rises on Oxford Street and an upgrading of the facades of the older blocks.[73] The halt of the advance of the CBD, the continued residential nature of the area, the existence of a range of premises fronting the street and able to cater for the population were the necessary preconditions for a gay and lesbian presence which does not prosper in high rises and shopping malls. In anticipation of the advance of high-rise offices up Oxford Street, the first South Sydney Council in the 1970s had bought one whole federation-style block on the northern end of the street. With local opposition and the imposition of 'green bans' there had been a stay on the demolition of the block:[74] saved and restored, it was eventually to provide offices for a number of gay and lesbian organisations (noted earlier) and was the focus of the furore over the 'privileges' accorded to gays in the 1990s.[75]

By the 1960s Oxford Street had become the site of illegal gambling and of prostitution, both of which fed the insatiable greed of the notoriously corrupt state government and police force. The Liberal premier, Sir Robert Askin, and Police Commissioner Hanson 'were paid approximately $100 000 each a year from the end of Sydney's gang wars in 1967/8 until Askin's retirement [in 1975]'.[76] In an early attempt to break the symbiosis of crime and bribery there was a clampdown on the illegal gaming houses and prostitution networks.[77] Deprived of their income, owners moved into providing gay venues. The Unicorn Hotel became the first visible sign of the gay presence.[78] From that point on, others followed. There was, however, no solidarity between the owners of these sites. When the Midnight Shift applied for a permanent late licence it was opposed by other bars. There are unproven but strong rumours of threats and actual violence directed against individuals who tried to set up in business on the street.

It is easy to romanticise the development of Oxford Street as a 'gay space', but the forces behind it were and are uncompromisingly commercial. There is much speculation about the degree of shady money involved. Gay premises are owned in three different ways. The first is the truly independently owned business; the second is the semi-independent business which is technically owned by an individual or group but which is financed by undisclosed parties; the third is the fronted business run by an employee but owned and controlled by a syndicate. In some respects, the 1960s tradition of dealing on Oxford Street has not changed.

Growth in the number of venues at the Darlinghurst end of the street killed off some of the longer-established, discreet bars such as the Apollo (now a Thai restaurant) that had catered for the professional classes of Paddington, and those for younger men and women such as Enzo's in Paddington and Chez Ivy at Bondi Junction — 'a sleazy little bar that had drag shows and rock bands' and was presided over by the owner, Ivy, 'a tall woman with a dark bouffant'.[79]

Oxford Street by the early 1980s had established itself as the gay heartland. The Mardi Gras parades helped consolidate that role, but it was not a straightforward gain. If the forces of capital and organised crime were quite happy to exploit the new market, the institutions of the state — principally the police — were not so amenable. The 1979–80 parades started from the heart of hostile territory. The march was routed through Saturday-night audiences coming out of the cinemas in George Street. It was channelled down one side of the street as if to declare that it would not be allowed to disrupt city life. Its disruptive element was further lessened by moving its start to the Domain, parkland tucked away from the city centre. As the size of the parade grew and overt hostility diminished, a new relationship began to be established between the organisers and the regulating police. It began to move from being protest to spectacular, in which spontaneity was limited. Bans were put on people standing on the awnings over the pavements after male strippers from the Flinders put on a show for the crowds below after the parade had passed. Barricades were erected, which meant that people in the crowd could no longer join in the parade, which is firmly marshalled by hundreds of volunteers supplementing a force of 100 police officers. The Mardi Gras organisers pay for the clean-up of the streets and there are demands that it pay the police costs of the evening. Understandably, the growth in size of the spectacle forces negotiation with the state authorities. This marks another stage in the way which the gay and lesbian community has learnt to deal with the institutions of the state — just as they have in the party political arena.

The extent to which Oxford Street is 'gay territory' is highly limited, at least topographically. The street stretches 3.5 kilometres from Hyde Park in the west to Bondi Junction in the east, where it peters out rather anticlimactically in a pedestrianised shopping mall. It is within four areas — Darlinghurst, Paddington, Woollahra and Waverley — each with its own character, respectively mixed residential–commercial–business; lower-priced housing and bohemian; wealthy professional; older, established; and mixed working- and middle-class. The gay area is overwhelmingly Darlinghurst with a spill-over into Paddington. If pubs and hotels are used as the principal landmarks we can move from the Exchange in the west to the Midnight Shift on the opposite side of the road; back across to the Oxford; across Taylor Square to JBF; up Flinders Street 300 metres to the Flinders Hotel and the Beresford; back to Oxford Street to the Beauchamp; then to the Albury, at which point 'gay' Oxford Street and its environs have come to an end. All in all, it is little over 750 metres in length measured from Oxford Square to the Albury Hotel.

What gives the feeling of greater space is that from the Albury east into Paddington there continues a range of stylish shops. One of the stereotypes of the gay and lesbian community is that it has a consumerist focus. It did, after all, raise money for the local AIDS charity in 1993 and 1994 by a 'Shop Till You Drop' day conducted mainly in Darlinghurst shops in which participating shops gave a percentage of their takings to the charity. This is the land of hairdressers with shops so minimalist that they look as though they have been designed by Le Corbusier. Clothes shops display garments fit for the voguish, the eccentric or the exhibitionist. There are three late-opening bookshops, record shops and several others catering to specialised markets; there is a range of coffee shops beginning to creep onto the pavement; there are delicatessens and expensive fruit shops; there are galleries for furniture and paintings; there is a New Ageish Saturday open market in the Uniting Church grounds in continuous occupation of the site since 1973.[80] From pre-gentrified Paddington come the RSL and the Police Boys' Club advertising the manly sports and martial arts that are considered to stop a young lad's thoughts lightly turning to crime. The fact that the fashionable shops give the illusion of an extension to the gay area picks up on the general perception that gays and lesbians are innovators and risk takers in fashion and self-presentation and that they have chosen to live their lives in a hedonistic way — and that they have money to spend. The justness of this impression is examined in the chapter on the economy.

Oxford Street, like Broadway, like Sunset Boulevard, like Wall Street, like The Lido is more than a topographically defined space. Each by a process of transfer becomes the shorthand for the individuals or the institutions and their values which occupy the space — be they the stars or the speculators: 'Give my regards to old Broadway', 'the Wall Street Crash'. Oxford Street operates more parochially, but nonetheless as significantly in its own sphere. Oxford Street for many gays and lesbians is the threshold between private and public recognition of their sexuality. 'As with other "minority groups", the gay and lesbian communities have their own distinctive universe of discourse which provides a means of entree to their social world and to its spatial constitution'.[81] Oxford Street provides the opportunity to make that crossover into 'Oxford Street'. There is no longer a rite of passage recognised by the dominant culture to mark the move from the straight to the gay world. At the annual Arts Ball in pre-Liberation days, there was the 'Imperial Court' presided over by two senior members of the community. Gays and lesbians who were new to the scene would be 'presented' wearing formal women's evening dress by an older gay or lesbian dressed in a tuxedo. It was taken very seriously. Newly out gays are no longer eased onto the scene. The most alienating thing for most gays and lesbians is to enter what seems to be a rule-less new world, a counter culture made all the more frightening by the sanctions, formal and informal, operated against it by the dominant culture. 'Coming out', the public declaration that one is gay or lesbian — is a move from the private space to the public.[82] There is no equivalent to the ceremonies of, say, tribal societies or the dubious initiations to which young soldiers are subjected. These happen at the behest of 'the elders' at a predetermined time. 'Coming Out' for a gay or a lesbian is ideally the result of a private decision to shun 'the safety, anonymity but stultifying confinement of the "closet" '[83] and to take one's place in a larger but more dangerous space.

Oxford Street is the most obvious place for gay men particularly to start the process of coming out. It is by no means uncontested territory, as we shall see.[84] Because of its symbolic importance to the community, the 'gay' health of Oxford Street is closely monitored. 'Is Oxford Street thriving or dying' is a none-too-coded way of asking: 'Is the gay community thriving or dying?'[85] Consequently, statistics are scrutinised. Reassurance comes in a 1993 end-of-year tally of the newcomers to the street which lists three new restaurants, two cafe–cafe-bars, one hotel–pub, one clothes shop and one sex emporium.[86]

SPACE CONCEDED

Threats to the space have to be resisted. At the end of 1992, three cases heard before the Land and Environment Court helped confirm a gay and lesbian interest in territory around Oxford Street. The first involved an appeal against the council's refusal of a Development Application to establish an amusement centre — Timezone — at the northern end of Oxford Street; the second involved a café; and the third was an appeal against South Sydney Council's attempt to close a gay sauna — Bodyline — on Flinders Street, off Oxford Street.

TIMEZONE AND OZ YEEROS CAFE

The Timezone[87] and Oz Yeeros Cafe cases were less significant in terms of public policy, though vital to the nature of the street. The issues around Timezone considered in the judgment were 'social effects, amenity of the neighbourhood and the public interest'. [88] The nub of the matter lay in the clientele who would use the centre. Experience elsewhere in the city showed that customers of such centres were predominantly men between 13 and 20 years of age. Police Sergeant Thompson noted: 'The patrons at these centres exhibit a high degree of anti-social behaviour and in the immediate area of such centres in George Street there is a high incidence of the following offences: assault and rob, steal [*sic*] from the person, assault and malicious damage'. Extra police were required in the area.[89] To one group of objectors, including the National Australia Bank, the Park on Oxford Hotel, Rogues Night Club and Streeton's, 'a widely acclaimed restaurant with discerning patrons',[90] the prospect of marauding gangs was obvious. To the gay community, the dangers were even more real. The site was on the fringes of gay territory. Adjacent to the Timezone site was a predominantly gay and lesbian bar, the Exchange Hotel, and a gay male sauna, King Steam. Police evidence noted that 'violence against gay persons is usually committed by persons of the same age group and sex as the persons who are commonly the patrons of amusement centres'.[91] The appellants stated that there would be 100 on the premises at any one time during their busiest period of 11 p.m. to 3 a.m. — coincident with the peak period for gay bars. The danger was real and clear. In finding against the appellants, the assessor stated that the centre would adversely affect the amenity of the area, produce an adverse social effect and would not be in the public interest. He did not refer to the gay factor, although it is implied in the last two of his reasons.

One point of entry for hostile young straights who have already begun to move into this part of the street was a fast-food takeaway, the Oz Yeeros Cafe next door to the Timezone site. The council had refused it a 24-hour trading licence following incidents of violence by its patrons against gays and lesbians. Judge Talbot of the Land and Environment Court rejected an appeal against the council decision. Among other considerations, he said that there was a real risk of injury to gays and lesbians after midnight.[92] Police had given evidence that customers at the café had viciously assaulted a lesbian and they feared further disturbance.

BODYLINE

The significance of the third case was that the judgment hinged on the acknowledgment of the gay character of the area.[93] Bodyline is a gay male sauna operating off Taylor Square in the heart of Oxford Street. The council sought to close it down on five grounds, falling into two categories: traffic management and residential amenity.[94] To these was added a submission that the use of the building constituted 'a common law misdemeanour of keeping a disorderly house, to wit, a bawdy house or brothel'.[95] Responding to criticism from the gay community, the council claimed that its barrister had exceeded his brief in making the submission of common law misdemeanour. Unintentional or not, its introduction allowed the judge to make significant comments on what constitutes 'the public'.

In determining the balance between nuisance and benefit for the residents, Judge Stein commented that as far as traffic was concerned, the area was already so heavily used both as a major thoroughfare and for parking, that the sauna would make little difference. In judging the benefits he commented that the Local Environmental Plan did not define 'resident' but that, 'applying a sensible and purposive construction it seems to me to embrace those people living in reasonable proximity to the proposal'.[96] Following from that and given the evidence of a very large gay community in the immediate area, he judged that for that community the existence of a sauna might well be seen to be an enhancement — as well as providing twelve jobs. In the wider area of public morality arising from the submission on the common law misdemeanour, he confessed his difficulty in determining what might outrage public decency — a matter for a jury not a single judge. He then added:

> And which public is to be considered? The general public of New South Wales or some smaller segment of them — the City of South Sydney or the environs of Darlinghurst? According to the evidence — and this is undisputed — the area around Darlinghurst has a population of between 18 000 and 30 000 gay men'. [97]

Judge Stein had already ruled that he was incompetent to decide the case on the charge of keeping a bawdy house and therefore would give no opinion on public decency, but his musings on 'the public' implicitly and his ruling on 'the residents' explicitly created a precedent in determining that the *use* and *perception* of an area are dependent on its demographic constitution. What is not appropriate in the grand residential environs of St Ives or Pymble may be in the gay area of Darlinghurst.

Both cases to varying degrees recognise the status and peculiar interests of the gay community. Such rulings give gays precedents and a tacit acknowledgment that part of Oxford Street at least is their space.

BEYOND THE GHETTO

Beyond the boundaries of the 'inner west' lies the 'outer west' an area which houses 45 per cent of Greater Sydney's population. The centre of the city has been moving steadily westwards and now lies beyond Parramatta, 20 kilometres from the GPO. To the resident of inner Sydney, the western suburbs represent 'the other', a vast, undifferentiated, stigmatised and largely unvisited area of suburbia. The gay press pays them scant heed. The inhabitants of the west, the 'Westies' recognise the slights of the 'Easties' and pursue a varied, but different style of life.[98]

What gay space is there beyond the confines of the inner city? From the gay Newtown Hotel in Sydney's inner west to the gay Midnight Factory in Penrith is approximately 60 kilometres. In this area between Newtown and Penrith there is no permanent venue for gays and lesbians. To gays and lesbians who live in the inner city and whose identity is at least partly predicated on the existence of social centres, it is difficult to imagine what it must be like to be gay or lesbian in an area which lacks those amenities. They doubt whether it is possible to operate openly and construct a satisfying life under the normative eye of heterosexual society.[99] There are indeed gays and lesbians out *there*: there are even some gays and lesbians who are *out* there, but they remain an unquantified group. Lacking a space, they lack visibility. If the area holds approximately 1.5 million people and we accept as the median figure 10 per cent of the population is engaged at some time in homosexual activity then we are looking at 150 000 individuals. On these people there is scant information: what we have falls under the headings of anecdote and highly specific statistics connected with AIDS work for men who use beats.

The one regular meeting place for gays and lesbians is the Golfview Hotel at Guildford, just south-west of Parramatta. It is advertised in the gay press and at the Women's Health Centre at Liverpool. A function room the size of a standard Oxford Street disco is hired once a fortnight and on average attracts about 100 people of mixed sex, age and dress. The atmosphere is sociable: everyone seems to know each other and because music comes from a record player in the corner and not from a sound system, people are able to talk to each other — quite unlike Oxford Street venues.[100]

Welcome though the Golfview is, it hardly caters for the gay and lesbian population en masse. There is a variety of social groups which advertise in the gay press: Gay and Lesbians Out West (GLOW); which meets in Parramatta and caters for men and women under 26; Westies Against Homophobia; Gays and Lesbians Penrith and Surrounds (GLIPS). To the south is the Cronulla Gay Group and at Revesby the South West Area Gay Society (SWAGS) and on the North Shore, Helix. 'Gaywaves', a gay radio program broadcast on 107.3 FM for two-and-a-half hours each Thursday; Queer TV broadcasts on UHF 31. The BBS computer network maintains links for some.[101]

For men, in addition to the social groups, there are the beats or, as an alternative, the sex bookshops where contact can be made. For women, these are not options.

Blacktown Lesbian Information Social and Support Group meets at the Women's Health Centre once a month. Liverpool Women's Health Centre holds a women's support group once a fortnight. It is mainly social but issues of sexuality are tackled. Lesbian events are advertised at the centre. Beyond that, there are women's dances and, again, the private networking of friends. Growing up in the suburbs is lonely. The pressures to conform are persistent.[102] Some lesbians and gay men do live open lives in a predominantly heterosexual milieu, accepted by neighbours and colleagues at work. By staying in the suburbs they avoid the danger of 'burn out' on the scene as well as the perceived homogeneity of the ghetto.[103] Others, however, suffer harassment. To most of those who have a choice, the east beckons either for evenings out or for settlement.

BEATS

So far we have been considering space that is used by both lesbians and gay men and which is generally open in some degree to the public — either by right, as in the streets, cafes and bars of the city — or by payment, such as by the purchase of a ticket to the Mardi Gras Party. Such space does not accommodate explicit sexual acts, beats do.[104]

A beat is a place used by men for unarranged encounters of fleeting, anonymous sex. A beat must have two characteristics. It must be public space, thereby giving right of access, and it must have areas which can 'become' private for the duration of the sexual exchange. Beats, typically, are to be found in public lavatories, in parks, in shopping centres and, in Sydney, on the beaches and along the cliffs.[105] Given the degree of homosexual activity recorded in Robert Hughes's *The Fatal Shore*, it seems likely that beats existed from the earliest days of the colony. The first public notice was in 1830 when parkland known as the Domain was noted as having become 'a resort for very unproper [*sic*] characters', although these were heterosexuals.[106] The first recorded homosexual incident occurred in 1882 in Hyde Park, and the area remained a favourite haunt.[107] Boomerang Street, opposite Hyde Park and the Roman Catholic Cathedral, was in operation certainly after the First World War and lasted until after the Second. It is now commemorated by the Boomerang Club, a fund-raising club for gay causes. The site of another beat — in Green Park, Darlinghurst, opposite St Vincent's Hospital — is to be the location of the Memorial to Gays and Lesbians who died in Nazi concentration camps. When the toilets were demolished, the Sisters of Perpetual Indulgence, in a pre-emptive move, rescued the urinal iconically left standing in a pile of rubble and spirited it away. It is preserved at a secret location as a relic and makes occasional appearances at Mardi Gras, most recently in 1994.

There are hundreds of beats throughout Greater Sydney, from the city centre[108] to the market area at Cabramatta and beyond. A beat may be one area, or a number of different locations that form a network.[109] They develop to meet a number of needs. If not the supermarket, then they are the corner store of sexual gratification. Being public, any sexual activity that takes place within them is against the law. For some men, the possibility of the rupture of the membrane of privacy is exciting in itself; for most, the risks that such a breach carries with it remain a cause of furtive anxiety. There are moments at which the beat becomes openly contested space. The public intervention can come from chance bystanders, innocent of what is going on; from groups of 'poofter-bashers' only too well aware of what is going on and determined to assert proper masculine values through violence;[110] from local residents who get wind of the use of a local area and who then take action by petitioning the council or, in one case, picketing the beat;[111] and from the police or shopping mall security guards.[112]

Beats as sites for sexual activity seem to be an exclusively male phenomenon. An attempt to breach this particular male preserve was made in Melbourne in 1974 when a group of lesbians set up a beat in the Edinburgh Gardens, Fitzroy, only to abandon it when they 'despaired of meeting anyone there except those same friends'.[113]

There is a suspicion, however, that the high incidence of dog walking by lesbians at Rozelle may be for more than their dogs' health. There is also a hint, judging by graffiti evidence, of some lesbian activity on the smaller beaches of southern Sydney.

How do you know when you are in a beat? Sometimes there are obvious signs which only the most innocent could misinterpret: phone numbers and dates for proposed assignations, boasts — sometimes accompanied by crude drawings of an individual's *membrum virile* and favoured sexual practice. 'What's going on here?' asks a graffito in the changing rooms at Balmoral Beach: the answer seems too obvious to state. Sometimes a beat has clearly been recognised by straight society. The cubicle doors in the lavatories of one shopping centre have been removed by the management, a case of going public with a vengeance. At one end of Lady Bay nudist beach a large graffito proclaims 'Poofter Free Area' — rather ineffectually it has to be said. Most beats, however, are more discreet. They are constituted in a space but not by that space. Rather, they are created by minute signalling that gives some truth to the cliché that 'it takes one to know one' — the fractionally-too-long-held gaze, the momentary, hesitating lingering; only occasionally is it done by outrageous but nonchalant flouting of society's rules as in the bold display of genitals.

To what extent are beats 'gay' spaces or indeed even 'homosexual' spaces? [114] In one novel, *The Beat*, all six characters are gay, ranging from the muscular physical education teacher to the now aged, toothless and bewigged former *flâneur*, all of whom take a part in a deeply satisfying act of vengeance.[115] Such a group, however, is not representative of beat users. Laud Humphreys, an early researcher into 'tearooms' (beats) in the United States, came up with findings that went against 'common sense'. He found that 62 per cent of his sample either were or had been married (8 per cent having divorced or separated).[116] This cross section is more representative than the characters in *The Beat*. Of course, some men marry to hide their homosexuality or in the hope that marriage will 'cure' it, but for a sizeable majority of the sample to have entered into matrimony alerts us to the fact that beat use is a complex matter.

No study similar to Humphreys' has been done in Australia but work around AIDS corroborates some of his findings. AIDS Council of New South Wales's (ACON) outreach workers carry out an educational program among users of beats. An unknown proportion of the patrons do not identify as either gay or homosexual: to cover these, the phrase 'men who have sex with men' has been coined. The 'contradiction of practice and identity is widely documented'.[117] One man, having inadvertently approached an outreach worker for oral sex, on being asked if he would rather talk about safer sex, swore and told the worker 'to talk to the fuckin' poofters' instead.[118] For some men the aim is simply to have sex and since it is easier to have casual sex with another man rather than with a woman, that is what they do. They see no complications in this; some even talk of it as a hobby or pastime.[119] An impression from a Sydney AIDS outreach worker is that a lot of the men have wives or girlfriends but 'don't get too hassled by the apparent contradiction'.[120]

VIOLENCE

There is a danger of writing a too utopian account of Sydney as a gay city. At a spatial level, it is easy to forget how small an area can justifiably be claimed as 'gay and lesbian'.[121] At a social level it appears that the concentration and visibility of gays and lesbians in Sydney does not alter public opinions of them either for or against. An opinion poll taken during the debate on the Anti-Discrimination (Homosexual Vilification) Bill shows attitudes in New South Wales to be identical to those of the Australian population as a whole.[122] Of those who do not accept the validity of homosexual relations, a few seek to show their disapproval violently. 'Poofter bashing' is a recurring feature of the gay and lesbian scene; fear of being bashed heightens tension among the patrons of Oxford Street and King Street in Newtown and haunts darkly on the way home.

It is not uncommon to refer to the areas of greatest gay and lesbian concentration as 'the ghetto', a shorthand term which may mislead as much as it enlightens. The traditional features of a ghetto are that it is sharply defined topographically, that it is exclusively given over to a particular group, that it is designed as a place of protection and security, that it is a focus for employment within that group and that it contains the institutions — social, religious, educational — of that group.[123] The ghetto may be created by the group itself or be imposed. The 'gay ghetto' in Sydney is similar to the classic form inasmuch as it bestows an identity and some degree of freedom. The most obvious difference is that it is neither tightly delineated nor exclusive. It is the porous nature of the 'ghetto' that renders its gay and lesbian *habitués* vulnerable. The Golden Mile can become a 'gilded cage' where the prey is easily identified and picked off — although attacks occur more widely than just in and around Oxford Street.

Commentators on the motives behind homophobic attacks distinguish the motivation for attacks on men from attacks on women. Both gays and lesbians share the stigma of difference but men are bashed as a punishment for not being 'real men' or as a demonstration by a 'real man' of the necessary attributes of that privileged status; women are bashed for failing to meet the sexual expectations or even demands of the propositioning male.

In one of the most horrific bashings of recent years, a gay man, Richard Johnson, was lured to a meeting at a public toilet in Alexandria in 1990 by a group of eight youths in their late teens who beat and kicked him unconscious. So badly injured was he that the pathologist said that the injuries to his brain were unusual even in boxers. Half an hour after the attack, the assailants returned to find Johnson still alive but did nothing to summon help. By the time a neighbour had discovered Johnson and had called an ambulance, he had died. The question of 'manhood' lay directly behind the actions of one of the defendants. Of 19-year-old Alex Mihailovic who received (with another) the heaviest sentence of eighteen years,[124] the judge said that his 'gentle and quiet behaviour had caused him to be teased over the years as a "poofter" ' and added: 'I have very little difficulty in accepting the opinion … that his involvement in this attack

... was ... attributable to peer pressure and to shake off his image as a sissy'.[125] The ferocity of the attack can partly be explained by a comment made by the judge: 'You give them [gay men] a label and dehumanise them', reflecting a remark by one of the accused: 'If he's a fag, bash the shit out of him'.[126] The case attracted the attention of mainstream newspapers two of which ran lengthy background pieces.[127]

The verbal ferocity that accompanied the attack on Johnson is echoed in an anonymous letter to the Anti-Violence Project:

> Words that come to mind [about gay men] include scum, filth, swine, vermin, faeces, maggot and rodent ... I shall refer to this lowly trash as faggots ... [which] ... in the old days would burn in fires and these scum today should burn in battery acid ... A national law should be enacted to shoot the faggot vermin on sight'.[128]

Renaming the object of hate anaesthetises the basher to moral considerations. In the period from 1989 to 1993, fourteen gay men have been murdered in New South Wales, all bar one in Sydney.[129] Six cases remain unsolved.

Just as gays are considered 'less-than-male', so too are lesbians considered 'less-than-female'. Just as gays are characterised as lacking the *active* principle of stereotypical masculinity, so lesbians are characterised as lacking the *passive* principle of stereotypical femininity. The former appear to be easy victims in the tradition of the school bully versus the school wimp; the latter, because they reject compliance with male demands to be brought back into line.[130] What is at work in cases of sexual harassment, be it against straight or lesbian women, is a refusal to acknowledge the woman's right to make her own choice. Even in the most inauspicious circumstances, certain men will persist. In past years, some of the straight men who have attended the Mardi Gras Party have waited outside the women's lavatories trying to pick up lesbians.[131] Stupefied by rejection — seen as a reflection on their masculinity — they become verbally aggressive. One of the four standard male responses on discovering that a woman is a lesbian is: 'You haven't tried me'.[132] To the penis-centred male, only the phallus has the answer. It becomes the elusive cure-all for the perceived sexual dysfunction of the lesbian.[133]

As a response to violence against gays and lesbians, the New South Wales Health Department in 1989 provided a grant of $55 000 for an Anti-Violence Project the main aims of which are to collect data, educate about violence and how to minimise risk and prepare recommendations for government. The project encourages victims of bashings to report to it.[134] It has produced four reports since 1989,[135] and ninety-four for the period covering June 1992 to June 1993. From the reports of the survivors of attacks in the latest survey, the following conclusions can be drawn: 51 per cent suffered physical injury; 17 per cent sustained serious injury; 75 per cent of attacks were to the head; 39 per cent of incidents occurred in the street: 22 per cent in the survivor's home; 30 per cent of incidents occurred in Oxford Street or its vicinity; 50 per cent of incidents took place in two months, January and February, at the height of summer; 42 per cent took place on a Friday, Saturday and Sunday; 83 per cent did not involve weapons; 19 per cent involved theft.

As far as the survivors were concerned, 26 per cent were female, 74 per cent were male; 17 per cent were lesbian, 71 per cent were gay; 56 per cent were aged between 25 and 39; 3 per cent were between 15 and 19; 65 per cent lived in the eastern suburbs or inner west. As for the assailants, 85 per cent were male and 13 per cent were in mixed sex groups; 14 per cent were estimated to be between 15 and 18; 36 per cent between 19 and 25; 21 per cent between 26 and 30; 45 per cent of incidents involved two to five assailants; five reports overall involved 15 to 17 assailants; 21 per cent of assailants were known to the survivors. As for witnesses to the incidents, 53 per cent of survivors were alone; 40 per cent of incidents were witnessed by others, but in 57 per cent of cases there was no intervention by the witness or witnesses. As for the attacks them-selves, 70 per cent of survivors said they believed they were attacked because they were gay or lesbian; 63 per cent said that anti-lesbian or gay remarks were made. As for action after the assault, only 36 per cent reported to the police and 22 per cent sought medical assistance.[136]

The unanswerable question is: what percentage of total assaults do these ninety-four cases represent? As in so much else in dealing with gays and lesbians, there is a failure of statistics, though the ninety-four cases are generally regarded as a vast under-reporting. What they tell us, however, is congruent with the experiences reported anecdotally.

Groups of straight men gather outside the Courthouse Hotel on the corner of Taylor Square, the centre of 'gay space'. They spread across the pavement, drinks in hand, expansive, leaving gaps through which other pedestrians must pass — as if run-ning the gauntlet. Gays and lesbians making their way down the street to their venues walk in single file trying not to catch their eye. It does not seem safe. There is a brief moment in the documentary *Feed Them To The Cannibals!* where, in the late evening on Oxford Street, a group of roistering and partly drunk straight young men, some with beer cans in their hands, some bare-chested, lay on a display of shouting and ges-turing for the camera.[137] Theirs is a confident, potentially threatening demeanour, mol-lified by the sense that their unabashed performance may find itself on television. Their use of space is expansive; their manner seeks to push aside others.

The implied threat becomes more explicit in what are known as 'Animal Buses' Typically these are buses privately hired to carry a sports team. After a game, the tradi-tional route is to Kings Cross for sex and alcohol followed by a journey to a gay area. The men tend to be in their twenties, although sometimes students from private or public schools are involved.[138] They travel around known gay areas, shouting abuse from the bus windows before parking and preparing for a night's violence. Appearance is everything. To be in the wrong place at the wrong time looking less than macho is an invitation to the gangs. You don't have to *be* gay; suspicion is all that it required.[139]

Seemingly innocent exchanges become fraught. Two gay men, Brown and Timmins, wait at a bus stop. They are approached by some men.

'Got a cigarette?', the first man asked Brown.

'No, sorry, I don't smoke.'

'What's that, then?' The man rapped his finger on Brown's shirt pocket.

Deep in the pit of Timmins's stomach, a muscle tightened. He knew what was going to happen.

What happened was a bashing that led to Timmins sustaining broken fingers, cuts and deep bruising that required four days in hospital.[140]

It is the random and unpredictable nature of the attacks, as well as the fact that the victim will always be outnumbered, that is most terrifying.

Measures to counter violence begin with the gay or lesbian. The 'Be StreetSmart' pamphlet issued by the Anti-Violence Project gives advice on how to avoid violence if possible, and face it if forced. There are self-defence classes, 'safe places', shops or other premises (even the Oxford Street McDonalds) displaying a pink triangle where someone who is being threatened can find refuge. Individuals are urged to carry whistles to attract attention and summon help. A police bus alternates between Taylor Square and Oxford Square at weekends[141] and officers patrol. There is, intermittently, a Volunteer Community Street Patrol.[142] Private security firms, including one, Eastside Security, founded by a gay former police sergeant, offer some reassurance as well as practical help.[143] Fred Nile opportunistically called in Parliament for the banning of Mardi Gras because it encourages gay bashing.[144] The Department of Schools Education has produced excellent material seeking to educate against violence of all sorts, be it domestic, against women or against homosexuals.[145] The module of six lessons on homosexuality starts with 'What We Know' and moves on to 'What We Want To Know'. It seeks to demystify homosexuality, to dispel disinformation; it requires students to recognise and question their attitudes. There is no central record of the use of the material in the public schools but at least it has been distributed.[146]

The demystification of homosexuality, the dispelling of disinformation and the need to recognise and question attitudes are as important among the general population as they are among school students. The marking out of territory in Sydney by gays and lesbians offers the opportunity for the general population to observe and form opinions from experience rather than from ignorance. For the gay and lesbian community, having its own spaces strengthens its sense of self gives it the confidence to push for equality.

Notes

1 This chapter was co-written with Iain Bruce. We are also grateful to Ken Davis for reading this chapter in draft and making helpful, detailed comments as both a thoughtful observer of and vigorous participant in gay politics in Sydney since the 1970s.

2 Andrew Leese 1993, 'The spatial distribution of subcultures: Gay men in Sydney', thesis submitted for the degree of Bachelor of Town Planning, University of New South Wales, figs 2.1 and 2.2. See appendix 1.5 for statistics by state electorates of men who, by 35, have never married — a crude indicator of gay concentration.

3 *Sydney Star Observer*, 10 July 1992, p. 5.

4 Peter Stallybrass & Allon White 1986, 'Bourgeois hysteria and the carnivalesque', in *The Politics and Poetics of Transgression*, Methuen, London, pp. 171–90. We are grateful to John Fletcher of the University of Warwick for this reference.

5 ibid., pp. 176 ff.

6 The state flower of New South Wales.

7 Interview in *Feed Them To The Cannibals!*, directed by Fiona Cunningham-Reid, Boabang Productions, 1993.

8 *Sydney Star Observer*, 21 February, 1992, p. 30.

9 D. Thompson 1986, *Flaws in the Social Fabric: Homosexuals and Society in Sydney*, Allen & Unwin, Sydney, especially ch. 1. See also G. Wotherspoon 1991, *City of the Plain*, Hale & Iremonger, Sydney, ch. 5. For a personal account which sets 1970s Gay Liberation in Sydney into a wider Left political context see Dennis Freney's 1991 autobiography, *A Map of Days*, Heinemann, Melbourne, ch. 17.

10 Ken Davis, cited in Galbraith, op. cit.

11 *Weekend Australian*, 27–28 February 1993, p. 20.

12 *Sydney Morning Herald*, 26 June, 1978, p. 3.

13 *Australian*, 26 June 1978, p. 1, cited in Wotherspoon, op. cit., p. 209.

14 *Sydney Morning Herald*, 27 June, 1978, p. 12. The disturbances at the court are reported on p. 3.

15 These three 1979 Acts were replaced in 1988 by the *New South Wales Summary Offences Act 1988*. Confusion can arise in dealing with the history of public protest in this period because acts from different periods bear the same name.

16 *Gay Community News*, no. 8 1980, p. 2 cited in K. Seebohm 1992, 'An Historical Geography of a Symbolic Landscape: the Sydney Mardi Gras', unpublished MA thesis, University of Sydney, p. 54 (Seebohm has published a digest of part of his thesis in Gary Wotherspoon & R. Aldrich, *Gay Perspectives II*, Department of Economic History, University of Sydney, Sydney, 1994.

17 *Sources*: 1980–90: Seebohm, op. cit.; 1991–93: Ian Marsh and John Greenfield 1993, *Sydney Gay and Lesbian Mardi Gras, An Evaluation of its Economic Impact*,

Australian School of Management, Sydney, p. 7; 1994: *Sydney Morning Herald,* 7 March 1994, p. 5 and the *Australian,* 7 March 1994, p. 3. Party figures are from Marsh and Greenfield except for 1994, which is from the *Sydney Morning Herald.*

18 *Sydney Morning Herald,* 1 March 1993 p. 5.

19 *Feed Them To The Cannibals!* op. cit.

20 Seebohm, op. cit. p. 105.

21 Observations on the 1992 parade are drawn from the photographs in G. North, (ed.) 1993, *The Night Of Your Life: Sydney Gay and Lesbian Mardi Gras,* Sydney, *passim.* The 1993 observations are from memory, prompted by media reporting and the booklet of the 1993 procession confusingly given the same title as the 1992 book by the same editor.

22 *Feed Them To The Cannibals!,* op. cit.

23 For a semiotic analysis of this event see Seebohm, op. cit. pp. 30 ff.

24 *Sydney Morning Herald,* 1 March 1993, p.18.

25 For the Order of Perpetual Indulgence, see *Campaign,* June 1992, pp. 16–19 and *Sydney Star Observer,* 24 January 1992, p. 21.

26 *Capital Q,* 12 February 1993, p. 22.

27 Set up to include lesbians more dramatically in the parade: see interview with Nora Savona in *Sydney Star Observer,* 5 April 1991, p. 4.

28 When asked what fags and dykes have to offer each other she replied: 'Fashion tips and motorcycle repairs'. *Capital Q,* 12 February 1993, p. 22.

29 Susan Sontag, Notes on 'Camp', in *Against Interpretation,* Eyre and Spottiswood, New York, 1964, p.275. For further discussion of camp, see M. Meyer (ed.) 1994, *The Politics and Poetics of Camp,* London, particularly Thomas A. King, 'Performing "Akimbo": queer pride and epistemological prejudice', pp. 23–50, where he rehearses some of the criticisms of Sontag.

30 Sontag, op. cit., p. 279.

31 The point at which simple exaggeration becomes parody — when muscles become cuirasses and greaves — is intelligently explored in Sam Fussell's 1991 *Muscle,* London, an account which plots his move from student of English Literature at Princeton and Oxford to runner-up in Mr Golden Valley (California). His obsession with his body convinces his friends that 'obviously he's gone queer' (p. 148), merely confirming a conversation he had when he started out: ' "Is this a gay gym?" I asked. / "Look honey," he replied. "*All* gyms are gay." / "But what about them?" I asked [pointing towards muscle hunks doing weights]. / Austin laughed out loud. "*Especially* them," he said. "They just don't know it yet!" (p. 38).

32 *Capital Q,* 18 February 1994, p. 1.

33 *Sydney Morning Herald,* 4 March 1994, p. 2.

34 Peter Baldwin (ALP) holds the federal seat of Sydney, covering the areas of greatest

gay and lesbian concentration: Balmain, Newtown, Erskineville, Glebe, Paddington and Darlinghurst with parts of Annandale and Leichhardt. He has appointed his Senior Electoral Officer, Kristine Cruden, as his Gay and Lesbian Liaison Officer; *Lesbians on the Loose*, December 1992, p. 16. He has supported the Anti-violence Project and the lifting of the defence forces ban on lesbians and gays.

35 *Sydney Star Observer*, 3 May 1991, p. 1.

36 *Sydney Morning Herald*, 21 June 1991, p. 6.

37 *Sydney Star Observer*, 31 May 1991, p. 1.

38 ibid. 17 May 1991, pp. 1, 2, 7 (Moore); p. 4 (Liberal); p. 6 (Labor); p. 9 (Democrat). Candidate interviews took up 1.5 pages (pp. 17–18); a survey of candidates' policies took up 1.5 pages (pp. 20–21) and a half page was given to the Legislative Assembly (p. 22).

39 ibid.

40 ibid, p. 6.

41 *Sydney Star Observer*, 31 May 1991, p. 15.

42 ibid. 22 March, 1991 p. 4.

43 *Eastern Express*, 13 October, 1993 pp. 1 and 5.

44 *Sydney Morning Herald*, 5 March 1994, p. 6.

45 M. Lauria & L. Knopp 1985, 'Towards an analysis of the role of gay communities in the urban renaissance,' *Urban Geography*, vol. 6, p. 159.

46 *Lesbians on the Loose*, February 1994, p. 6.

47 *Feed them to the Cannibals!*, op. cit.

48 *Sydney Morning Herald*, 27 June 1978, p. 12.

49 For example, a magistrate's opinion that a gay man had 'more likely than not' been assaulted by a plain-clothes officer at the Cleansing Rally organised by Rev. Fred Nile on 1 October, 1990, *Sydney Star Observer*, 15 November 1991, p. 5. The officer was charged with causing actual bodily harm and brought to trial on 15 June 1992; *Sydney Star Observer*, 12 June 1992, p. 6.

50 *Campaign*, July 1993, pp. 34–9.

51 *Feed Them To The Cannibals!*, op. cit.

52 *Campaign*, July 1993, p. 36.

53 ibid.

54 ibid., p. 37.

55 *Sydney Star Observer*, 18 October 1993, pp. 6–7, describing violence at Fred Nile's 7 October Jesus Jericho March to claim victory over homosexuality, abortion, drugs and prostitution.

56 *Weekend Australian*, 27–28 February 1993, p. 20.

57 *Feed Them To The Cannibals!*, op. cit.

58 *Body Politic*, produced in Toronto, was one of the most influential newspapers on the gay scene. It had wide circulation in the English-speaking world.

59 The pioneering legislation on decriminalisation of some aspects of homosexual behaviour in Australia was in the state of South Australia. The debate and the final form of the legislation drew heavily on Britain's Wolfenden Report (*Report of the Committee on Homosexual Offences and Prostitution*, London, 1968). For a full discussion of this, see Tim Reeves, 'The 1972 Debate on male homosexuality in South Australia', in Aldrich & Wotherspoon, op. cit..

60 Peter Walsh, West Australian Labor Senator (1973–93), bemusedly remarked of the decision of the Commonwealth Parliament: 'We have just voted to allow poofters to bring their boyfriends into this country'. *Sydney Star Observer*, 28 June 1992, p. 12.

61 J. Morris 1992, *Sydney*, Viking, New York, p. 153.

62 ibid., p. 110.

63 When asked in an ABC TV arts program why she had not mentioned Mardi Gras, she somewhat sheepishly admitted that she had not heard of it. But, then, she did not mention the state's most heavily promoted sport — football (Rugby League) — either. *Sydney Star Observer* 15 May 1992, p. 25.

64 For the widespread occurrence of homosexuality — forced and voluntary — in the colony, see the account in R. Hughes 1988, *The Fatal Shore*, Collins Harvill, London, pp. 264–72 and 536–8. For an early convict homosexual love-letter written anonymously in 1846 see Robert Dessaix (ed.), 1993, *Australian Gay and Lesbian Writing*, Oxford University Press, Melbourne, p. 20. Robert French 1993, *Camping by a Billabong*, Hale & Iremonger, Sydney, 1993, contains accounts from the days of the penal colony to the beginning of gay liberation in the 1970s. Garry Wotherspoon 1991, *City of the Plain*, Hale & Iremonger, Sydney, gives a comprehensive account of the twentieth century.

65 These data can be found in Kym Seebohm 1990, 'An Historical Geography of a Symbolic Landscape: the Sydney Mardi Gras', unpublished MA thesis, University of Sydney, maps 1–4.

66 Sydney's longest running gay bar was in Kings Cross — the Bottoms Up at The Rex.

67 John Pilger 1990, *A Secret Country*, Vintage, London, pp. 254, 260.

68 Susan Geason's 'Syd Fish' novels are among the best descriptions of the work of corruption and the local crime syndicates, centred around land deals. See, for example, *Shaved Fish*, Allen & Unwin, Sydney, 1990. The same forces are at work in P. Carey 1991, *The Tax Inspector*, University of Queensland Press, St Lucia. The Liberal government of Nick Greiner, elected in 1988, sought to curb the endemic corruption in state bodies by establishing the powerful Independent Commission Against Corruption (ICAC).

69 See Paul Ashton 1993, *The Accidental City: Planning Sydney since 1788*, Hale & Iremonger, Sydney, ch. 6; ICAC 1991, *Report on Investigation Into the Planning*

and *Building Department of South Sydney Council*, Sydney; *Sydney Morning Herald*, 3 December 1981, pp. 1, 2, 6; 18 April 1985, p. 1; 13 March 1987, p. 3.

70 *Sydney Morning Herald*, 13 March 1987, p. 3.

71 ibid., 11 March 1987. The Liberal leader, Nick Greiner, called the postponement the 'ultimate corruption of the democratic process in New South Wales'. When he was returned to power in 1988 and set up ICAC it fundamentally shifted the culture of government and administration in the state. Greiner was the commission's first and most spectacular victim. Although he was cleared of wrongdoing by a superior court he had resigned by then.

72 *Sydney Morning Herald*, 25 October 1982, p. 8.

73 ibid., 26 November 1986, p. 3.

74 The Builders Labourers' Federation refused to demolish buildings which served individuals to allow the building of others which served companies or institutions. The Rocks area of Sydney, now lauded as a quaint piece of original Sydney, was the most significant and valuable Green Ban.

75 See 'It pays to be gay', *Eastern Express*, 13 October 1993, pp. 1, 5.

76 Pilger, op. cit., p. 255.

77 We are grateful to Gary Dowsett of Macquarie University for the following information and for the convivial evening in which it was transmitted.

78 For the bars, see Wotherspoon, op. cit., p. 191.

79 Gail Force, 'Love Is All You Need', in M. Bradstock & L. Wakeling 1986, *Words from the Same Heart*, Hale & Iremonger, Sydney, p. 140.

80 M. Margold 1993, *Paddington Bazaar*, Sydney, p. 3. The name 'Paddington Bazaar' is registered by the Eastside Parish of the Uniting Church.

81 Peter Jackson 1991, *Maps of Meaning*, Routledge, London, p. 121.

82 'Coming out' to others is not a once-and-for-all act. A gay or lesbian will have to decide whether to 'come out' at every new encounter with the straight world.

83 Jackson, op. cit.

84 See section on violence.

85 *Campaign*, May 1993, p. 38.

86 *Capital Q*, 14 January 1994, p. 8.

87 Land and Environment Court of New South Wales, Case Number 10215 of 1992 before Assessor G. Andrews; *Mirella Raffaele and Orlando Grippa* v. *The Council of the City of South Sydney*: judgment date, 1 December 1992.

88 ibid., p. 10.

89 ibid.

90 ibid., p. 13.

91 ibid., p. 12.

92 *Sydney Morning Herald*, 3 December 1993 p. 6.

93 We are grateful to Gary Dowsett of Macquarie University for his suggestion that

we look at the papers for this case in which he was called as an expert witness for the appellants.

94 Land and Environment Court of New South Wales, Case Numbers 40031 of 1992 and 10204 of 1992 before Stein J.; *Bodyline Spa and Sauna (Sydney) Pty. Ltd v. South Sydney Council*: judgment date, 3 Novembe, 1992, p. 2.

95 ibid., pp. 2, 10.

96 ibid., p. 16.

97 ibid., p. 13.

98 For a persuasive account of the western suburbs, see D. Powell 1993, *Out West*, Allen & Unwin, Sydney.

99 See S. Hodge 1994, 'No fags out there: gay men, identity and suburbia', paper delivered at the Places In The Heart Conference, Geography Department, University of Sydney, 17–18 February.

100 Interview conducted January 1994.

101 *Campaign*, November 1993, p. 20.

102 For an account of adult life in the suburb of Green Valley, see Shannon Simons, 'A Nice Girl Like You', in Margaret Bradstock & Louise Wakeling (eds.), *Words from the Same Heart*, Hale & iremonger, Sydney, 1986, pp. 33–47.

103 *Campaign*, November 1993, pp. 18ff.

104 The Australian usage combines two terms current in the United States and in Britain. A 'beat' (Aus) may be either a 'cruising ground' (USA and UK) or a 'tearoom' (US) or 'cottage' (UK).

105 All beats are dangerous, and the standard gay guide to Australia warns off using them: *Sydney and Beyond, A Gay Guide to Sydney, Australia and New Zealand*, 1989 edn, p. 98. Beats on the beaches and cliffs are considered particularly dangerous. In the incidence of violence to gays, beats have accounted in 1989, 1992 and 1993 for 19 per cent, 15 per cent and 8 per cent respectively of incidents reported to the Anti-Violence Project. G. Cox 1994, *The Count and Counter Report*, Sydney, p. 34, table 16.

106 *Sydney Star Observer*, 15 May 1992, p. 12.

107 ibid.

108 ibid., 1 October 1993 p. 4.

109 M. D. Davis, U. Klemmer & G.W. Dowsett 1991, *Bisexually Active Men and Beats: Theoretical and Educational Implications*, Macquarie University AIDS Research Unit, Sydney, p. 20.

110 The case of Richard Johnson, discussed later, was one such example.

111 This happened at Ashfield Park on the boundaries of the inner west. *Capital Q*, 19 November 1993, p. 5. It was closed by the Council: *Sydney Star Observer*, 10 December 1993, p. 5.

112 The police officially deny any use of *agents provocateurs* to incite breaches of the

law, but their denials are countered by evidence from Marsden's, a company of Sydney solicitors. See *Sydney Star Observer*, 1 November 1991, p. 4, where Police Commissioner Lauer denied having a policy of selective entrapment. The *Star*, 29 May 1992, p. 3, reported the commissioner's declared determination to act on cases of entrapment.

113 Graham Carbery, 'Some Melbourne beats: a "map" of a subculture from the 1930s to the 1950s', in R. Aldrich & G. Wotherspoon, op. cit., p. 131.

114 Throughout this chapter, we have used the words 'gay' and 'lesbian' to describe individuals who acknowledge their sexuality in a politico-social way. We have used the word 'homosexual' of those whose practices involve sexual relations with members of the same sex but who do not acknowledge their sexuality. AIDS workers now use the term 'men who have sex with men' for those on beats who deny any homosexual impulses.

115 S. Payne 1985, *The Beat*, London. It is set in Melbourne.

116 L. Humphreys 1970, *Tearoom Trade*, Aldine, London, p. 112, table 6.1.

117 Davis, Klemmer & Dowsett, op. cit., p. 13.

118 ibid., p. 11.

119 We are grateful to Gary Dowsett for his observations on beat sex. See also Simon Nicholas, 'Men, sex and public places', in *Campaign*, July 1991, pp. 37–9.

120 Nicholas, op. cit., p. 39.

121 No figures exist for Sydney. B. Weightman 1981, 'Towards a geography of the gay community', *Journal of Cultural Geography*, vol. 1, p. 109, makes estimates of 'gay space' in four major American cities.

122 In NSW 12 per cent (12%) of those polled were 'very' accepting of people having homosexual relationships and a further 39 per cent (39%) were 'somewhat' accepting, as opposed to 39 per cent (38%) who were 'not at all' accepting; 11 per cent (11%) had no opinion. The *Bulletin*, 13 October 1992, p. 12. (Figures in brackets are for Australia as a whole.)

123 B. York, J. Jupp & A. McRobbie 1990, *A Working Paper on Multiculturalism. Paper No. 1 Metropolitan Ghettos and Ethnic Concentrations*, Office of Multicultural Affairs, Department of the Prime Minister and Centre for Immigration and Multicultural Studies, ANU, Canberra.

124 *Sydney Star Observer*, 19 April 1991, pp. 1, 3. For a report of the unsuccessful appeals against sentence and comments on the salutary nature of the sentences, see the *Sydney Star Observer*, 13 November 1992, p. 1.

125 ibid.

126 *Sydney Star Observer*, 8 March 1991, p. 1.

127 *Sydney Morning Herald*, 6 April 1991, p. 39; *Sun-Herald*, 14 April 1991, pp. 22 f.

128 G. Cox 1994, *The Count and Counter Report: A Study into Hate Related Violence Against Lesbians and Gays*, Sydney, p. 4.

129 *Sydney Star Observer*, 2 October 1993, p. 9.

130 For an account of one attack and the reactions of the men she had to deal with — from attacker to father to police — see Petra Alexander, 'Recharting the Terrain', in Bradstock & Wakeling,op. cit., pp. 146–61.

131 Interview about the 1993 Mardi Gras Party.

132 Bradstock & Wakeling, op. cit., p. 12. The other three responses are: 1. How come a good-looking girl like you is a lesbian? 2. How do you do it?; and 3. Can I watch?

133 A lesbian who was physically attacked at Rockdale Station was told by her assailant: 'You fucking dyke. All you need is a good man'. *Lesbians on the Loose*, July 1993, p. 6.

134 For example in the *Be StreetSmart* pamphlet.

135 Streetwatch 1989, *Off Our Backs*, 1991 on lesbians; and *Count and Counter* 1992 and 1993.

136 Cox, op. cit., pp. 8–11 and *passim*. We are grateful to Bruce Grant of the Anti-Violence Project for discussing the issues with us.

137 Directed by Fiona Cunningham Reid, Boabang Productions, 1993, broadcast ABC TV, Sunday, 28 February 1993, 8.30 p.m.

138 See, for example, *Sydney Star Observer*, 12 November 1993, p. 20.

139 Of survivors reporting to the Anti-Violence Project 6.4 per cent were straight. Cox, op. cit., p. 21. For an example of straight bashing, see *Capital Q*, 18 February 1994, p. 3.

140 *Sydney Morning Herald*, 'Good Weekend', 12 January 1991, pp. 8–11.

141 *Sydney Star Observer*, 17 April, 1992, p. 4.

142 See, for example, *Sydney Star Observer*, 15 May 1992, p. 19, and 2 October, 1993, p. 9.

143 *Sydney Star Observer*, 14 June 1991, p. 6.

144 *New South Wales Parliamentary Debates*, session 1991, 41 Eliz. II, 3rd series, vol. 225, pp. 3274–78.

145 *Resources for Teaching Against Violence*, n.d., NSW Department of School Education, Sydney.

146 We are grateful to Dr Lesley Lynch, Director of Curriculum at the Department of Schools Education, for discussing this issue with us.

5 FRAGMENTS AND DIVISIONS

Cities are microcosms of the wider economies and societies of which they are part. Social differences of gender, sexuality, income, age, religion and ethnicity are mapped onto cities. Some suburbs are populated mainly by the rich, others by the poor, although even behind the seeming social homogeneity of places there is greater complexity. Cities are mosaics of fragments and divisions. The forces driving residential choice are mainly economic, although cultural and social issues matter too, particularly for minorities. Localities which are accessible to jobs, services or good amenities are obviously more sought after, so in a bidding war the rich are the winners. Over time the perceived values of places may change. Neighbourhoods which formerly did not attract higher income people, such as inner city areas of nineteenth-century workers' housing, now do so. You would, for example, be hard pressed to find a house in Balmain under $400 000, yet Bill, in Glenda Adams's *Our Town*, reminisces how in 1962 'hardly any of the Balmain kids had hot water and some didn't have bathrooms. Art's house didn't have running water inside, only out the back.'[1] Conversely, once popular places may lose their charm, such as suburbs in the inner west suddenly affected by aircraft noise. Older long-term residents in localities which have gone 'up market' may be poorer in income (although not necessarily in assets if they own their homes) than more recent purchasers and renters of housing. Even a suburb where mostly rich people live may contain pockets of less sought after housing which enables lower income earners to gain or retain footholds.

Though cities have been the stage for novels from Dickens to Joyce, and an analytic site for geographers and sociologists for decades, the 1970s and 1980s saw rekindled academic and political interest in the social geography of cities. In Australia, a federal Labor government took office in 1972 and a major part of its appeal to the electorate was its promise to address problems in the larger cities, especially Sydney and Melbourne. Under Prime Minister Gough Whitlam a new Department of Urban and Regional Development (now referred to affectionately as DURD, while the bureaucrats from that time are the DURD 'Mafia') was set up. The brief was to devise policies to redress urban inequalities, since there was a growing fear that Australian cities might go down the path of American and British cities where unemployment and social discontent were on the rise.

Unlike American cities, where it is the inner areas which are populated by minorities — especially black and Latino people — and where much of the urban inequality and deprivation is concentrated, it is in the Australian outer city, the raw new suburbs on the edge, where incomes are relatively low and there is a lack of services and jobs.

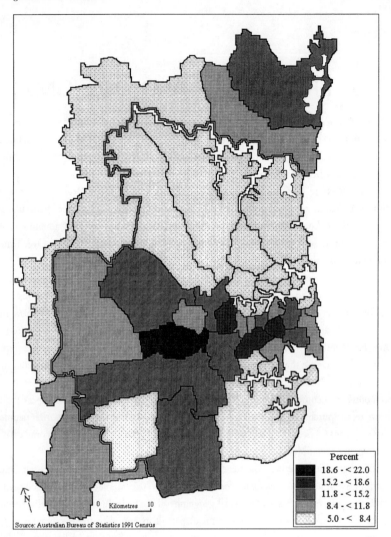

Percentage of resident workforce unemployed, 1991.

The massive suburbanisation of the 1950s and 1960s provided an opportunity for many people to own property and to escape from high density inner city living — often from suburbs which were perceived as slums forty or fifty years ago. But the negative side of suburban living was often poorer access to jobs and services and, for women, isolation. By the late 1960s these problems had become widely publicised and equity in the city was a political catchcry. The idea that where people live has a significant bearing on their welfare had taken root. In the 1990s the outer city remains a region in which jobs are far fewer than the resident population,[2] and with a growing deficit despite some increased provision of social services, an improvement in access to hospitals, universities and major recreational facilities.

The contrast between the outer city in Australia and the United States is striking. Richard Kirwan explains the difference thus:

> *[In the United States] for a variety of reasons, including more extensive investment in urban highways, the lack of low density sites close to the city centres and racial or ethnic antipathies, it was the middle to upper income groups which during the early post-war period moved to the outer suburbs. The problem for lower income households was conceived to be the poor quality housing that the high price of inner area sites entailed, not the lack of access to facilities — such as schools, hospitals and public transport — with which inner areas were generally better endowed.[3]*

By the late 1970s, unemployment had emerged as a major concern in Australia. Rising unemployment, from less than 2 per cent of the work force in 1970 to around 10 per cent in the mid-1990s, has been the result of turbulent changes in the global economy buffeting Australians, although it was not until the 1980s that the sociospatial structure of cities began to be explicitly interpreted as the outcome of the powerful forces of global economic restructuring since the early 1970s. These restructuring forces and their social outcomes are central to understanding representations of Sydney's contemporary social geography.

The unemployment map of Sydney divides the city roughly into two contrasting parts. Western and south-western suburbs have the highest rates, especially of youth unemployment, while suburbs to the north and north west of Sydney Harbour have the lowest incidence. This dichotomy has become more marked since the mid-1970s with much of the increase in unemployment being in areas where there were more unemployed than the regional average.[4] Areas of high unemployment are also areas where the work force is younger, less well educated, more likely to have been born overseas and more likely to work, or to have worked, in factories. While many jobs have been created in Sydney's economy since the early 1970s, most of these have been in services and thus less suited to the skills of the unemployed. Higher paid service jobs are also concentrated in the northern and north-western parts of Sydney, as well as in and near the CBD, and so are relatively inaccessible to people living in the suburbs where unemployment is highest. The unemployment map thus largely mirrors factors which predispose people to remain or become unemployed. Affluent households are more likely to encourage and be able to support their children to stay on at school and to obtain post-secondary qualifications, which means better chances in the job market. Being unemployed obviously implies a usually dramatically lowered income. Affluent workers tend to be concentrated in the higher paid segment of the service economy where there is less susceptibility to the job shedding which has been so marked in manufacturing.

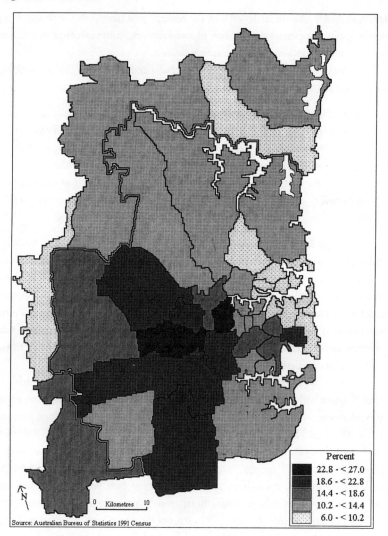

Percentage of resident workforce working in manufacturing, 1991.

Although an individual's class position, skills and education levels are the primary predictors of the risk of unemployment, where she or he lives in the city can also matter. In most of the east, 50 per cent of the population is unqualified whereas in the west the figure is 68 per cent.[5] In Sydney, because there is a marked lack of jobs in the outer areas, when people get jobs they typically have to travel long distances to work, and for low paid jobs this simply may not be worthwhile.[6] Low paid jobs in factories and shops are often only advertised locally, so that people searching for jobs are unaware of them. There is also a certain historical stigma attached to Sydney's outer western and south-western suburbs, so that a 'Westie' going for a job in the eastern part of Sydney faces potential discrimination from employers. People living in the west are also ironically stigmatised by some of their own political representatives. A councillor on Fairfield Council argued, for example, that:

> no-one in Fairfield wants to work any more because it's too easy not to … I work in the high school and I see the kids and they just want to leave school so they can go on the dole. I knew a careers adviser who was very cynical about the whole thing too. The kids wanted to do what the parents wanted to do and that was nothing.[7]

ECONOMIC RESTRUCTURING SINCE THE 1970s

Australian economic restructuring since the early 1970s has been defined by the decimation of manufacturing jobs, growth of employment in the service sector and rising unemployment. A sharp decline in manufacturing employment in Australia since the early 1970s has largely been the result of the shift in factory production from a national to an increasingly international scale, especially through the agency of TNCs. A combination of high tariffs and limited foreign competition in the 1950s and 1960s, propelled by burgeoning domestic demand, drove growth in the number of Australian factory jobs to a peak of 1 215 570 by 1971. In that year manufacturing comprised 23 per cent of the Australian work force. But by the beginning of the decade the outside world had begun to change radically. Most significantly, East and later South-East Asian nations had started to industrialise rapidly, using cheap and politically docile supplies of labour with TNCs integrally involved. In technologically advanced sectors, especially motor vehicles and white goods like refrigerators and washing machines, Australia's domestic market was too small to absorb the output from modern, large-scale factories. Local manufacturers were thus increasingly exposed to competition from imports at cheaper prices. High local production costs and growing international pressures led to the dismantling of tariffs from the early 1970s, which continued at an accelerating pace through the following decade. The growing foreign competition meant that over a quarter of a million Australian factory jobs were lost and not replaced between 1970 and 1990. Cities which had been most dependent on manufacturing were the hardest hit.

Sydney had the largest number of factory workers of any Australian city, with 30 per cent of Australian manufacturing jobs in 1971, a fraction ahead of Melbourne. Between 1971 and 1991 Sydney lost some 140 000 jobs compared with Melbourne's 100 000. But the effect on unemployment in Sydney has been less marked because the city's economy was more diversified at the onset of job loss with thus a greater potential for job growth. Excluding Canberra, Sydney's unemployment rate by 1991 was, despite the job loss, lower than all other major cities except Brisbane's which was much the same. Within Sydney those parts of the city where the largest numbers of factory workers lived in the early 1970s, the west particularly, when manufacturing employment was at a maximum Australia-wide, experienced disproportionate growth in unemployment over the next two decades.[8] A Fairfield community worker described the link between decline in manufacturing jobs and rising unemployment thus:

> Employment trends here are similar to trends across Australia. Like the absolute destruction of youth employment opportunities. And because we've got such a high rate of increase in numbers of young people, it's really problematic ... The other group that's a real concern are the men older than 45. Their employment opportunities are destroyed as well because of the manufacturing decline. And once again if their first language is not English and they've been doing unskilled work, they don't have any qualifications, they've been tied into a corner. There are not going to be many opportunities for them. Unemployment is around 40–50 per cent among refugees. So I'm pretty disillusioned by the employment situation up here.

In his view efforts to alleviate high immigrant unemployment in this part of the city needed to recognise that:

> Our local work force has disadvantages which are multiply layered: English as a second language, torture and trauma background, knowledge of and access to labour market and training networks. Traditionally, people who came to Australia to seek a new life found work. That post-Second World War experience in a growing, burgeoning and protected manufacturing environment has totally gone.[9]

Manufacturing was established in Sydney's inner city around Port Jackson and south from the CBD to the north shore of Botany Bay in the nineteenth century. This concentration continued, with some dispersal to Silverwater and Bankstown and other areas, between the First and Second World wars. As Sydney's economy grew during the 1950s and 1960s factories decentralised within the Sydney region as workers increasingly moved to the suburban home on the quarter-acre block. Decentralisation was also precipitated by the fact that the relatively fixed supply of centrally located industrial land was becoming more expensive and the roads more congested. Coupled with the widespread use of trucks for goods transport, which made central locations close to Port Jackson and railheads at Central and Darling Harbour less essential, the effect was to reduce the importance of the old manufacturing areas. In about 1970 the so-called 'central industrial area' thus accounted for only 40 per cent of Sydney's factory jobs.[10] By the onset of de-industrialisation the inner city was no longer the sole concentration of factory workers. While the inner city was affected, the brunt of the impact of job loss was thus distributed across the wider Sydney region. This is one reason why there is less entrenched inner city deprivation on the scale of the cities in the United Kingdom and United States.[11] Unemployment is nevertheless serious in places like South Sydney and Marrickville, although to a much lesser extent than in the west and south-west.

Loss of factory jobs and the inner city's diminished although continuing role as a residential zone for recent immigrants are at work here too. The words of local people capture the shifts. A Marrickville social worker observed that:

> the large old industrial manufacturers, the knitting mills, foundries and all those larger manufacturers disappeared, but what's replaced those are factory-unit type developments. And they're not so much factory units either, they're more small ware-housing operations that are servicing the airport and the port area.[12]

Asked where immigrants to Marrickville work now, a local resident said:

> I've got a couple of thoughts. There's a lot of home industry, particularly amongst the Asians, there are a lot of people working basically in sweatshops, sewing. That's certainly very much the case. I think the industry that required totally unskilled labour doesn't really exist in Marrickville as it used to.[13]

Youth unemployment in Marrickville is also perceived to be very significant. A community worker noted: 'There's a whole lot of unemployed youth growing up that are becoming a social problem. There's no hope for them to get a job'.

Yet even though decline in manufacturing has been a major cause of rising unemployment in Australia, factory production has not been withering on the vine. As Ross Gittins explains:

> between 1982–83 and 1990–91, the amount of goods produced by manufacturing increased by 20 per cent. That's just another way of saying that the productivity of our manufacturing increased greatly ... In the jargon, manufacturing is becoming more capital intensive ... Which means it's going down the road already travelled by our rural sector. At the turn of the century, agriculture provided employment for a third of the work force. Today the proportion is 5 per cent.[14]

Also pointing to a bright side to de-industrialisation is the enhanced export performance of Australian manufactures which now constitute 24 per cent of exports by value. Exports of hi-tech goods, the so-called elaborately transformed manufactures (ETMs), such as telecommunications equipment, medical and pharmaceutical products, have grown particularly strongly. Economics commentators agree that Australia's economic future depends significantly on enhanced exports of manufactures. The roles of cities in this are not readily measured but Sydney and Melbourne remain dominant.

As manufacturing declined as a source of jobs so employment in the service economy grew, although not at a rate great enough to compensate for the jobs lost. The service economy now employs four-fifths of Australian workers but growth has not been even across all categories.[15] Between 1983 and 1992, the big four growth sub-sectors were: community services; wholesale and retail trade; finance, professional and business services; and recreation, personal and other services. Community services — education,

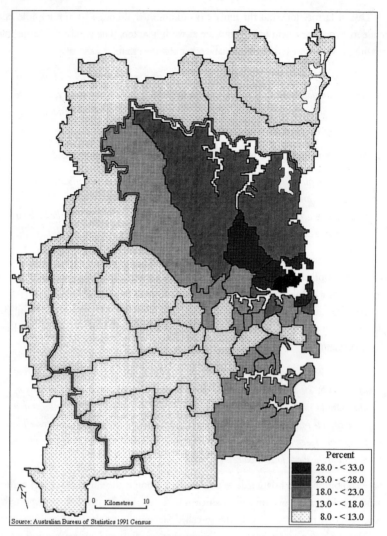

Percentage of resident workforce working in finance, property and business services, 1991.

health and the like — accounted for almost one-third of the job growth in services over the period. Wholesale and retail trade accounted for a further quarter. Finance, property and business services contributed just under a quarter, while recreation, personal and other services accounted for less than a fifth. Although some of the growth comes from providing more services (particularly retail) to consumers, much of it comes from providing services to business. Just over half of these extra jobs in services were part-time of which the majority were done by women. The service economy thus consists of a highly diverse set of jobs with matching variations in incomes and security of tenure. There have been fundamental shifts in the service economy since the early 1970s in the western, industrialised world and the Australian economy has reflected these trends.

Robert Reich, an American economic historian and Bill Clinton's labour secretary, classifies growth jobs in the service economy into two groups which he calls 'symbolic analysis' and 'in-person services'.[16] The first, relatively small group, although growing rapidly, includes highly skilled, well-remunerated work. The second, with many more people involved and also growing rapidly, provides generally lower skilled, lower paid and less secure jobs. Symbolic analysts (roughly coincident with professional–managerial workers as defined by the Australian Bureau of Statistics) drive the so-called 'information economy'. The production and transmission of information in all its myriad forms has become a very lucrative field for business investment and employment. Symbolic analysts work in all sectors of the economy but may be loosely categorised into technical — like engineering, industrial design and legal — and advertising and market research and business services. These workers typically provide what are known in the trade as 'producer services'. These contrast with services provided direct to consumers, such as hairdressing, medical attention and education. Businesses have always needed producer services but these have become more diverse and complex and are increasingly provided outside rather than within businesses. Integral to much growth in the information economy are global networks for the production and trade of goods and services which are dominated by TNCs. These networks depend crucially on reliable and fast flows of information.

Australian official statistics are produced in such a way that it is impossible to track precisely the growth in the numbers of symbolic analysts. But the FPBS category used by the Australian Bureau of Statistics gives some idea of trends. Two questions are interesting. First, how does Sydney compare with other Australian cities?, the answer to which shows how much Sydney has been incorporated into the global economy compared with its national competitors for business investment. Second, how has restructuring in the service economy contributed to social polarisation in Sydney? The 1991 shares of Australian FPBS jobs in Sydney and Melbourne were 31 and 21 per cent respectively. This exceeded their national shares of the population, which were 21 and 18 per cent respectively. Perth and Brisbane, the capital cities of the 'sunbelt' states, increased their shares of producer services jobs at rates equivalent to their increased shares of national population. High numbers of producer service jobs in Sydney and Melbourne are consistent with those cities' roles as headquarter sites for national and international businesses and associated producer services. Although FPBS does directly measure all command and control functions and producer service jobs, these trends clearly reflect the new dimensions of competitive advantage which favour attraction of global business activity.

People employed in FPBS jobs live in all parts of Sydney but there is a pronounced and growing concentration in the north and north-west arc where regional incomes are highest and unemployment rates, proportions of recent immigrants and dependence on manufacturing are lowest. These workers also live in the inner areas of mainly nineteenth-century workers' housing, like Paddington, Glebe and Balmain, which have become gentrified since the 1960s. Gentrification of inner Sydney, like elsewhere, has been driven partly by nostalgic interest in older housing — and a new cultural capital associated with these sites — and partly by a desire to live close to entertainment and cultural facilities which are typically found in the inner city. An important part of the explanation of gentrification has been growth in demand for symbolic analysts to fill private sector and government jobs in Sydney's CBD. In this way gentrification is linked to economic restructuring and globalisation of Sydney's economy.

Two contrasting inner city localities, Waverley and Marrickville, illustrate the emergence of gentrification in rather different contexts.[17] Waverley is east of the CBD and on the ocean, while Marrickville is in the inner west adjacent to, indeed incorporating, industrial areas. In Waverley the impact of gentrification on housing prices, particularly around Bondi, is a major concern for low-income people. According to a Waverley real estate agent:

> The prices in this area are unbelievable. The average Joe can't afford it out here, so you've seen a change in the people that are buying in. The ones that are buying into the area for the first time or wanting to for the first time, can't afford it. They're the ones that are being pushed out to Redfern or down south, around Gymea, those areas. They're looking at totally different areas and lifestyles. That's something that bothers me, because I would like to think that my children have grown up in the Eastern Suburbs and if they wished to live here, that they could afford to do it. And I think it's very sad that this is not happening ... I think we're driving our young families out of the area, and the moment you've done that, you've lost the plot ... Look how schools are closing ... They're closing our hospitals.[18]

But the picture is too simplistic. Bondi may be less a place for young families than it once was, though many who can afford it still live there. Instead it offers a city space to heterogeneous households of single people, gays, single women with children and old people who delight in its gentrified seediness and lack of convention. At Gusto's on Hall Street the demarcation between shoppers and coffee drinkers evaporates as inside becomes outside and outside in. Gentrification has brought with it a claiming of public space where anything goes. And even though rents are high, for many the costs are worth the escape and pleasure.

This picture of widespread gentrification is leavened by a Waverley community service worker's recognition that: 'there are certainly real socioeconomic extremes. There are little pockets within suburbs that are quite exclusive. Then some Housing Commission houses down the road, a real contrast.'

Marrickville gentrification tells a different story. A local government councillor commented:

Post-gentrification, Brighton Boulevard, Bondi Beach, August 1995.

Pre-gentrification, Blair Street, Bondi Beach, August 1995.

There are no uniform changes in Marrickville over the last ten years, in fact they are very divergent changes ... You can almost put a line through the middle of the municipality ... On the Newtown side of the municipality there's a new group of people moving into the area that tend to be either in shared households or single; some of them are gay. They tend to be better educated with better jobs and they've forced change on a whole range of areas ... On the other side of the municipality, Dulwich Hill, and in the south Marrickville area ... you've got a few people described as yuppies ... because there's big houses over there. But more significantly you've got all the Arabic speaking people.[19]

It is a tale of at least two cities, where Newtown, to many Marrickville residents, is another world. A community service worker observed:

We know that Marrickville goes all the way up to Missenden Road but it certainly doesn't feel like it ... You just don't relate to the people up in Newtown in the same way ... I've noticed, in Newtown, a lot more young mothers with young children who don't have to go out to work, who seem to be fairly well off and their whole social attitude is that they're fairly well off. This seems like a simple explanation, but for example, we provide fruit and things for the children and they think nothing of tipping it all in the garbage bin, whereas our mums would make sure that every bit was eaten.[20]

Apart from, and indeed closely linked with, rising unemployment — the most dramatic and politically charged aspect of social change in the last quarter of the twentieth century — has been the divergence in incomes and economic opportunities available to people in different social classes.[21] Throughout most of the twentieth century trends were in the opposite direction. But just what this notion of a growing gap between rich and the poor actually constitutes is technically complex. Depending on the statistics used it is possible to support or deny, or at least to qualify, the proposition that the rich are getting richer and the poor are getting poorer.

The media have had a field day on the topic. In a cover story in the *Bulletin* magazine of 28 February 1995, the then deputy leader of the federal opposition (now federal treasurer), Peter Costello, flagellated the Australian Labor government for its 'shameful legacy'. His figures supported the proposition that the gap between rich and poor in Australia grew wider in the 1980s and 1990s.

Two years earlier, in a *Sydney Morning Herald* article headlined, 'Our egalitarian society is just a debating point', the economist Frank Stilwell also suggested that, 'contrary to the popular myth about an egalitarian society, there is a striking and growing degree of inequality in income and wealth in Australia,' an ironic meeting of Left and Right.

In response to Peter Costello, the then Labor minister for social security, Peter Baldwin, argued that improvements to social security and the social wage in the 1980s meant that the poor, while increasing in number, were actually better off in the 1990s than they were a decade earlier. A year earlier the economic commentator Ross Gittins had said much the same thing:

> *Something you wouldn't be surprised to be told is that the rich are getting richer and the poor are getting poorer. But you won't hear that from me because it's not true and it is not what the research is saying. [In the 1980s] the gap between the rich and poor widened — the distribution of income became more unequal — not because the poor got poorer, but because the rich got so much richer ... But what did the growing inequality of wages do to the distribution of families' disposable income? In the US and Britain, changes in other sources of family income (including welfare benefits) did little to prevent the greater inequality of wages leading to greater inequality of disposable income. In Canada, the Netherlands, France, Sweden and Australia, however, changes in other sources of family income (including welfare benefits), significantly offset the greater inequality of wages, so that the widening of the distribution of family income wasn't as great.*[22]

Economic restructuring in Australia since the early 1970s is the root cause of the growing gap due to rising unemployment and shifts in the occupational structure. Not only has restructuring shifted the sectoral balance of the economy it has also shifted the occupational structure. Bob Gregory encapsulated this trend in the phrase, 'the disappearing middle'.[23] His research showed that in 1980 there were 406 000 fewer jobs in the middle fifth of the earnings distribution of adult, male, full-time, non-managerial workers than if the proportions as at 1976 had remained constant; 118 000 actual jobs were lost. The reasons for this marked trend are not fully understood but Gregory concluded that technology and product demand patterns are changing the way in which work is organised and creating many more low-pay, fewer high-pay and no middle-pay jobs. The phenomenon of the disappearing middle has been widely identified in other advanced capitalist countries.[24]

Discourses on the shifts in income distribution and occupational structure are dramatic. Under the headline, 'Forecast: a nation of servants and masters', the *Sydney Morning Herald* reported the social researcher Hugh McKay as believing that Australia will split into an 'upstairs' and 'downstairs': 'We are on the brink of a service class', he said. The business analyst Phil Ruthven, while predicting a boom in domestic services, expects a discarding of old prejudices towards certain occupations: 'the word "servile", applied to service occupations is wrong, it is stupid, it is offensive'.[25] Another feared outcome of income polarisation, linked to rising unemployment, has been the emergence of a so-called 'underclass'. Under the headline, 'Locked Out', the *Sydney Morning Herald* proclaimed:

> *No work, no hope, no escape ... this is the prospect facing a growing number of Australians. Call it a welfare society, a workless class or an underclass, it is the same: a group of people excluded from mainstream society. It is a way of life that is being passed down from one generation to another.*[26]

Discourses of fragmentation (Source: Sydney Morning Herald, 1993–95).

This discourse of the 'underclass' implies a group of people who are hermetically sealed off from the social mainstream and who have no prospect of crossing the divide. In the United States, images of the underclass derive most potently from black and Latino ghettos and from people living on the street. While there is certainly homelessness in Australia, unemployment is the far greater problem. Because the level of unemployment is so high, even high rates of economic growth would take many years to reduce it. The social trend to formation of single-parent households since the early 1970s is also deployed in discourses of the underclass:

> *When Gloria Swift goes shopping, she looks for the pictures on the labels. Unable to read or write, it may be the only way she can distinguish a bottle of detergent from a bottle of cordial. Swift, 40, is a sole parent with five children. Three of them have serious reading problems … The family is part of a debilitating cycle of illiteracy and unemployment: it is a cycle that is passing from generation to generation.*[27]

More sympathetically, and less punitively, journalist Adele Horin bemoans the link between single parenthood and poverty:

> *The term sole parent is almost synonymous with poverty in Australia. But elsewhere the story is different. A woman would be better off taking her kids to Britain, France, Germany — just about anywhere in the West except the US ... nearly 50 per cent of sole parents were poor by the end of the [1980s] decade compared to 40 per cent at the start. Their living standards [fell] further and further behind the living standards of two-parent families, Canberra academics Ann Harding and Deborah Mitchell discovered. This was because two-parent families increasingly earned two incomes.*[28]

Labor governments in the first half of the 1990s decade tackled the problem, with the result that the number of sole parents living under the poverty line has halved since 1990 because of a sharp increase in social security payments. But this contraction, from 60 to 30 per cent, while a move in the right direction, is not far enough. In the overall population, 12 to 15 per cent of all Australian households fall below the poverty line. Where single-parent households cluster in Sydney reflects the location of public housing — a mere 5 per cent of all housing — and of households with lower than average incomes. It is another vignette in the contemporary story of a growing welfare gap between those living in the more, and those in the less, affluent parts of Sydney. But perceptions of that gap derived from statistical discourse can miss the heterogeneity of many areas. In Waverley, for example, there are many single-parent households. According to a Waverley community worker, many of the women who use the local refuge come from nearby:

> *They like to stay in the area but it's extremely difficult when the Department of Housing is offering them Mount Druitt, in the outer west, as a first option for available housing. And they don't seem to be addressing the problem in the Department of Housing, of building more housing for people in this area. So it's extremely difficult. We're looking at them going out to Maroubra or Matraville if we can or otherwise into the high rises in Surry Hills or Redfern. The women prefer that to Mount Druitt. But there are so many problems involved with those high rises: isolation, suicide, people get agoraphobia living up there. The government actually pulled down the high rises down in Canberra. So it's not an appropriate option to offer a woman who's been through a crisis.*[29]

In Marrickville the scale of the welfare-dependent population is much greater than in Waverley, and more diverse. As a community service worker said:

> *We are having a growth in welfare dependent people generally in the community. One of the actors in that has been the Department of Housing which has moved people with welfare based problems into our area from other places. The other thing*

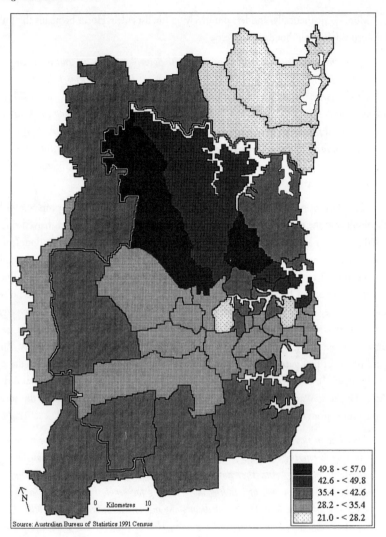

Median household incomes, $ per annum 1991.

has been that particularly in the Greek community, the more successful ones [the immigrants from the 1950s and 1960s] have been moving away and we've been left with the ones coping less well. We're also getting more people with mental health problems in the area. The mental health facilities in Marrickville are fairly good and that's also tending to attract people needing support to live in the area; there's not a lot of community based support.[30]

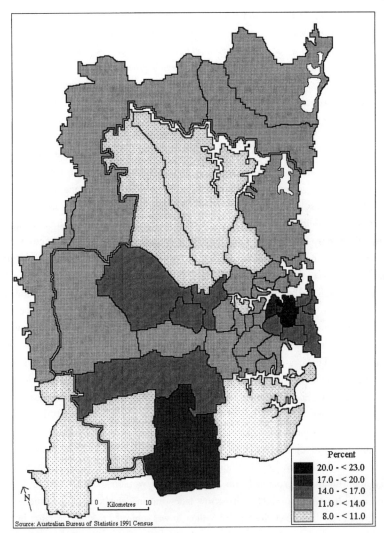

Single parent families as a percentage of all families, 1991.

And a Marrickville resident added:

Over the last few years I've seen a lot of these fringe people that we're talking about. There's many of those who are mentally sick, and the government has virtually dumped them out on the street. My local church is just invaded with people that really should be in hospital; they're walking the streets of Marrickville. I'm involved

with St Vincent de Paul and things ... like the government puts in thousands of
people in the Warren into public housing and I think that's terribly wrong. Even
before they built it, we knew at St Vincent de Paul we were going to be there full-
time ... I don't know how many thousands are living there but it's appalling. Many
of these are people coming from outside the area. They have to live somewhere and I
don't mind having those sort of people living in our group but for God's sake please
provide the services that they require so they can rehabilitate.[31]

It is arguable whether the notion of an 'underclass' has much analytical, as opposed
to political, use, but there are undoubtedly segments of the population in Australia at
the bottom of the income spectrum who have little chance of improving their position
and their numbers have grown as the outcome of economic restructuring. In this group
Australian Aborigines undoubtedly stand apart as the most long-term disadvantaged.
Australia's history in dealing with the massive problems inflicted on its indigenous population by invasion and settlement has paralleled other colonised spaces. Yet while superficially analogous to the American minorities (blacks, Latinos, native Americans), the situation of Australian Aborigines is different in several ways. Most obviously, their numbers
are small — so many having been killed by disease brought in by white settlers or by
more violent methods. The most visible concentration of Aborigines in Sydney is in
inner city Redfern, although there is another Aboriginal community at La Perouse on
Botany Bay. The area lies on Eora country where the original inhabitants were the
Cadigal people. Given its proximity to the site of early invasion the group was virtually
wiped out at the time through killings, a denial of access to food areas, and disease.[32]

Redfern went through a series of social shifts over the next two centuries. In the
early years of European settlement the high ridge where Cleveland Street now runs was
popular with Sydney's landed gentry and with William Redfern and his family in particular, who were given large landholdings. By the end of the nineteenth century the
neighbourhood had expanded into a settlement of workers' cottages and low-cost,
poorly built terrace housing, with narrow lanes and inadequate sanitation and other
facilities. Like other inner city areas of Sydney, it was subjected to slum clearance in the
1930s as people were relocated to the outer suburbs. In the fashion of the time, high-
rise blocks of flats were constructed by the Housing Commission in the early 1960s,
despite resident action to retain the old workers' cottages and terraces. In the ensuing
years the original landowners — the Aboriginal people — returned to the area, partly
in search of employment and housing, partly to avoid the isolation or racism they were
subjected to in rural and outer suburban areas. Ruby Langford describes her life in a
Green Valley Housing Commission house in 1972: 'There were so few black families
there in 1972 ... you weren't able to have anyone come and stay without permission
from the Commission. It reminded me of the missions. The rule was useless in our culture, where survival often depended on being able to stay with friends and relatives.'[33]

At the 1991 Census there were approximately 1100 Aboriginal people in the South Sydney local government area, representing 1.4 per cent of the population. Aboriginal people in Sydney refer to themselves as Kooris — which is a south-eastern New South Wales term or Murris, a northern New South Wales and Queensland term. Redfern has the most concentrated urban Aboriginal population in the country; overall only 27 per cent of Aboriginal people live in major urban areas compared with 62 per cent of the general population. Yet the population is not static. Many Aboriginal people spend some time in the city and some time in the country. The expectation is that relatives and friends can stay whenever they turn up, which at times might mean fifteen to twenty people staying in one house. The majority of Aboriginal people live in the Housing Commission dwellings of Waterloo and Surry Hills as well as in privately owned houses. The Aboriginal Housing Company, a federally funded housing authority, owns a block of houses bordered by Eveleigh, Caroline, Hugo and Vine streets, which is referred to locally as 'the Block' or the 'Country' ('coon country') by the police.

The area is characterised by urban inequality and deprivation. Welfare indicators — incomes, unemployment, single-parent households, health — are poor and upward social mobility is very limited for most people. The *Sydney Morning Herald* on 22 March 1996 described the situation thus:

> *The Block looks like a display centre for urban black misery … Last November a black African journalist, Vuyo Mvoko, also found similarities to his homeland. He'd heard plans for a $35 million 'Black Chinatown' replacing urban despair with a 'tourist friendly district' of shops and Aboriginal culture and industry. He wrote: 'For a while I forgot I was in Sydney. I saw a conglomeration of South African townships … I found abandoned dwellings, litter and torn clothes hanging shabbily from part- ly ripped balconies, broken windows tinted by a thick and foggy layer of dust.*

On the other hand, housing tenures are relatively secure, transfer payments under the Hawke/Keating Labor government at least were relatively high, and there are a num- ber of local health and other advisory services. Most of the organisations in the area — such as the Aboriginal Medical and Legal services, the Murawina Pre-School and the Tony Mundine Gym — are Aboriginal run and controlled. These represent important sites of resistance to white Australia's policies of colonisation and the prevention of Aboriginal self-determination. Through the Commonwealth-funded Community Development Programme people are employed in jobs ranging from demolition work to vegetable gardening as a way of learning new skills and gaining self-esteem to enter the mainstream labour market. This is important in the context of a national Aboriginal unemployment rate of 30.8 per cent. With no Aborigines as managers and only 4.2 per cent as professionals, compared with 11.2 per cent and 21.3 per cent respectively in the wider community, there is a long way to go. Under the Howard coalition government, the federal programs for Aboriginal people are under tremendous threat.

White spaces are also being contested. Paralleling the emergence of gay pride, marked by Sydney's annual Gay and Lesbian Mardi Gras, are tribal markings, flags and other flamboyant signs in the streetscape. Space in inner city Redfern has been symbolically as well as physically expropriated. The locality is well marked with conflicting signs of social dislocation on the one hand, and black pride on the other. Yet despite increasing self-determination and resistance and considerable advances in recent years in support services, political mobilisation and social mobility, the entrenched processes of marginalisation continue to act forcefully.

In the media Redfern continues to be represented as a ghetto and a place of crime, violence and threat. Local Aboriginal people report media incitement to racist violence. On one occasion in the 1980s the Willessee television program allegedly entered the area without permission and began abusing and filming local residents. The residents reacted, police were called, a riot ensued and Willessee triumphed with a sensational programme at the cost of the local people who were arrested and charged. Levels of police intimidation and occupation of the area remain high. The TNT office towers adjacent to Redfern Station have been used as a vantage spot for the streets in the Redfern patrol, a strategy reminiscent of police tactics in the South Central area of Los Angeles. Police incursions and operations in the area are regular occurrences.[34] In the Redfern Raid, code named 'Operation Sue', of 8 February 1990, thirteen police from the Tactical Response Group, the Anti-Theft Squad, the Rescue Squad and other officers moved into positions around the 'the Block' at 4 a.m. Some seventy police led by the Tactical Response Group raided at least eight houses with sledgehammers and iron bars and sealed off the area. Adults and children were hauled from their beds in nightclothes and taken off to the police station. One woman reported having to use her husband as a shield to dress, since the police would not leave her bedroom. At least eight arrests were made. Yet while there is petty crime, alcoholism and drug dependence in the locality, violence of the kind and level emerging from the ghetto areas of American cities is virtually unknown.

Recent immigrants, especially from non-English-speaking backgrounds, who have obtained visas on humanitarian grounds, are also sometimes argued to form an incipient underclass. Some have suggested that residential concentrations these immigrants have formed in places like Cabramatta in Sydney constitute ghettos. One of the last studies concluded by the recently axed Bureau of Immigration, Multicultural and Population Research (axed in 1996) summarised the situation:

> *The three Australian cities most impacted by immigration in the past twenty years have been Sydney, Melbourne and Perth and this is reflected in settlement at the neighbourhood level within the cities although significant residential concentrations do exist in other cities. No major birthplace group can be shown as being segregated in Australian cities although strong residential concentrations exist. Not only is there*

no situation in which anywhere near all of a given birthplace group resides in a single Statistical Local Area, but there is no grouping of the smaller census collection districts in which more than 30–40 per cent of the total population is comprised of the same birthplace group.[35]

There has at times been sharp debate over the significance of ethnic concentrations and whether some of them may be ghettos in the process of formation. The evidence is at best equivocal on this point. This is not to say, however, that socioeconomic disadvantage is not associated with ethnic concentrations in Australian cities. Such associations, if they exist, do not mean that the ethnic concentrations in themselves cause disadvantage.

Recent, especially non-English-speaking, immigrants nevertheless make up a disproportionate share of economically marginalised groups in the capital cities. Further moves to deregulate labour markets, to the extent that they contribute to the growth of secondary labour markets in the cities, may disadvantage these groups even more.

Rather than taking jobs from the Australian born, as some have argued, immigrants seem to have borne a disproportionate share of the impact of economic and political restructuring in the cities. The patchy evidence suggests that longer established immigrants, even from the most vulnerable communities, have improving employment experiences over time, are recognised widely as hard working and highly motivated (for example, towards home ownership), and have higher rates of self-employment than the Australian born.

Unemployment in Australian cities has been one of the uneven outcomes of globalisation and de-industrialisation. Governments have implemented strategies purposefully to facilitate and encourage restructuring either in the knowledge that its impacts will be socially uneven, commonly arguing that this is a temporary problem of adjustment to necessary change, or misunderstanding the importance of local process in determining outcomes. Because of this, recent arguments that immigration should be curtailed because of high rates of urban unemployment are simplistic and verge, at worst, on blaming immigrants (usually those from non-English-speaking background groups) for labour market problems. Such arguments also distract attention away from the complex combinations of global, national and local forces which cause unemployment in the work force at large.

Solutions to unemployment in the cities will require not just further job creation through economic growth but serious attempts by federal and state governments to come to grips with social infrastructure deficiencies in the rapidly growing outer suburbs. If the Australian government's immigration policies are to contribute to the search for solutions to unemployment, then they could be coordinated with industry policy (for example, in planning the skill composition of the annual intake) and constructed with greater regional and local sensitivity. Yet because of the difficulties in connecting immigration intake to economic issues, immigration policy should be decided on grounds other than assumed difficulties faced in urban labour markets by people born overseas.

Reports such as those provided by the Bureau of Immigration, Multicultural and Population Research provided vital resources to counter the racist claims of Pauline Hanson, the federal MP from Queensland, and her ilk, who simplistically blame immigrants for problems in the economy.

SYDNEY, LONDON AND NEW YORK?

Sydney is often represented as going the way of large cities in other advanced capitalist countries. But how apt is the comparison? Broadly speaking, processes of economic restructuring, accentuated by economic rationalist governments, are at work as much on cities like London and New York as they are on Sydney and there are parallel but contrasting social outcomes. One obvious difference is that in most American and British cities the inner city is the focus of growing social polarisation, while in Australia the concentration of urban inequalities lies in the outer suburbs.[36] In Sydney and other Australian cities there is much less visible evidence of inner city de-industrialised wastelands on the one hand, or beggars, homeless people and drug users on the other. Several things combine to polarise the lives of the rich and the poor socially and spatially in the outer urban areas. Despite policies to encourage the decentralisation of employment, which have had some success — notably the movement of various state government departments and manufacturers — many places still have very limited employment opportunities.[37] One effect is that most outer suburban residents face long travelling times. Another effect is higher unemployment than the rest of Sydney, particularly among single parents, notably women, and young people.[38] Such inequalities are less marked in Melbourne, which has been less affected by global forces in the 1980s. The contrast with American cities is particularly acute. There it is the upper- and middle-income earners who inhabit the metropolitan edge, where many well-paid jobs appear to be a driving force in the development of 'edge cities'.[39]

A second and related issue is transport. Sydney's low-density urban form means that people are very reliant on private cars. Public transport is restricted in many localities and operates effectively only in times of peak use. Where households have either no car, or one car which is used by the main earner during the day, many people are rendered immobile. Again, youth, old people and women with small children are particularly affected. Third, there is a lack of public and community services in many places. Expenditure cuts within the hospital system are threatening the resources of some of the major hospitals,[40] but less visible services, such as child-care centres, community centres, immigrant resource centres, cultural facilities and the like, are also absent. The lack of services and transport compounds exclusions from the labour market, especially for women. Fourth, because land is relatively cheap many people are

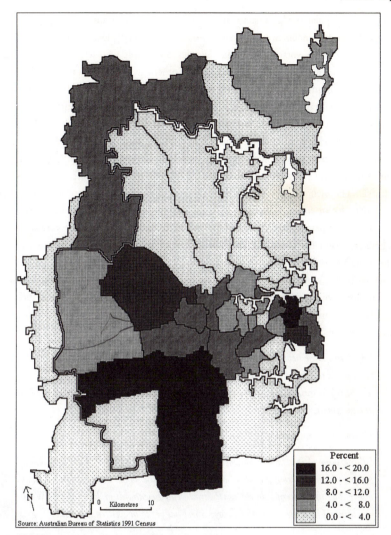

Percent	
■	16.0 - < 20.0
▨	12.0 - < 16.0
▦	8.0 - < 12.0
▒	4.0 - < 8.0
░	0.0 - < 4.0

Source: Australian Bureau of Statistics 1991 Census

0 Kilometres 10

Public housing as a percentage of all housing, 1991.

attracted into these areas by the lower house prices. Infrastructure costs associated with these new developments have led to great controversy about who should bear the costs, and also to policies to increase residential densities to deter ever more urban sprawl. Many public housing tenants have also been housed in the outer areas since the mid-1970s, again due to the relatively low cost of land and the buying policies of the public land owning authority, the Land Commission, which in the 1970s and 1980s bought land out west to provide low-income housing options, both public and private.

In the popular media western Sydney is characterised by images of deprivation, cultural lack, low incomes, poor amenity, social homogeneity, locational disadvantage, alienation and the worst of suburbia. 'Westies' are people who wear ugh boots and have no sense of styles. The west is Sydney's 'other', its poor relation reclaiming its otherness even unto itself. A poster on the lawn in front of Liverpool Hospital during a staff protest against funding levels in October 1996, read: 'The West: East's Poor Cousin'. As McCann-Erickson advertising agency's Dave McCaughan puts it: 'the only time Sydney's elite see the west is through the windscreens on the annual trip to the snow'.[41] The east is represented as wealthy, as having cultural richness, city life, beautiful houses, good location, high incomes, good services and schools, and a yuppie lifestyle. The dichotomy is simplistic. Radio programs reporting that crime rates and debt defaults are lower in the west than the east can disrupt such binaries.[42] There is clearly greater heterogeneity within both areas than is reflected in these caricatures.[43] There are fragments within the divisions. In particular, quite a few rich people live in the west. Not only are there wealthy parts of the urban fringe, notably the 'Hills' district in Sydney's north-west, but rich households are interspersed with poor households, notably in rural 'exurban' residential environments.[44] Fairfield residents, such as this factory worker, castigated what they saw as an unjust depiction of their locality in the metropolitan media:

> I don't think the newspapers really understand this area. You got a reporter comes in here, put a microphone to ask: 'What do you think of Cabramatta?' They just want something to talk about, something to sell the papers ... They want something always simple.[45]

Another resident added:

> I think some of it is lack of knowledge on the part of the reporter. They don't know one part of Sydney from the other, so they just group the whole western suburbs. Now, where does the western suburbs start? Strathfield, Leichhardt or Parramatta? When you think of it, anything west of George Street has got to be western suburbs.[46]

Despite assumptions that racial and ethnic minorities are affected in a uniform way by the processes of social and economic change, ethnic differentiation is a key component of post-industrial cities.[47] Here Sydney differs from New York and London. In inner city Sydney there are concentrations of several ethnic groups, notably Italians and Greeks, who were part of the 1950s and 1960s non-Anglo migrations to Australia. Most recent immigrants (60–70 per cent) still settle in the established inner and middle ring parts of the city.[48] Yet unlike American and British cities there is also a significant minority of more recent arrivals who move directly to the outer areas, partly because the receiving migrant hostels are located there, in Fairfield particularly, and partly because of access to public housing, cheaper home ownership and family members already living there.[49] Like in New York, some immigrants move into inner city areas of good housing quality like Marrickville. Here the new wave of recent immigrants takes the place of earlier immigrants who are shifting to outer areas in search of more space and supposedly greater amenities.

There has been a much larger refugee component in the migration to Australia in the last twenty years than to the United Kingdom and the United States. Also, an active policy since the mid-1980s of encouraging business migration has produced large inflows of capital, much of which is invested in property. Family reunion migration is another major component. The diversity of recent immigrants is therefore very important in Australia. The fact that there are many immigrants who are relatively wealthy and who have more political clout, and immigrants from so many countries, leads more to debates around multiculturalism than around racism. Notwithstanding racist responses, overall there is greater, if ambivalent, tolerance of non-Anglo groups, at least compared with the United Kingdom, because they comprise such a large proportion of Sydney's population. There are also no visible inner city ghettos, with the exception of the small, predominantly Aboriginal locality in Redfern. The most visible non-white group are immigrants from South-East Asia who are concentrated instead in an area one hour's drive from central Sydney. There is significantly less racial violence and fewer hostilities.[50] For immigrants the social security system matters. A Marrickville council worker said that: 'in fact it provides for a family now something like 70 per cent of the average weekly earnings which contributes to people being able to establish themselves without that incredible pressure, needing to find a job to feed yourself'.[51]

Sydney and Australia's location within the Asia–Pacific region sets Australia apart from the United Kingdom and United States.[52] Its orientation is less and less towards the United Kingdom or Europe and more and more towards the countries in this region. This means that most of Australia's offshore manufacturing takes place in East and South-East Asia while at the same time tourism from the region is booming. A large and increasing share of Australia's exports go to these countries, matched by a large part of foreign investment in Australia coming from Asian investors. Political and economic shifts in Asia are therefore likely to have a greater impact on Australia than changes in Europe. After several clashes between Dr Mahathir, Prime Minister of Malaysia, and then Labor Prime Minister Paul Keating in the early 1990s, both leaders in 1995 declared an interest in cementing a more stable relationship to avoid any continuing threat to two-way trade and investment as well as security in the region. The worry is that this increase of Asian influence and exchange may be leading to new arenas of racism, which are still relatively latent. It is not uncommon to hear references to having beaten the Japanese militarily in the Second World War but now losing economically. Bus loads of Japanese tourists to Bondi Beach are derided for their camera shots of groups standing by the edge of, but not surfing, the waves.

The role of the public sector and social policy in Australia has differed from those of the United States and the United Kingdom in various ways. The Australian welfare state superficially looks like that of both the United States in some respects, and the United Kingdom in others. That is, a less extensive version of the British welfare state was adopted with considerably less public housing and a lack of public provision in some localities, which approximates the American system more closely. The more limited welfare state in Australia is not, however, directly comparable since it derives from different historical roots. Here the welfare state has largely been seen, until recently, as a safety net, or as Castles described it, 'the workers' welfare state' [53]. The emphasis in Australia historically was on providing full employment through industry protection rather than on bolstering those out of work. This has led to a relatively impoverished welfare and non-government voluntary sector. Similarly, home ownership was considered the right and preference of all citizens, and therefore large levels of subsidy have bolstered this sector and assisted households trying to buy rather than providing low-rental accommodation as a feasible alternative.

During the same period that has witnessed a decline in public expenditure in the United States and the United Kingdom, Australia had a Labor government in power at the federal level which, in spite of its economic rationalist policies, increased the relative proportions of gross national product expenditure on various forms of public provision, such as housing, childcare and labour market training. During the 1980s there was no residualisation of welfare and disinvestment in public housing in the British sense. Federal–State relations led to different forms of political responsibility and provision of services and infrastructure from those of the United Kingdom and United States. There is much less local provision of goods and services than in those two countries. The major services are either provided by the states or through the Commonwealth, or some combination of these. This means there is less reliance on local tax bases and thus inequality deriving from this. Australian local government has less autonomy and financial power, traditionally being the site of the three R's: rates, roads and rubbish.

Australian cities not only show little visible inner city decay but also less significant major urban redevelopment. The redevelopment in the late 1980s of the Darling Harbour railway yards into a major tourist attraction only approximates the London's Docklands redevelopment in its tourist sites, not its investment in office buildings, financial investment and private housing initiatives. The space was contested by local residents and activists demanding more public housing in the locality, but there was no massive decimation of public housing and a local community as in Docklands. Most of Darling Harbour was built on disused dock areas. There has not therefore been an equivalent collapse with huge sums of money lost and lives destroyed.

The beach, the great outdoors, the pleasures of sun, sea, surf and bodies are central to the construction of Australian identities, particularly Sydney identities. Although some people are excluded from these pleasures, since most are free the main access constraint is distance and transport. Many places in and close to the central city have been designated for pleasure. Leisure resources in London and New York are for those with money and thus reinforce and produce other forms of sociospatial inequality. Australia's largest cities also have far fewer people than many British and American cities. The population of Sydney is only 3.7 million which, according to Sydney's metropolitan strategy, is expected to rise to 4.5 million by 2006. Although the causal connections between city size and inequalities are unclear, if inequalities resulting from economic restructuring are more muted for Sydney than for cities like London and New York then Sydney's much smaller size may be part of the explanation.

The statistical narrative dramatises social and economic contrasts across Sydney. But while a growing gap in the average welfare levels of people living in more and less affluent parts of cities is obvious enough, the statistics fail to signify the emergence of residential forms which are qualitatively different from before. Peter Marcuse is one writer who has attempted to reconceptualise urban sociospatial structure more qualitatively.[54] Taking social division as a starting point, he argues that representations of social polarisation, particularly the idea of cities splitting into ever richer and ever more impoverished parts, is too simplistic. Instead, he suggests that in typical large cities in the United States there are five types of residential areas. He calls them the dominating city, the gentrified city, the suburban city, the tenement city and the abandoned city.

Marcuse's *dominating city*, 'with its luxury housing, [is] not really part of the city but [consists of] enclaves or isolated buildings, occupied by the top of the economic, social, and political hierarchy'.[55] Gated suburbs, such as those dramatised by Mike Davis for Los Angeles,[56] or in Paul Theroux's futuristic, fortressed, inner city, high-rise apartments for the wealthy, with their foundations in a seething underclass,[57] exemplify the dominating city. In Australia there are some early signs of these trends.[58] But these experiments are sensationalised in the mass media and the actuality of a dominating city is vestigial rather than an unambiguous part of the urban social landscape. In Sydney, even the wealthiest areas are not gated and people can still walk openly in the streets of the affluent suburbs of Bellevue Hill and Vaucluse, or Hunters Hill and Mosman, without being watched and harassed as potential invaders — at least for now.

Marcuse's *gentrified city* denotes spaces which are 'occupied by the professional–managerial–technical groups, whether yuppie or muppie without children'.[59] Gentrification is easily found in Australian cities and for the same reasons. In Sydney it has similar effects of displacing earlier working-class populations from suburbs like Paddington and Glebe who were unable to pay inflated housing costs deriving from competition by the symbolic analysts.

The notion of the *suburban city* which, for Marcuse, 'sometimes [consists of] single family housing in the outer city, [at] other times apartments near the center, occupied by skilled workers, mid-range professionals and upper civil servants'[60] does not wholly map onto Australian cities. Here average incomes in residential areas generally decline from the centre of the city to the outer suburbs, whereas the reverse holds in the United States. In Sydney, Melbourne and other capital cities there have been relatively few apartment buildings near the CBDs and those that there were, unless public housing, were occupied by the rich. In recent years, however, there has been a strong trend to inner city living in Sydney. Statistics from Sydney City Council show that in 1992, 1464 residential units were approved for construction and in 1993 the figure was 2122.[61] A substantial proportion — up to 30 per cent — of these units, are being sold to buyers from Singapore, Hong Kong and Malaysia, the apartment blocks close to Chinatown in the Haymarket area especially. Away from Sydney's CBD, both within and beyond the gentrifying inner city, there are masses of 1920s blocks of flats and 1960s 'three-story walk-up' apartment buildings but these, as around Bondi, are more likely to house lower income earners, except where they have been gutted, renovated and repackaged with glitzy facades.

Marcuse's *tenement city* refers to 'cheaper single family areas, most often rentals, occupied by lower paid workers, blue and white collar, and generally [although less in the United States] including substantial social housing'.[62] This residential type is echoed in the Australian inner city, although in a much more muted form. There is no massed high density tenement housing as is common in older American cities. Perhaps the closest analogy in Sydney are areas of relatively recent — post Second World War — inner city public housing such as in Redfern and other parts of the inner city where environmental quality is perceived to be low. So far gentrifiers have barely begun to colonise these neighbourhoods.

Marcuse's *abandoned city* is 'the end result of the failure of economic growth benefits to trickle down to the bottom of the social hierarchy. Areas of the city left for the very poor, the unemployed, the excluded, where in the United States home-less housing for the homeless is most frequently located'.[63] Homelessness unquestionably exists in Australian cities, and is particularly visible in Surry Hills and Kings Cross, but it bears no resemblance to the scale of the problem in London and New York and there are no tent cities of alarming proportions like in the Lincolns Inn Fields of London or in the shopping fronts of the Strand. The Australian inner city lacks the ghetto concentrations of deprivation of Ammerican cities. Australian government welfare provisions so far have limited the number of people who might be forced to occupy these spaces through lack of alternatives. But welfare in the late 1990s political climate is under threat.

DISCOURSES OF DIVISION

Mapping social differences in the city matters because maps have social policy and political implications. Richer areas are typically better supplied with parks, sporting sites, hospitals, schools and cultural facilities. Unequal access to these facilities may relate to the differing capacity of people to pay. It may also reflect bureaucratic and political inertia. Inequalities between areas in a city also have political ramifications.

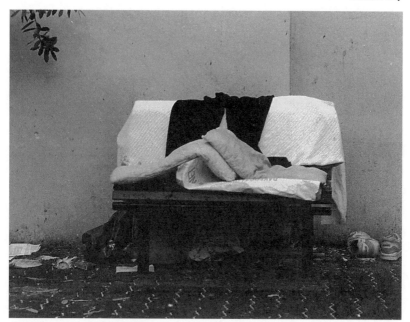

Kings Cross 'home', August 1995.

Point Piper waterfront, August 1995.

Rich areas are usually safe for conservative political parties while poorer electorates tend to return Left or social democratic candidates. Mixed areas become the focus of heavy political manoeuvrings and campaigns at election time.

Discourses of division and fragmentation shift across the political spectrum. On the traditional Left the city is represented as an arena for class conflict, with notional advantage accruing to the rich and disadvantage to the poor. Higher income areas, it is argued, tend to have better amenities and public and private services than low-income areas. Many lower income people live towards the edge of Australian cities in the newer suburbs, where average incomes tend to decline and accessibility to jobs is low because jobs remain quite highly centralised. And though most people living in the outer city are home owners, this is often through lack of choice and the higher costs of housing in the inner areas. A counter discourse suggests that while where people live may influence their welfare it does not matter all that much; such effects are marginal to those deriving from someone's labour market position, ownership of assets, health and so on. Here people are assumed to choose where they live and the densities at which they live. A higher density city would have been produced had people wanted it. The picture is more complex. A 1992 survey suggested that people buying houses in the outer city were much more diverse than the stereotypical struggling first home buyer.[64]

In the 1970s it was commonly thought that equity problems in the city were the outcome of maladministration and domestic policy.[65] Solutions could thus be found in innovative urban policies. Since the 1980s there has been a shift from this simple optimism. With the rise of unemployment and homelessness, which derives in part from forces outside the national economy, it has become ever harder for governments to solve the problem at a local level. Access to further education cannot simply solve the problem of unemployment amongst the unskilled. Urban problems are complex; solutions likewise. Space is contested and interests are fragmented. Sydney has entered the global stage — a stage characterised by sociospatial divisions and fragmentation the world over.

Notes

1 H. Daniel (ed.) 1989, *Expressway*, Allen & Unwin, Sydney.

2 NSW Department of Urban affairs and Planning 1996, *The Journey to Work*. Sydney.

3 R. Kirwan 1991, *Financing Urban Infrastructure: Equity and Efficiency Considerations*, Background Paper No. 4, The National Housing Strategy, AGPS, Canberra, pp. 60–1.

4 Joan Vipond has examined the main factors underpinning these patterns. See, for example, J. Vipond & C. Beed 1986, 'A Sydney and Melbourne comparison of intra-urban differentials in unemployment rates', *Australian Geographical Studies*, vol. 24, pp. 41–56.

5 *Sydney Morning Herald*, 5 October 1996.

6   Numbers of jobs per resident worker in sub-regions of Sydney vary from fewer than sixty-five in the outer west and south-west to over eighty in the more affluent and accessible areas of the North Shore and eastern suburbs: Department of Urban Affairs and Planning, op. cit., note 2.

7   From B. Hanna, P. Murphy & S. Watson 1995, *Snapshots of Sydney: Marrickville, Waverley, Fairfield, Baulkham Hills, Blue Mountains Locality Studies*, Department of Urban and Regional Planning, University of Sydney.

8   F. Stilwell 1989, 'Structural change and spatial equity in Sydney', *Urban Policy and Research*, vol. 7, pp. 3–14.

9   B. Hanna, P. Murphy & S. Watson, op. cit.

10 R. V. Cardew & D. C. Rich 1982, 'Manufacturing and industrial property development in Sydney', ch. 6. in R. V. Cardew, J. V. Langdale, & D. C. Rich (eds), *Why Cities Change*, Allen & Unwin, Sydney.

11 P. Murphy & S. Watson 1990, 'Restructuring of Sydney's central industrial area: process and local impact', *Australian Geographical Studies*, vol. 28, pp. 187–203.

12 B. Hanna, P. Murphy & S. Watson, op. cit.

13 See, for example, the excellent study, of this and other aspects of immigrant business activity by J. Collins, K. Gibson, C. Alcorso, & S. Castles 1995, *A Shop Full of Dreams: Ethnic Small Business in Australia*, Pluto Press, Sydney.

14 *Sydney Morning Herald*, 12 August 1992.

15 ibid.

16 R. Reich 1991, *The Work of Nations: a Blueprint for the Future*, Simon & Schuster, London.

17 B. Hanna, P. Murphy & S. Watson 1995, op. cit.

18 ibid.

19 ibid.

20 ibid.

21 See F. Stilwell 1993, *Economic Inequality: Who Gets What in Australia*, Pluto Press, Sydney.

22 *Sydney Morning Herald*, 11 November 1992.

23 R. G. Gregory 1992, 'Aspects of Australian labour force living standards: the disappointing decades, 1970–1990', Copland Oration, 21st Annual Conference of Economists, University of Melbourne.

24 Manuel Castells 1991, *The Informational City*, Blackwell, Oxford, summarised American research on this phenomenon. It is also discussed by Reich, op. cit.

25 *Sydney Morning Herald*, 7 December 1992.

26 ibid., 17 July 1993.

27 ibid.

28 ibid., 3 November 1992.

29 B. Hanna, P. Murphy & S. Watson 1995, op. cit.

30   ibid.

31   ibid.

32   The research of Nicole Salimbeni of Sydney Girls High School contributed to this section of the chapter.

33   R. Langford 1988, *Don't Take Your Love to Town*, Penguin, Melbourne, p. 174.

34   C. Cunneen 1990, *Aboriginal–Police Relations in Redfern*, Human Rights and Equal Opportunities Commission, Sydney.

35   P. Murphy, I. Burnley & R. Fagan 1996, *The Effects of Immigration on Australian Cities. Bureau of Immigration*, Multicultural and Population Research. Consultant's Report. (To be published in revised and expanded form, by Federation Press.)

36   See S. S. Fainstein, I. Gordon & M. Harloe 1992, *Divided Cities: New York and London in the Contemporary World*, Blackwell, Oxford; and S. Sassen 1991, *The Global City: New York, London, Tokyo*, Princeton University Press, New Jersey.

37   B. Fagan 1986, 'Industrial restructuring and the metropolitan fringe: growth and disadvantage in western Sydney', *Australian Planner*, vol. 24, pp.11–17.

38   Vipond & Beed, op. cit., note 4.

39   J. Garreau 1991, *Edge city: Life on the New Frontier*, Doubleday, New York; P. Murphy & R. Freestone 1995, 'Towards edge city: business recentralisation and post-suburban Sydney', ch. 8 in K. Gibson & S. Watson (eds), *Metropolis Now: Planning and the Urban in Contemporary Australia*, Pluto Press, Sydney, ch. 8.

40   *Sydney Morning Herald*, 14 October 1991.

41   ibid., 5 October 1996.

42   For example, ABC Radio 2BL, 8 October 1991.

43   D. Powell 1993, *Out West*, Allen and Unwin, Sydney.

44   P. Murphy & I. Burnley 1993, 'Socio-demographic structure of Sydney's perimetropolitan region', *Journal of the Australian Population Association*, vol. 10, pp. 127–44.

45   B. Hanna, P. Murphy & S. Watson 1995, op. cit.

46   ibid.

47   S. S. Fainstein, I. Gordon & M. Harloe, op. cit.

48   I. Burnley, 1996, *Atlas of the Australian people — 1991 Census: NSW*, AGPS, Canberra.

49   I. Burnley & P. Murphy 1994, *Immigration, Housing Costs and Population Dynamics in Sydney*, AGPS, Canberra

50   For example, *Sydney Morning Herald*, 10 December 1992.

51   B. Hanna, P. Murphy & S. Watson 1995, op. cit.

52   M. Daly & M. Logan 1989, *The Brittle Rim: Finance, Business and the Pacific Region*, Penguin, Melbourne.

53   F. Castles 1985, *Working Class and Welfare*, Allen & Unwin, Sydney.

54   P. Marcuse 1989, '"Dual city": a muddy metaphor for a quartered city', *International Journal of Urban and Regional Research*, vol. 13, pp. 697–708.

55 ibid., p. 703.

56 M. Davis 1992, *City of Quartz*, Vintage, New York.

57 P. Theroux 1986, *O-Zone*, Penguin, London.

58 See, for example, J. Hillier & P. McManus 1994, 'Pull up the drawbridge: fortress mentality in the suburbs', in K. Gibson & S. Watson (eds) *Metropolis Now*, Pluto Press, Sydney, ch. 6.

59 P. Marcuse, op. cit., p. 704.

60 ibid.

61 Sydney City Council 1995, *Living City: Sydney City Council Blueprint for Sydney*.

62 P. Marcuse, op. cit., p. 705.

63 ibid.

64 R. Burgess & N. Skeltys 1992, *The Findings of the Housing and Location Choice Survey*, Background Paper No. 11, National Housing Strategy, AGPS, Canberra.

65 K. Gibson 1994, 'Restructuring difference and social polarisation', paper presented at Institute of Australian Geographer's Annual Conference, September.

6 GENDERED SPACES

Women and men inhabit cities differently. Not only do they do different jobs and have different patterns of responsibility, they also weave different shapes as they move through the spaces of the city, living in the interstices and disrupting boundaries between public and private. Women's imaginings and fantasies take on their own particular form reflecting and constructing the lives they lead. Drusilla Modjeska's book *Inner Cities*, on women's sense of place, captures some of this:

> *Our memories, our stories, like the ways we live, are formed in movement between inner and outer, past and future, centre and margin, between the physical environment and the social world. We shape our cities, and re-shape them from the edge, we always have; just as our cities shape us.*[1]

The city is gendered in both obvious and hidden ways. Because women are still the primary carers of children, older dependent relatives and others in the family, the lives they live in the city are often more complex, fragmented and arduous than those of men. Many women combine paid employment with unpaid domestic responsibilities. Twenty-two per cent of married women work full-time in Sydney but with considerable variations across the city; there are more employed married women in the wealthier parts. Other women work part-time to enable them more easily to combine their domestic and paid work lives: 26 per cent of married women in Sydney work part time. This ranges from over 27 per cent in affluent inner city suburbs like Waverley and Woollahra to less than 23 per cent in poorer outer suburbs like Blacktown and Campbelltown. There are also a large number of single parents with dependent offspring in Sydney — now about 8.5 per cent of all households. About nine out of ten single parents are women, which reflects the tendency of children to remain with their main carer when a marriage or cohabiting relationship ends, and the continuing primacy of men's careers over women's in many households.

Women's incomes remain on average lower than men's, with the average female median income in 1991 being $13 800 compared with $23 600 for men. There is considerable variation in incomes depending on with whom a woman lives, her age, employment and where she lives. Median income levels for women in the Blue Mountains in 1991 were $11 500 compared with $18 200 in Waverley, where many single 'yuppied' professional women live. It is interesting to compare these figures to those in Baulkham Hills, a wealthy suburb in the Hills District. Here women's average median income was $15 000 while men's was $29 500, which shows how men in this locality are benefiting more than women from the shift since the mid-1980s to high-paid service sector employment.

Between 1976 and 1991 the proportion of women in paid work has only risen in the top half of neighbourhoods ranked by socioeconomic status. In lower socioeconomic areas the gains made by women between 1976 and 1991 — in dollar terms, $996 a year — were not enough to compensate for real falls in their household income. At the same time, the income gains made by women in the top 5 per cent have substantially added to the real income of high-income neighbourhoods. In the top half of neighbourhoods in Australia the proportion of employed women increased by 10 per cent between 1976 and 1991 whereas in the bottom half their employment fell by 40 per cent.[2] This represents a stark gendered variation across space which has only recently been recognised. What seems to be going on is that middle-class women are taking up the new jobs in low-skilled service occupations through lack of alternatives, while poorer women are opting out and relying on social security payments.

If women are married or cohabiting with children the crucial issues they face are how to interweave their multiple responsibilities and how to negotiate their textured lives. Many women, and some men, have to negotiate taking children to school or child-care, going to work, doing the shopping, possibly taking a child or relative to the doctor, collecting the kids, preparing evening meals, ferrying the children to sport or other activities, dropping in on friends or family — all in the space of one day. What matters here is transport; if there are two cars in the household life may be manageable. If there is only one car, invariably it is used by men to go to their place of work. Given that the average vehicle ownership per household for Sydney in 1991 was 1.35, there are still many households with one or no car. Fewer women than men drive, particularly among more recent immigrants. For women without access to a car the public transport system is the lifeline. A train thus offers a point of connection, an escape, the possibility of other places and other lives. Susan Dermody describes her childhood memories of the buses on routes 389 and 390:

> Either number still has the power to slightly unsettle your heart. They signalled a touch of luck, of grace, a small way forward, a short respite from waiting … Every arriving bus was an augury that you were, for the moment, connected with other things. It offered a place to settle with the smoothed over panic of life for a while and to look from safe cover.[3]

Yet the outer suburbs where many people with children live — since houses are cheaper, and more space is desired for bringing up children — are precisely the areas where public transport is poor. These are the women who are trapped and isolated at home, and for whom the materiality of daily life becomes a nightmare. The more dispersed a city is, and Sydney is one of the most dispersed cities in the world for its population size, the harder the situation is to remedy with public transport solutions, since the cost of providing services becomes prohibitive.

There has been a dramatic shift in the proportion of married women in the labour force since the mid-1970s. In part this reflects gains made by feminist struggles for greater equality for women and changing assumptions about gender. But it also reflects the growing necessity for two incomes to pay the mortgage and survive. An immigrant in Fairfield described it thus:

> I remember again, my wife never worked and I came here with two children. Now I've got five, they've all grown up and I'm the only one who was a breadwinner in the family. And I managed and I worked well. I had everything I wanted, and whatever my wife wanted from the shops. The only thing we went without was the lottery, the poker machines, the club — that was the only thing. Other than that, we lived comfortably ... Now today, it's impossible — it's the cost of living. A hardship really, very hard.

Married women's labour force participation increased from 43.9 per cent in 1978 to 53 per cent in 1991, with 48.0 per cent and 49.0 per cent as the respective figures for immigrant women.[4] House prices in Sydney have risen strongly in the same period. Even in Baulkham Hills, where there is a concentration of white-collar workers, business owners, executives of large companies and bankers, many couples both work in order to meet the high cost of housing repayments necessitated by the house prices there. For those who stay at home there is tremendous isolation. As one social worker there said: 'There has been a shift in what's happened to women in the last 20 years ... now there are no neighbours, they have all cleared out by Monday morning and so you're trapped with a young baby or whatever — you're alone'. This echoes the bleakness and depression identified by Betty Friedan in *The Feminine Mystique*, in 1963.

SINGLE PARENTS

The number of single-parent households living in Sydney has risen dramatically since the mid-1970s as a result of divorce law reform and changing attitudes to women bringing up children on their own. Single mothers are concentrated in some parts of the city rather than others. This reflects women's lower incomes, which means that they either move to areas where home purchase and rentals are cheaper, or their incomes are low enough to make them eligible for public housing.[5] Social security constitutes 70 per cent of the income in the poorest quarter of households in Sydney, and most of these are women.[6] Cuts to social security payments proposed by the Howard government can only make matters worse. Public housing policies in New South Wales have been oriented towards the acquisition of land in the cheaper parts of the west and outer west, such as Campbelltown and Liverpool, over the development of denser high rise housing in the inner city (as is more characteristic in British and European cities) or the purchase of existing property from private owners or landlords. There is some high rise development, notably in Redfern, but it represents a fraction of the public housing stock.

Old and new (foreground) styles of inner city public housing, Waterloo, August 1995.

In the inner city areas of Glebe, Woolloomooloo and The Rocks there is old terrace housing and there are newer purpose-built medium density developments in the public sector. These attractive and popular sites are a legacy of the Whitlam government's urban policy initiatives in 1972–75, when the Australian Department of Urban and Regional Development saved inner city housing from destruction by rampant development interests. In The Rocks, the Builders Labourers' Federation supported local residents in their fight to save the area in 1973 and imposed Green Bans which prohibited their members from working on these sites. In Victoria Street, Kings Cross, this resistance to the incursions of property developers, in which women played a central part, met with violence and arrest. Yet the numbers of people gaining from these significant low-income housing initiatives are small and most single mothers remain consigned to the far-flung suburbs of the west.

Single parents constitute 17.7 per cent of all households in Campbelltown and 16.2 per cent of all households in Liverpool. This represents a dramatic increase since the mid-1970s and is in marked contrast to the number of single parents in Baulkham Hills (5.2 per cent), and Ku-ring-ai (9.1 per cent). For women in western Sydney life is not easy. Public transport is limited due to the dispersed nature of the city. There are many poorly serviced streets with either no buses at all or irregular services. Trains exist in some parts and not others, and taxis are expensive. There are also limited child-care services, while access to employment opportunities for women without cars, or for those whose children are young, is extremely limited. Many of the new industries and service sector jobs which have decentralised to the outer fringe are inaccessible by public transport. The skills required are also often not those of the women living there. Proportions of women with associate diploma or higher qualifications in areas like Liverpool, Blacktown and Campbelltown are less than 8 per cent. Jobs which may be viable in terms of skills or qualifications required are often located in the inner city, which is inaccessible to women whose hours are restricted by child-care responsibilities. A vicious circle is established which keeps many such women unemployed and trapped.

Similarly, at the same time as the more alternative, and sometimes lesbian, women reside in the mountain towns, particularly Katoomba, a growing number of poor single parents are living there: 13 per cent of households in 1991. This represents the welfare migration of those who cannot afford to live in the city and find rentals or cheap houses to buy in the mountain towns. Poverty is such that a garage sale may have little more on display than a few tattered toys and crockery that is recycled. But, like the west, endlessly homogenised as a bland and uniform place, Katoomba's changing relation to Sydney 'proper' makes it a textured and liminal place — a space where women who are poor can manage to live. For Brian Castro:

> *Katoomba is libidinal, pleasurable, exciting, depressing. They used to come up here for cures, the mentally ill, the pulmonary, the artistic. Entrepreneurs made it sound as though the place was spuming with spas instead of mud baths ... They come up now to eat ... displaced, cosmopolitan wealthy, buying their illnesses. Sniff. They wear furs flavoured with moth balls ... you stand here in one of the last decaying boarding houses, hungry, naked, with only a handful of memories.[7]*

Women who live in the Blue Mountains with children and without a car, including women who have a partner, are very cut off. Public transport is unreliable so people can get stuck in the wrong place. Children over 12 are ineligible for after-school care and are thus often at a loose end, particularly in the lower Blue Mountains towns like Winmalee. Housing developments have been built at considerable distances from the transport routes, as in Yellow Rock, so women with small children are landlocked during the day with a scarcity of services.

IMMIGRANT WOMEN AND ABORIGINAL WOMEN

Ania Walwicz writes of Australia:

> *You big ugly. You too empty. You desert with your nothing. You scorched suntanned. Old too quickly. Acres of suburbs watching the telly. You bore me. Freckle silly children. You nothing much. With your big sea. Beach beach beach. I've seen enough*

already. You dumb dirty city with bar stools. You're ugly. You silly shopping town ... Road road tree tree. I came from crowded and many. I came from rich. You have nothing to offer. You're poor and spread thin ... You silent on Sunday. Nobody on your streets. You dead at night.[8]

Women who have migrated to Sydney from other parts of the world, particularly from non-English-speaking countries, find a city built on Anglo–Australian assumptions and norms. Often there is a severe clash of culture. The notion that it is reasonable for women to work, to enter public life, to display their bodies and so on, is not one shared by all cultures. Women from Muslim countries may be expected to go out in purdah. The support systems on which women relied in their country of origin, be it extended family networks or local communities, are often absent on arrival in Sydney. Isolation and stress can precipitate domestic violence. Social workers in Marrickville report that a high incidence of domestic violence among the Vietnamese is exacerbated by stress, alcohol and gambling.

The treasurer for the Chinese Women's Support Group in Baulkham Hills reported that she knew many women who felt very isolated and were reluctant to mix with people locally. She herself was called: 'a banana — I'm yellow on the outside and inside white'. One difficulty is that the reluctance of Asian women to integrate with established Australian culture is seen as rude, which leads to hostility and harassment. Many Asian women in this part of Sydney are products of the 'astronaut' syndrome. The president of the Australian Chinese Association in a *Sydney Morning Herald* article headed 'Family Grounded as "astronaut" shuttles', describes it thus: 'Chinese space travellers, astronaut, that's what we call those people who travel from place to place'.[9] One pattern is for men from South-East Asian countries to buy a house in which to install their families, and in some cases set up a business, while simultaneously continuing to live and work in Singapore, Malaysia or Hong Kong. The women left behind may only rarely be visited by their husbands and often are seriously isolated. For some immigrants from Hong Kong the move was precipitated by the Tiananmen Square massacre, and fear as to the future of Hong Kong. But in the early 1990s the economic situation in Australia deteriorated at the same time as opportunities for work in Hong Kong improved, with men able to find higher paid and status jobs there.

Isolation is one problem, lack of language skills is another. This can mean difficulties in getting to employment on the one hand and difficulties in negotiating the transport system or accessing services on the other. A Vietnamese woman told of her mother's fear of taking the bus since all the streets and houses looked the same to her so it was easy to miss the stop. Such is the visible homogeneity of suburban environments. Almost 17.5 per cent of women from non-English-speaking backgrounds are unemployed. Others, through lack of alternative opportunities, work part-time in home-based industries for low and below-award wages. This is reflected in the growth in home-based small industries in Fairfield in residential areas, many of which employ local immigrant women with children. The story of a Housing Commission house where the guts of the dwelling were ripped out and filled with sewing machines, and where four shifts were taking place each day, is typical. Garages are also used as small factories and not declared as such to the local council. Another pattern is for immigrant women to do piecework at home using their own machines. Employers are either unaware of the industrial and planning regulations or conveniently forget them. This extra money is used to supplement the dole or a paltry income of the main breadwinner. Traditionally, home-based industries were also prevalent in Marrickville but many of them have declined or moved to other areas.

Migration is an uprooting, literally. That which was home, though still in the imaginary marked as 'home', no longer is. Home has been disrupted, disturbed and dislocated. Given the central place of the domestic for many women, particularly those from more traditional cultures, housing represents a powerful site of affective as well as material investment for immigrant women. Home signifies belonging and its importance. Susan Thompson talked to immigrant women in Sydney and explored the culturally embodied meanings of home.[10] She found that it represented a safe place for the display of difference facilitating the celebration of cultural festivals, religious practices and traditional entertaining. Behind the traditional suburban facade of houses belonging to Vietnamese Buddhists can be found shrines, pictures, statues and framed verses. The garden takes on a particular significance when plants that are evocative of the place of origin can be planted, or vegetables and herbs can be grown that are unavailable here. Home can evoke a sense of belonging and achievement for those who have been uprooted by war or poverty. Dwelling design also matters. The spatial arrangements of the house and local council regulations can constrain culturally specific domestic practices like meals that are traditionally cooked on a wood-burning fire rather than on electricity or gas.

Women in low-income Aboriginal households, like other poor women, have limited access to home ownership and private rental, but their problems can be exacerbated by racial discrimination. At the 1991 Census Aborigines and Torres Strait Islanders had the lowest rate, 13.5 per cent, of owner occupation compared with any other households. Of the rest, half were public tenants and half private. For many Aboriginal households housing is inappropriate in its design, location and materials.[11] It is customary for Aboriginal people in Sydney to have visitors from the country passing through for a day, a week or longer, so space needs to be flexible and adaptable.

Ruby Langford tells of being allocated a Housing Commission house in the 1970s in Green Valley in Sydney's west and her sense of extreme isolation there: 'I used to die to see another black face like mine, I got so lonely, I'd keep coming back to the city to Eveleigh Street'. This was the only way she could get a four-bedroom house to bring up her children. Yet the neighbours continually harassed her when she had friends or relations staying overnight.[12] After moving back to Redfern while her children grew up, she moved to a hostel set up for older Aboriginal Australians called Allawah, which means 'stop, sit down and rest awhile'. And, as she puts it: 'we are like family here and always look out for each other. I've come to this conclusion that I've found my belonging place at last, and here's where I'll stay for the rest of my days'.[13] There are some special housing projects for Aboriginal people in Redfern and more recently attempts have been made to include the community in the consultation process from the start, to avoid establishing forms of housing which does not address cultural practices. This kind of consultation is important for women, since in Aboriginal households also it tends to be the women who define the domestic.

OLDER WOMEN AND YOUNG WOMEN

Women still live longer than men. The average life expectancy for a woman is 80.4 years compared with 74.4 for men. Women's housing problems when older may thus go on for longer and can be more acute. Women who have relied on men to look after the dwelling in terms of its financing and maintenance can find it difficult to cope when their partners die. If the house is owned there are problems with finding tradespeople, knowing how much to pay them and dealing with the potential or imagined threat of having strange men visit the house; inhabiting older housing stock also means more expensive repairs. Many older women in Sydney therefore opt to live in public housing if they can get it. But, like single parents, this can mean being consigned to suburbs which are far from places they have lived in before. Some of these developments, in Mount Druitt for example, are cut off from public transport and at some distance from services and shops. Taking a taxi may be the only way of getting about. For others, a private rental flat near to the centre of town, despite its expense and lack of security, means the pleasures and sense of belonging of city life. These, perhaps, are the new *flâneuses* abandoning planned suburbia or anaemic city spaces for the anonymity and bustle of the streets of colour.[14] Many older women live alone in places like Kirribilli or Neutral Bay on the North Shore or Potts Point and Elizabeth Bay in the eastern suburbs.

Others who have equity from a house sale, choose retirement villages and are attracted by the promise of security, support and maintenance and a ready-made social life. Some of these retirement villages are themselves in isolated suburbs while others are connected to local shops and amenities. Some are located in the inner city areas of Glebe and Randwick where buses are easier to find. Retirement villages to many older women are completely anathema and living in the houses they have owned for years, whatever the problems, is infinitely preferable to any move. Several local councils have initiated dual occupancy provisions which means that 'granny flats' can be built on the sites of already established dwellings, thus enabling older people to live near relatives or friends while retaining independence. In longer established areas like Waverley there is a large older population, though it is increasingly difficult to live there on limited incomes as it becomes more trendified and expensive and older women living in large houses are being forced to sell out. Others remain totally isolated from neighbours.

Young women's housing problems parallel many of those facing women on low incomes and with few resources. Private rental accommodation is often the only option and the cost of rental bonds and rents can simply be too prohibitive to enable them to set up independently. It is more and more common for young women to join with friends and set up shared housing in inner city areas like Newtown and Chippendale, but this is a greater possibility for students or young women in work. Unemployed and lowly paid younger women often have little option but to remain living with their parents, with the lack of freedom and privacy that implies and, for some, the risk of domestic or sexual abuse. There are very few hostels or refuges for homeless young women in the city, with the result that the more vulnerable are forced onto the streets and into prostitution through lack of work or accommodation. Kings Cross is particularly notorious for its prostitution and sex industries, but in parts of suburbs like Fairfield and Liverpool prostitution by the young is prevalent but simply less visible. Once on the streets young women are vulnerable to abuse, drugs and ill-health and the route out into stable employment or housing is not an easy one.

WOMEN AND SAFETY IN THE CITY

For women all over the world the safety of the streets, public spaces, parks and the public transport system matters. Sydney presents a heterogeneous picture. A study conducted by the Safe Women Liverpool Project in 1994 found railway stations to be a site of fear and anxiety.[15] All the 136 women surveyed avoided Liverpool Station at night and over one-quarter avoided going there in the daylight because of drunks, intimidation by local youths 'hanging out', poor lighting, and desolation. The walkway under the bridge near the station was particularly feared, while other sites identified were car parks, parks, laneways and hotels. What was striking was the level of self-surveillance generated which made many women reluctant to go out at night, a Foucauldian panopticon effect. In Marrickville residents reported an increase in street violence over the previous ten years, with one real estate agent preventing his wife from walking alone to their car in the street. In Fairfield there were reports of increasing harassment of young girls on the streets and blatant attempts to intimidate women. Despite and before the Hagland murder, women in Bondi were attracted to the locality because it felt safe. As one woman said: 'I'm happy to walk on the beach or Bondi Promenade at night up to midnight. There are so many people about'.

A concern for women out west, particularly those who travel long distances to the Blue Mountains, is safety on trains, especially when travelling alone in a railway carriage. There are regular accounts of attacks, making women feel on their guard, or discouraging them from taking trains at all at night. The alternative is a taxi which many women can ill afford.

On the domestic front, since the early 1970s there has been a growing recognition of domestic violence, which has been partly addressed by the provision of refuges for battered women. There are now many refuges in Sydney, and few localities have no refuge at all. The first of the refuges to be established was Elsie in Glebe. A major problem for battered women is how to find more permanent accommodation for themselves and their children once they are back on their feet again. Homelessness is widespread. When women are rehoused from inner city refuges they are usually allocated public housing far from friends, family and other support systems. For example, in Waverley there are limited options for re-housing in the eastern suburbs and, usually, women are offered public housing in Mount Druitt even when they have expressed a preference for the high-rise blocks in Redfern after having first been to a refuge out west which they found isolated and grim. But it is not just poorer areas where domestic violence is manifested; it is a city-wide phenomenon but with some differences according to the socio-economic status of the locality. Rates of Apprehended Domestic Violence Orders sought in 1989 ranged from 204.5 per 100 000 in Campbelltown to 8 per 100 000 in Ku-ring-ai.[16] There has been an increased reporting of domestic violence in higher income places like Baulkham Hills in recent years; a local policewoman was unsure whether this reflected a higher incidence of domestic violence or a greater propensity to report it.

WOMEN ON THEIR OWN

In the inner west lie Newtown, Stanmore, Erskineville, Redfern, Leichhardt, Annandale and Balmain — places chosen by many women living alone or with other women. Women alone or living with a partner or friends share impulses, needs and desires with gay men: proximity to work, a community with which to identify, a neighbourhood which is friendly to non-traditional households and affordability. Housing, both for rent and for purchase, is cheaper the further it is from the eastern suburbs, hence the popularity of the inner west.[17] Barbara Brooks explains the appeal of the city for women, particularly those on lower incomes:

> *An urban or semi-urban environment gives more variety, more chance to move around between different groups and get lost in between ... I like the lost spaces — the back lanes with frangipani trees and cats sleeping on rusty iron roofs, the ends of streets along creeks and railway lines with fennel growing wild, overgrown backyards with jasmine and bush lemon trees. The city can give you the anonymity to be what you want.[18]*

Leichhardt, Newtown and Erskineville are sometimes referred to as the 'lavender triangle', representing another space of lesbian and gay settlement in Sydney, while in local discourse Leichhardt is dubbed 'dykehardt'. Balmain and Rozelle are popular with higher paid women bureaucrats and professionals and women who got into the housing market early. In the eastern suburbs it is Bondi and Waverley where more single women are found than in Paddington and Darlinghurst, partly because of affordability, and diversity of smaller dwellings and flats, and partly because of the attraction of living in an area where there are other single people, which makes it both safe and congenial to live alone. But also important is that women who do not live in traditional families desire spaces of consumption where cafes and restaurants are found, since eschewing more domestic life goes hand in hand with eating out and socialising. No children or dependents also implies fewer financial constraints and more disposable incomes for culinary pleasures.

In choosing inner city areas there is a repetition of the process of gentrification which occurred in the eastern suburbs in the 1960s and 1970s. Paddington and Darlinghurst had declined from housing the bourgeoisie into often divided working-class and migrant housing serving the sweatshops and other industries that thrived in and near the city centre. In the massive building program that saw Sydney expand into the Western Plains in the 1950s and 1960s there was a decanting of the inner city population to the west. Partly this was a willing move by individuals to houses with gardens in a supposedly healthy area with space for children to play, partly it was a forced move to allow for demolition — sometimes resisted, as in the case of areas of Redfern.[19] Into these working-class areas with low property values moved, first of all, individuals or groups who needed cheap rental accommodation in divided large houses. A number of these incomers were single people looking for housing in which they could live an independent and unsupervised life near the heart of their alternative society. They were soon to be followed by wealthier groups, including gay gentrifiers, as purchasers.[20] The 1960s put a premium on the suburbs but even as the west was being settled the reconstitution of the inner city had begun. In Paddington, those employed in professional and technical work rose from 6 per cent in 1966 to 20 per cent in 1976; for those in administration the figures rose from 4.6 per cent to 10.8 per cent; while those involved in labour and trades fell from 53.5 per cent to 29.2 per cent.[21] The period from the late 1960s saw a return 'by the young upwardly mobile professional generation [to] the accessibility and flexibility of the inner city.'[22] In later years, as eastern suburbs prices rose pushing aspirant households of young couples, gays and women out of their preferred areas, the terrace houses of other working-class suburbs became the target, raising prices and driving the original population further west.[23]

Alongside single mothers there are also women on their own who are living in the Blue Mountains and are involved in a great diversity of cultural and work practices, both paid and unpaid. The mountains are well known as a place where writers and artists live. They also attract 'new age' women and men, alternative health therapists, masseuses and naturopaths, recreating a hippy 1970s ambience deplored by sceptical inner city dwellers. There is a joke in the Blue Mountains that women run the teashops and men the restaurants. Strong activism and persistent lobbying among women in the mountains has resulted in more services specifically for women, like women's health centres and child-care centres, than in other parts of the west.

LESBIAN SPACE

The advent of coalitionism and the decline of separatism as the defining characteristic of the relationships between gays and lesbians began to reshape the lesbian and gay community in Sydney in the late 1980s. What had been monopolised by men had now begun to be shared. Women began to take leading roles in a number of organisations such as the Gay and Lesbian Rights Group and the Gay and Lesbian Counselling Service — until 1992 regarded as 'a bastion of male chauvinism'.[24] The Board of Mardi Gras Limited is balanced between the sexes.[25] In the use of space, too, there has been a greater mixing. In Oxford Street, for long a virtually exclusively male bastion, there have been some breaches. The Exchange Hotel, under its licensee Elizabeth Court, sought to establish in the Lizard Lounge a space where lesbians could feel comfortable in a mixed environment. In a community where 'lesbians had always been offered second rate things', she has countered with professionalism and with an eye for style. A September 1996 exhibition there explored local lesbians' iconic fantasies from Patty Hearst to Joan Sutherland.

There remains however, a world of difference between provision for lesbians and for gay men. There are no longer any dedicated lesbian bars to match the Albury, the Oxford, Midnight Shift or other gay male spots, although the Leichhardt Hotel, the Bank Hotel at Newtown, the Imperial in Erskineville, Delaney's in Redfern and the Bridge at Pyrmont have at various times hosted the growing band of pool-playing dykes,[26] following the lead of the iconic k d lang and her pool partner, Martina Navratilova.[27]

In some cases it seems as though lesbians are fitted into non-lesbian bars and other venues either as a gesture or to boost trade on a quiet night. Another characteristic of the lesbian social scene is the transient nature of its venues.[28] Whereas the major gay bars have been running continuously for over a decade, a survey of the venues page of *Lesbians on the Loose* over the four years of its publication[29] shows only one venue to have survived from 1990, Clover Women's Club founded in 1972.[30] It seems a matter for comment when lesbian venues last more than six months. Some close without warning before popping up in the same or in a new guise elsewhere. The Other Side closed without warning in January 1993 and moved from Kings Cross to Kinselas in Taylor Square. Oblivion at the Black Market near Central Station, closed and disappeared for a few months and then reappeared at JBF on Taylor Square. The clientele, loyal to the people who run the events, follow them around. Sometimes, however, a seemingly successful venue will suddenly and without obvious reason lose popularity, forcing a closure. This was the case with The Freezer in Oxford Street, numbers at which fell from over 200 to fifty in a period of weeks.

Commonly, women's bars are begun by entrepreneurs in property rented for the nights in question. Disputes with the owners are a continuing problem which inhibits development and may bring the closure of the bar[31] although the same entrepreneur may subsequently open another in a new location under a new name. Lack of a secure tenancy, sufficient capital or income from a community that shares the comparative poverty of all women, or a combination of all three, renders the survival of such lesbian nightclubs precarious. One entrepreneur, the exception, who has gained financial independence and has secured her own property is Dawn O'Donnell. Beginning in the 1960s with the Trolley wine bar, in which lesbians would gather upstairs after closing time,[32] she ran Ruby Red's in Oxford Street from 1975 to 1985 as 'an institution for dykes: back bar was the rough end and at the front cocktail bar were the lipstick dykes'.[33] Her commercial empire now includes the Toolshed sex shops, the Newtown and Imperial hotels and Marcy's, though each with a predominantly male clientele. 'A room of one's own and 500 pounds a year', were Virginia Woolf's requirements for an independent woman.[34] Allowing for inflation, they remain the two basics.

'Safety' and 'security' are recurring discourses in the lesbian community. Safety from violence, safety from insult, security of tenure, financial security, the security that comes in a supportive environment — all lay behind the launch of the Lesbian Space Project at the Lesbian Feminist Conference in December 1992 which set itself, and reached, the target of raising $250 000 by December 1993[35] to buy a disused factory in Leichhardt or Newtown for a lesbian cultural and community centre.[36] For the aquatic who wants to travel beyond familiar territory, weekends can be spent at Coogee Women's Pool,[37] or at softball in Centennial Park on a Sunday morning on a turn-up-and-play basis with or without hangover.

It is cafes, however, that are considered real lesbian territory. Although not all are lesbian-owned, the Bella Bar in Newtown, Beth's Place in Annandale, Cafe Brontosaurus in Erskineville, the Bar Italia in Leichhardt (which also caters for the local football team) have all been popular at one time or another. One of the common epithets deployed in relation to lesbians is 'invisible'. It is manifested in the lower-profile venues — the noisiest cafe is quieter than the quietest of gay bars; it is implied in Adler and Brenner when they talk of the common fronts that are created with other women which broaden the range of concerns beyond that of sexuality; it is stated explicitly by Castells when he says that lesbians are 'placeless' and 'tend to create their own rich, inner world'.[38] It is stated by Winchester and White when they consider the lesbian population of Paris, provision for which is 'discreet and virtually anonymous'.[39] The stereotype is simplistic and absurd, but where it exists, this anonymity stems from two sources: the desire of some lesbians to remain anonymous; and the perverse refusal of straight society to acknowledge gay women's lives.

Just as Sydney can be mapped across cultures so also it can be mapped across genders and bodies. Returning to our point of departure — some of these spaces are only imaginary. But most are not. Sydney, like other cities of the world, is differently lived by women and men. It is also differently lived by women and women, depending on whether they are rich or poor, old or young, black or white, with children or without, established or recent immigrants, gay or straight. Sex/gender forms part of the warp and the weft of the city. There is no static sexed/gendered urban subject in relation to urban space. The patternings, interconnections, disjunctures of women's lives are formed within, and themselves form, the geography and shape of Sydney. Sexed bodies are produced in the very skin and bone of its built environment, and the patterns they make can at once be fleeting and temporary, contingent or seemingly locked in disadvantage and marginality.

Notes

1   D. Modjeska 1988, *Inner Cities*, Penguin, Melbourne, p. 2.

2   Professor Bob Gregory's study was reported in the *Sydney Morning Herald*, 27 April 1995.

3   Quoted in Modjeska, op. cit., pp. 43–54.

4   Australian Bureau of Statistics, cat. 6203.0.

5   S. Watson 1988, *Accommodating Inequality: Gender and Housing*, Allen & Unwin, Sydney.

6   *Sydney Morning Herald*, 27 April 1995.

7   B. Castro 1991, *Double Wolf*, Allen & Unwin, Sydney, p. 2.

8   Ania Walwicz, 'Australia', in Modjeska, op. cit., p. 241.

9   *Sydney Morning Herald*, 17 January 1994.

10 Susan Thompson 1994, 'The meaning of home for migrant women', in K. Gibson & S. Watson (eds) 1995, *Metropolis Now*, Pluto Press, Sydney, pp. 37–41.

11 B. Cass 1991, *The Housing Needs of Women and Children: The National Housing Strategy*, AGPS, Canberra, p. 56.

12 Ruby Langford, 'The Koori way: belonging places', in Modjeska, op. cit., p. 2.

13 ibid p. 179.

14 E. Wilson, 'The invisible flaneur', in S. Watson & K. Gibson (eds) 1995, *Postmodern Cities and Spaces*, Blackwell, London, pp. 59–79.

15 L. Reedy, M. Hickie, et al., n.d., *Ask Any Woman*, Liverpool: Safe Women Liverpool Project.

16 Cass, op. cit., p. 57.

17 For an account of a lesbian couple in Surry Hills and Redfern in the 1950s and 1960s, see Paddy and Robbie Byrnes 1956, *La Vie en rose*, and M. Bradstock & L. Wakeling 1986, *Words from the Same Heart*, Hale & Iremonger, Sydney, 1986, pp. 23–32.

18 B. Brooks, 'Maps', in D.Modjeska, op. cit., pp. 29–42.

19 D. Powell 1991, *Out West*, Allen & Unwin, Sydney, gives an excellent account of this process.

20 See the illustrated page from *Oz* magazine, March 1964, printed in Gary Wotherspoon, *City of the Plain*, Hale & Iremonger, Sydney, 1991, p. 151 in which a gay advertising executive manifests the camp gentrifier. See also the comment: 'Homosexuals are not a separate group of white Anglo Saxon Paddington poofters who own their own interior decorating business. We exist in every corner and community group'. *Gay Task Force*, 1981 cited in Andrew Leese 1993, 'The spatial distribution of subcultures: gay men in Sydney', Bachelor of Town Planning thesis,

University of New South Wales, title page. See, too, the estimate from San Francisco that '90% of the houses in San Francisco's Victorian Alliance Program are being rehabilitated by gay individuals or couples'. Barbara A. Weightman 1991, 'Towards a geography of the gay community', *Journal of Cultural Geography*, vol. 1, p. 109. House prices in Paddington in the years 1960–65 rose by 206 per cent compared with 67 per cent in Redfern. H. Kendig 1979, *New Life for Old Suburbs*, Allen & Unwin, Sydney, p. 128, cited in Leese, op. cit., p. 26.

21   Kendig, op. cit., p. 128, cited in Leese, op. cit.

22   H. P. M. Winchester & P. E. White 1988, 'The location of marginalised groups in the inner city', *Environment and Planning: Society and Space*, vol. 6, p. 44.

23   M. Lauria & L. Lawrence Knopp 1985, 'Towards an analysis of the role of gay communities in the urban renaissance, *Urban Geography*, vol. 6, p. 160. A Sydney example is the Alexandria area where the locomotive works were closed and where former workers now rub shoulders with their new middle-class neighbours.

24   *Lesbians on the Loose*, March 1993, no. 39, p. 18.

25   After the 1991 elections to the Committee, women actually held the majority of senior positions within the organisation. See *Sydney Star Observer*, 20 September 1991, p. 1. 'The Board is extraordinarily coalition in how it does its business': Sue Harben, Mardi Gras president, *Lesbians on the Loose*, October 1992, p. 16.

26   *Lesbians on the Loose*, November 1983, p. 18 ff, 'A woman's right to cues'.

27   *Sydney Morning Herald*, 29 January 1994, 'Spectrum' p. 5A.

28   This is true, too, of other centres such as cafes. *Lesbians on the Loose*, January 1994, pp. 16 ff.

29   Taken at December 1990, 1991, 1992 and 1993 (12, 24, 36 and 48).

30   For its history see *Lesbians on the Loose*, January 1992, no. 25, pp. 12 ff.

31   For an account of the career of one entrepreneur, Gigi Legenhausen, and her bars Freezer with Girl and On the Other Side see *Capital Q*, 7 January 1994, p. 9.

32   See the interview in *Feed Them To The Cannibals!* dir. Fiona Cunningham-Reid, Boabang Productions, 1993.

33   *Lesbians on the Loose*, January 1992, p. 14.

34   Virginia Woolf 1984, *A Room of One's Own*, Chatto & Windus, London, p. viii.

35   *Sydney Star Observer*, 12 November 1993, p. 5. For a history of earlier attempts and an account of the last-minute bid to meet the target, see *Lesbians on the Loose*, January 1994, pp. 1, 2, 6, 7, 10.

36   *Sydney Star Observer*, 22 December 1993, p. 5.

37   For an account of the comparatively recent adoption of pool by lesbians, see *Lesbians on the Loose*, April 1992, pp. 14 ff.

38   Manuel Castells 1980, *The City and the Grassroots*, University of California Press, Berkley, p. 140.

39   Winchester & White, op. cit., p. 49.

7 CITY BATTLES

Cities are battlegrounds on which interests compete. Some conflicts are associated with sex, gender, ethnicity and social class. Others derive from unequal access to social resources and revolve around the location of government infrastructure and services such as roads, parks, schools, hospitals and jobs. The problem in Sydney is that in the outer areas of the city where population growth is rapid, state and local government services typically lag behind housing development, mainly as a result of bureaucratic inertia in the metropolitan planning process, coupled with the politics of relocating established facilities such as schools, universities and hospitals from the older parts of the city.

Local government funded infrastructure — notably libraries, child-care centres and recreational facilities — is limited by the financial capacity of councils in what are typically lower to middle-income areas with high proportions of first home buyers. While councils may require land developers to contribute to the costs of services, these tend to be passed on to home buyers who are struggling to purchase their own homes, so any extra costs will be resisted. Historically, jobs have decentralised more slowly than have workers in the Sydney region. In the long economic boom of the 1950s and 1960s that did not matter too much since unemployment was low, journey to work distances were shorter (because the outer suburbs were not so 'outer') and people's expectations about government services were more modest.

Other conflicts in Sydney are grounded in the negative impacts, or social costs, which are incurred by producers and consumers of goods and services. On the metropolitan canvas there is air and water pollution, traffic congestion and the like. These affect the whole or large parts of the city and derive from a myriad of scattered sources. On a more regional but still broad-brush scale are the impacts of major elements of urban infrastructure, such as airports and freeways, which create considerable problems for people across a wide area. At a more localised level are issues associated with environmental change which influence people more on aesthetic or minor nuisance grounds, as in places next to proposed apartment and town-house developments

The degree to which Sydney's residents experience unacceptable living conditions is substantially related to their economic power; the rich, not surprisingly, buy into the suburbs which are least affected by the negative workings of the city. Their spending power in turn draws private sector services, while their capacity to mobilise political power also ensures a better stock of public infrastructure. There is nothing new in this situation, although recent deepening of social polarisation exacerbates it. But economic power does not totally insulate people from problems. The relatively affluent are, for example, more exposed to beach pollution since they live near the beaches and use them more often because they are close; the new third runway at Sydney Airport has exposed large numbers of inner city yuppies and wealthy residents of the North Shore to unacceptable levels of airport noise. So, although conflicts over land use and resources in Sydney have a basis in class differences, at the same time important issues cut across class to produce new political alliances that transcend socioeconomic lines.

Five arenas of urban conflict in Sydney are of particular contemporary significance because they are driven by economic change and reflect the increased incorporation of Sydney into the global processes described elsewhere in this book. First, there is environmental deterioration, in particular the impacts of Sydney's population on air and water quality. The discourse of ecologically sustainable cities reflects a much broader — indeed global, set of considerations. Second, there is the strengthening shift towards privatised provision of urban services and cost-recovery pricing of those services: the so-called 'user pays' debate. This trend is also the outcome of global economic factors but its adoption by governments as a panacea for present day ills also reflects the imperatives of environmental management. Third, there are serious conflicts over population densities in residential areas; the 'urban consolidation' debate. This debate is related to the first two inasmuch as higher densities may result in improved environmental quality and may also make the provision of urban infrastructure more financially manageable. It also illustrates the intrinsic conflicts deriving from local versus regional political interests. Fourth, conflicts have arisen over the re-use of large areas of the inner city, whose original economic foundations have atrophied, specifically the Pyrmont–Ultimo area to the west of the central business district and the Central Industrial Area between the CBD and Botany Bay. Fifth, the 2000 Olympics raise questions of debt, which all New South Wales residents will face, but also environmental impacts, accelerated gentrification, and opportunity costs in terms of other spending priorities.

A GRIM FUTURE

As in any large city, environmental quality in Sydney is less than most people would want although some are particularly affected because of where they live. Air and water pollution constitute one set of concerns: traffic and aircraft noise, waste disposal and loss of agricultural land to housing another. The main sources of water pollution are domestic waste water — sewage and other household waste — and stormwater run-off from the land. Sydney's sewage is discharged via treatment works into water bodies. Provided that sufficient funds are spent on the latest technology, and in the past they have not been, such 'point sources' of pollution are in principle controllable; pollution is more or less able to be eliminated. Polluted run-off from the land is far more difficult to control and takes many forms. This matters in Sydney because rain can bucket down, turning the streets into rivers in an afternoon — especially in summer. From the built-up parts of the city, stormwater runs off into drains and collects oil, dog droppings, paper, plastic and all sorts of other rubbish. Apart from screening for solids, such waste goes directly into water bodies. Agriculture at the edge of the city uses fertilisers and pesticides and these too get into the water.

Waste water and sewage goes into either the Pacific Ocean or the Hawkesbury–Nepean River on Sydney's western perimeter. While disposal to the ocean has adverse impacts on aquatic fauna and flora, it also threatens Sydney's beach culture. Many are the mornings after a storm when the beaches from Manly to Maroubra are declared too dirty to surf. The growing threat to water quality from sewage, and to a lesser but still significant extent stormwater drainage, became a major political issue in the 1970s. The state government committed millions of dollars to build deep-water ocean outfalls at North Head, Bondi and Malabar. These were (and are) the main sewage treatment works on the coast. Before the outfalls were commissioned, raw sewage — screened only for 'solids' — was dumped into the ocean at the base of sand-stone cliffs. Sun and salt were left to kill bacteria and viruses and to dilute effluent in the water. Nothing is done to strip plant nutrients although this is less of a problem than in inland waterways where algal blooms can result. In certain wind conditions undiluted sewage would drift into the beaches. As Sydney's population grew after the Second World War, conditions gradually worsened with more effluent being discharged to the ocean. It included toxic effluent from factories which proliferated in the industrial areas in the 1950s and 1960s. But it is not only people in Sydney who find pleasure at the beach, so increasingly do international tourists. The maintenance of high environmental quality is, and will increasingly be, crucial in sustaining the tourism expenditure which has come to be so important to Australia — and especially Sydney.

How effective the ocean outfalls are likely to be was seriously questioned by environmental activists in the mid-1980s. Under a headline 'Sydney's toxic waste dump — the Pacific', Richard Gosden put it this way:

> The Sydney Water Board is currently embarked on the first stage of a multi-million dollar publicity campaign aimed at convincing the public that the solution to the sewage pollution of beaches is in hand. The days of faecal lumps on the sand and chemical stinks in the waves are almost over. Television ads show surfers performing in pristine, sparkling waves. Double page colour spreads in magazines display bikini girls and high divers.
>
> The solution this wasted hyperbole is trying so desperately to sell is the extension of the ocean outfalls at Malabar, Bondi and North Head. Construction work has commenced on all three projects. The total cost in 1985 figures is put at $450 million and commissioning is expected for Malabar and Bondi in 1990–91 and North Head in 1992. The question is will it work and if it does, for whom? [1]

Water quality at the main Sydney beaches was officially recognised to be poor in the monitoring period, 1983 to 1987, with significant bacterial contamination. [2] The deep-water outfalls commissioned in 1990–91 have, according to official assessment, markedly alleviated this situation and beach users have noticed a major improvement in water quality: 'of 32 beaches sampled, 25 beaches in summer 1993–4 met the NHMRC guideline for recreational water quality for fecal coliform (bacterial) pollution at any time'.[3] Yet sewage grease is still sometimes found on beaches and the level of grease in beach sands has not fallen to natural background levels. Pollution can still happen after heavy rains when treatment plants cannot cope with the volume of water. Stormwater pollution remains a serious problem with over 200 outlets between Palm Beach and Cronulla. Environmentalists contest that levels of treatment are no higher and maintain that, while visible pollution has been reduced on especially Bondi and Manly beaches, damage to the aquatic environment persists — with fish toxicity being a real worry — while beaches in areas to the south, notably Cronulla, are now subject-ed to higher levels of pollution displaced from the coastline between Bondi and Maroubra.

The Hawkesbury–Nepean River supplies most of Sydney's drinking water. It is pre-cious habitat for aquatic flora and fauna and a popular recreational resource. The river draws on a very large catchment — about 22 000 square kilometres — bounded by Goulburn to the south-west, Lithgow to the west of the Blue Mountains and the Broken Bay Plateau to the north between Hornsby and Gosford. The catchment is 65 per cent forested but there are extensive agricultural uses and increasing urban and industrial development.

Sydney's population growth is now almost entirely contained within the catchment of the Hawkesbury–Nepean River, which means that sewage and waste water will increasingly be disposed of in the river. For several years environmental activists have been vociferously drawing attention to worsening water quality, especially problems of viral and bacterial pollution. There is also the problem of plant nutrients, nitrogen and phosphorous, getting into the river from sewage and run-off from market gardens located on the river flood plain. These cause plant growth, notably of the toxic blue-green algae, and threaten eutrophication of the river with fish kills and strong odours of decaying vegetation.

The state government has responded by deferring large areas of land designated for urban development and implementing much higher technology effluent disposal. New housing at Rouse Hill in Sydney's north-west — an area which will be developed over thirty years and will ultimately yield 70 000 housing allotments — will, for example, have two water supplies, with separate plumbing. One will be potable water for house-hold drinking, cooking and washing. The other will be recycled water for toilet flush-ing, car washing and garden watering. This is the first time such a recycling system has been available in Australia on anything but a trial scale. It will help reduce the demand for potable water, thus delaying the need for further dams, and will reduce the volume of waste water entering the Hawkesbury–Nepean River system.

Homes and hazards, Port Botany, August 1995.

A new sewage treatment works is also being developed at Rouse Hill. De-watered sludge will be sold to fertiliser manufacturers and the treated water will be recycled or treated in wetlands and riffle zones being developed on site. As well as reducing the treatment plant's environmental impact, the wetlands riffle-zone system will provide a sanctuary for birds and small wildlife and a recreation site for residents. These systems are expensive to construct and are arguably only possible because the land releases will attract predominantly upper- and middle-income buyers. In the generally cheaper areas of the west and south-west such technology may mean higher costs to lower income earners unless they compensate by buying smaller parcels of land and living at higher densities.

Sewage effluent has been the major source of pollutants that affect water quality in Sydney. In the 1980s the levels of nutrients and plant growth measured by the Environmental Protection Authority (EPA) showed reductions. But excessive levels still exist in sections of the Hawkesbury–Nepean that receive discharges, with phosphorous, nitrogen, faecal coliforms and algae sometimes exceeding guidelines. The EPA believes that there is a general downwards pressure on pollutant levels, especially with improved water treatment with long term effluent quality objectives expected to be achieved by the year 2000. Diffuse sources of water pollution continue to be a problem and the state EPA is shifting its focus to these. Environmental groups distrust the sanguine rhetoric of government and call for a ban on further urbanisation of the catchment. The problem is that there are as yet no clear alternatives. To ban development would lead to price increases and these would especially affect first home buyers who are struggling to get a foothold in the housing market. Politically, the state government is caught between the devil and the deep blue sea.

The main air pollutants in Sydney are lead compounds, nitrogen oxides, carbon monoxide, ozone, particulate matter, sulphur dioxide and other acid gases. Sources, levels and trends have been monitored by the EPA for many years. In 1993 the EPA presented the following information:

Acid gases: Since 1980 levels have fallen and are well below long term health goals. Industry contributes 77 per cent.

Particulates (basically dust): Levels peaked in central and suburban Sydney in 1985 and have declined since then to below the National Health and Medical Research Council (NHMRC) annual average goal. 40 per cent are from motor vehicles. Suburban levels are well below World Health Organisation guidelines; CBD levels are higher but still below.

Nitrous oxides: 80 per cent from motor vehicles. Of this, heavy-duty, diesel powered vehicles account for 25 per cent. Levels have exceeded NHMRC guidelines for years but introduction of three-way catalyst technology in new cars appears to have been effective. Trend has been down but not clear for future.

Ozone and smog: In the 1970s, Sydney was Australia's most smog-bound capital. The situation has improved in recent years and the occurrence of photochemical smog has decreased. Future trends are unclear.

Lead: Unleaded petrol was introduced in 1985 and lead levels have declined below the NHMRC standard. 60 per cent of petrol sold is still leaded.[4]

Sydney suffers from levels of air and water pollution similar to those of other large cities in the developed world. It is hard to disentangle fact from fiction, with marked contrasts between the official and environmentalist discourses. Official reports suggest improved trends, while the Total Environment Centre referred to an:

emerging air pollution crisis in western Sydney ... Air protection in Western Sydney has a history of neglect and secrecy by all New South Wales Governments over the last two decades. In an educated and progressive society the public have a democratic right to be properly informed of matters that affect their health and lifestyle. With regard to air quality, this right has not yet been recognised by our politicians and bureaucrats.[5]

Air pollution in Sydney is largely the product of motor vehicle exhausts. There are no electric power stations operating in the region and, while industry is a significant source of pollutants, Sydney is not a specialised heavy industries city. The problem is exacerbated by high levels of motor car ownership and the regional topography. High levels of car ownership, especially in the western and south-western areas of highest population growth, is linked — in a chicken and egg manner — to low residential densities. Although the quarter-acre block, which gave Australian cities among the lowest densities in the western industrialised world, is for most home buyers long gone, the massive suburbanisation of the population which began in the 1950s has not abated. The outer areas of the city remain poorly served by public transport and numbers of jobs remain significantly lower than resident populations. Journeys to work are thus long and typically by car. Cars, which were initially luxuries, have become necessities.

The situation is exacerbated by topography. Sydney is ringed by higher terrain: the Southern Highlands south of Campbelltown; the Blue Mountains west of Penrith; and the Plateau country between Hornsby and Gosford. The effect is that that much of the region is poorly ventilated by prevailing winds. Instead of polluted air being dispersed away from the city, it tends to accumulate for long periods. Concentrations are especially high to the south-west which is one of the major growth axes. From a global perspective, even if wind clearance of pollutants was high, pollutants produced by Sydney's car-dependent population would be an environmental problem of considerable magnitude.

Deteriorating air and water quality in the Sydney region has become one of the more significant political issues for state and local governments, with community concern at its peak in the late 1980s. The coincidence of rising public awareness of the state of the environment, increased official scientific monitoring and high immigration levels to Australia, especially to Sydney (which now takes 40 per cent of immigrants), led to the simplistic assumption that the latter caused the former. The election of a Labor government in New South Wales in 1995, with a premier, Bob Carr, noted for his green sympathies, has thrown issues of population size and environmental quality to the forefront of political debate. In part Carr was naively proposing a quasi-apartheid or forced settlement policy of directing immigrants to settle away from Sydney. Not only would the proposal not work (as most of the earlier experiments of decentralisation under the Whitlam government of 1972–75 had not worked either) but Carr had given little thought to how the policy could be enforced or the likely political uproar from the immigrant lobby. Newspapers at the time displayed provocative headlines. In an article headlined, 'Carr wants migrant intake cut', David Humphries and Michael Sharp wrote:

In line with the Premier, Mr Carr's views that Sydney is 'bursting at the seams', the New South Wales Government will take a proactive role in trying to cut the number of migrants settling in the city. The Department of Urban Affairs and planning will directly lobby the federal Government over the annual immigration targets,

suggesting migrants be encouraged to settle elsewhere. 'I want Sydney interests to fig-
ure larger when the national immigration targets are considered', Mr Carr said yes-
terday, 'it might suit Perth or Adelaide to have maximum intakes, but it's not in the
interests of Australia's largest city.'[6]

In another article David Humphries reported a 'Grim future forecast for crowded
Sydney':

A Premier's Department briefing paper, prepared for Mr Carr, portrays a Sydney
where, on current projections, the quality of life has been much reduced. The
gloomy scenario has fuelled Mr Carr's enthusiasm for population control in Sydney
on economic and environmental grounds, prompting remarks such as his weekend
urging of disincentives for immigrants to settle in the city.[7]

Carr's statements provoked a passionate response. Many people immediately took
Carr's comments as being anti-immigration, reflecting the difficulty of publicly debating the urban implications of immigration, and specifically immigration's contribution
to population growth. Australia runs an immigration program much higher, on a per
capita basis, than anywhere else in the world. Some 40 per cent of Sydney's population
is now either born overseas or the children of the overseas-born. There is no question
that immigration drives Sydney's, and indeed Australia's, population growth. There is
too, no doubt, great difficulty in cutting back immigration since 40 per cent of immigrants are in the family reunion category. To cut immigration is to risk the fury of overseas-born Australians who wish to bring their close relatives to the country. In response
to Carr's comments the chairwoman of the Ethnic Communities Council of New
South Wales, Mrs Angela Chan, said Mr Carr's proposal 'ignored the importance of
family reunion as a motive for migrating to Australia'. 'There was no way migrants or
anyone else could be forced to live in regional areas,' she said.[8] In reply to these and
other comments from the state political Opposition accusing him of having offended
ethnic groups, Carr said: 'Nobody could be offended by it. What I'm talking about is
getting sensible planning policies that protect Sydney'.[9]

The then minister for immigration, Senator Bolkus, also criticised the Premier but
on different grounds. Writing in the *Australian*, Catherine Armitage said:

New South Wales Premier Mr Carr's call for a curb on immigration to ease Sydney's
population pressures put the city's claim to be a regional headquarters for multina-
tionals in the Asia Pacific at risk, the Minister for Immigration, Senator Bolkus,
said yesterday. In a carefully worded rebuke to the Premier, Senator Bolkus noted
that of the 130 regional headquarters established in Australia since September
1993, investing $2.3 billion in the economy and creating 2000 jobs, 70 per cent
had gone to Sydney. 'In this era of globalisation, we can't say to the rest of the world
we want your money but we don't want you.'[10]

It is ironic that, as was pointed out in chapter 3, multiculturalism has been used by the New South Wales government as a city marketing tool.

In the popular imagination it seems that the more people there are in a city like Sydney, and living as they do now, the greater the pressures there will be on the environment. So politicians wishing to improve environmental quality face a dilemma. They are caught between the apparently conflicting interests of green politics and the immigration lobby. But the dilemma is more apparent than real once it is recognised that it is not population numbers in themselves which cause environmental deterioration. It is how people behave which matters. The solution is to influence behaviour, essentially to reduce car usage, and to improve technology to treat waste water to higher standards.

These strategies, though, imply constraints on behaviour and higher costs for sewage and waste water disposal, and such costs and constraints impact most strongly on people living in the newer growth areas in the outer city, people who for the most part have the least capacity to absorb higher costs. So there is a political problem here exacerbated by equity considerations. The reality though is that current patterns of behaviour and assumptions about what we can do need to be changed if environmental quality is to be improved. In principle equity problems need not be severe. If people are to be encouraged to use their cars less, especially for work trips, then public transport will simply have to be provided as an alternative. If people have to pay more for waste water disposal they can keep their costs of living constant by living on smaller blocks of land. The technical solutions to Sydney's air and water pollution are obvious enough. The political balancing act is much more complex.

GOOD MANAGEMENT

State Rail Warns of 139 per cent fare rise
Fairs for peak hour train travel would need to rise by up to 139 per cent and off peak fares by 40 per cent were the Sydney rail network to be placed on a commercial footing and lose some of its public subsidies, State Rail warned.[11]

Urban sprawl hit where it hurts
The cost of developing land will rise by 20 per cent — and drop by up to 60 per cent in the inner established suburbs — under a radical overhaul of developer charges designed to review the real price of the city's burgeoning sprawl.[12]

Cities consist of residential, commercial and industrial land uses but they also function as economic and social systems due to the provision of various types of infrastructure: roads, ports, power stations, airports, railways, water and sewerage systems, schools, hospitals and so on. In Australia, urban infrastructure has mainly been financed and managed by governments (predominantly state — about 62 per cent, and to a much lesser extent local — 24 per cent) through taxation, alongside varying levels of cost recovery from users (household and firms).[13] Roads, for example, excluding toll roads, have been financed directly by taxes, while water has been partially funded by charges on users but with large cost elements financed through taxes. In short, governments have been the main providers and much of the infrastructure in cities like Sydney has been supplied at either no direct cost to users or else at prices that are less than the costs of supplying it. This arrangement sustained the great wave of low-density suburbanisation in the 1950s and 1960s and continues, although at a slower pace, today.

Since the mid-1970s governments worldwide have sought to reduce the burden on themselves of financing urban infrastructure. They have done so by involving the private sector in infrastructure provision (privatisation) and by charging users prices which more closely approximate the costs of provision. Yet both these strategies are hotly contested, usually on equity and accountability grounds. Three arguments are used by governments to justify privatisation and the political opprobrium of cost-recovery pricing.

First, there has been a long-term increase in interest rates to levels which will be sustained well into the future. This is a global phenomenon which reflects high levels of demand for loan funds — notably from the East and South-East Asian growth economies — and a relatively restricted supply of capital. In Australia domestic savings rates are very low so loans have to be raised internationally and this has implications for macro-economic management. During the mass suburbanisation of the 1950s and 1960s governments could readily borrow to finance infrastructure for long periods at very low interest rates and did not have to worry too much about paying for loans with user charges. That strategy of debt financing has not been viable for many years although the reality has yet to enter popular discourse.

A second factor argued to have disabled the capacity of governments to supply and price urban infrastructure in the traditional way has been increasing per capita demand. In the 1950s and 1960s, after the austere 1930s and Second World War periods, many people buying into their suburban dream homes were prepared to accept low levels of services to the site (notably sewerage) and vicinity (hospitals and libraries for instance). This is no longer the case. Collective expectations of the good suburban life have increased. Much of the new demand arises from necessity. Child-care facilities, for example, are needed to enable two working parents to sustain a family and home purchase whereas in the 1950s and 1960s married working women were unusual and one household income was considered enough. More libraries are needed now because far more students are staying on at high school. Most significantly, improved environmental quality inevitably means increased expenditure on state-of-the-art pollution control technology and public transport.

The third reason articulated for the privatisation of, and increased cost recovery for, urban infrastructure derives from massive requirements for maintenance and replacement of old infrastructure. In cities like Sydney much of the urban fabric is old. Some drains, sewers and waterpipes date to the nineteenth century. Roads designed before the 1960s were not predicated on the traffic loads now carried. Government agencies worldwide have failed to plan for maintenance and refurbishment and now the chickens are coming home to roost.

In the 1990s Sydney saw increasing numbers of examples of cost-recovery pricing being implemented and urban services being privatised. Notable examples of privatisation are the Sydney Harbour Tunnel, the M4, M5, M6 and proposed M2 motorways, and the Rouse Hill Development Area in north-west Sydney. The privatisation of Kingsford Smith Airport by its owner, the Australian government, is also looming.

Each case of privatisation generates issues of economic and political principle. Privatisation is highly politicised because it is part of the broader economic rationalist debate. The sale of government assets, deregulation of the Australian economy, and microeconomic reform strike at the heart of social democratic ideology. Alternative ways of financing and supplying urban infrastructure are thus caught up in the broader politics of economic management which themselves are driven by the imperatives of globally sourced economic restructuring.

The tunnel under Sydney Harbour was one of the first cases of privatised infrastructure. It was financed and constructed by Transfield-Kumagai in the late 1980s but reverts to state government ownership after thirty years. This is not, however, a purely commercial venture. Tolls on the Harbour Bridge were increased by the state government to part-finance the project. If revenue from the tunnel falls below a specified level the state government has to subsidise the developer and this has already happened. So it has been a matter of considerable public controversy as to whether the people of New South Wales are getting a fair deal.

The same issue has arisen in relation to the privatisation of urban motorways. But here there are other serious concerns. Commuters travelling from the North Shore and northern beaches complained about increased charges, while people living in western Sydney argued that they had a greater need for transport infrastructure and that arrangements for the tunnel's financing would preclude that need being met. The pro-public-transport lobby pointed out that the tunnel would just encourage more cars into and through central Sydney. Local government discourse stressed that their burden of the costs of road building needed to accommodate traffic entering and debouching from the tunnel. The political heat was raised by the way in which the deal was pushed through by the then New South Wales minister for public works, Laurie Brereton, the same man who gave Sydney the very controversial Darling Harbour redevelopment. It is notable that the state government's own Department of Planning (as it was called then) made a scathing technical attack on the Environmental Impact Statement (EIS) prepared for the tunnel by the Department of Public Works. In ignoring the issues raised in this technical attack, which was unquestionably the department's responsibility, Minister Brereton reinforced community perceptions that the state's environmental laws would be flouted when they threatened to inhibit government action. The EIS was seen to be supporting a decision that had already been made.

Similar issues have arisen in relation to the privatisation of motorways. The same imperative — the need to reduce traffic congestion — applies and the same constraints on governments financing the roads is in force. One such road is the M5 motorway which partially links central Sydney with the far-flung suburbs and businesses of the south-west. In 1948 the Cumberland County Council, Sydney's then de facto regional planning authority, reserved land on which the M5 was to be built, as it turned out over forty years later. The M5 was entirely financed by Interlink Roads with loans from the New South Wales Roads and Traffic Authority and the Commonwealth Bank. Interlink funded the construction of Stage 3 of the motorway by issuing infrastructure bonds. These were a federal Labor government initiative in 1992's *One Nation* package and were designed to expedite important public works projects which had a life-span longer than twenty-five years. Interlink is repaying loans and funding maintenance and operation via user charges and advertising.

Charges come in the form of tolls. The new state Labor government of 1995 had to grapple with the company after its election promise to abolish tolls on the M5, M4 to Sydney's west and the M6 to Wollongong. Financial arrangements entered into by the previous Liberal–National Party government precluded this promise from being honoured and Labor sustained considerable political damage as a result. A year later, the Carr government did a back-flip and announced that Sydney motorists would be reimbursed for using the M4 and M5 tollways, at a cost to taxpayers of $74 million. While politically and socially advantageous, the commitment stands to reduce the state's credit rating and this will make government borrowings more expensive.[14]

Equity issues are regarded as being more central to the western and south-western motorways than to the Harbour Tunnel since they service the outer areas of the city. In the outer city people travel the longest distances to work and tend to be on the middle to lower ends of the income spectrum. A competing discourse suggests that people have not been forced, but have chosen, to live in the outer city for detached houses on larger blocks of land, and thus they should not expect the tax base of all Sydneysiders to pay for their infrastructure costs. This is complicated by the fact that the rest of Sydney uses infrastructure which was originally supplied on a subsidised basis, although many people who live in the older parts of the city now effectively pay for their access to infrastructure in the form of higher property prices. The problem here is that there are all sorts of 'cross-subsidies' from one part of the city to another and they are not at all easy to quantify.

Apart from questions of equity and the government subsidisation of private developments, the environmental impacts of motorways are highly controversial, leading to considerable local political resistance. This is the case in Wolli Creek, in Sydney's near south, and has erupted in relation to the soon to be built M2 servicing the north-west growth sector of the city. With the Harbour Tunnel a similar paradox emerges, namely that new and less congested roads actually encourage more vehicle use and thereby cause more air pollution and therefore reduced demand for public transport. One of the problems here is that the National Roads and Motorists Association (NRMA) has always acted as a powerful lobby group in favour of car owners whereas environmentalists have far less influence financially, politically and in the number of their supporters. A good sign perhaps is the recent greening of the NRMA via its Clean Air 2000 initiative.

Sydney's lateral expansion has been along a western corridor through Penrith and a south-western corridor through Campbelltown. In the *Sydney Region Outline Plan* of 1968 a further north-western growth axis was identified, the so-called north-west sector. In the 1980s, after serious investigation this area began to be brought under large-scale urban development. The Rouse Hill Development Area, near Blacktown, was selected for the first stage of development brought onto Sydney's *Urban Development Program*, which is run by the state government. The process was speeded up because a deal was struck to allow a consortium of private landowners and the state government's land development agency, Landcom, in return for their investment in certain infrastructure development, to go ahead far more quickly than was possible under the traditional government-financed approach. As well as relieving the state government of the financing burden, the deal enabled government, as a major landowner in the area, to benefit from early sales. Apart from the broader issues over privatisation, conflict over the north-west sector has been tied up with further development accelerating environmental deterioration. There is a similar proposal for South Creek Valley between Campbelltown and Penrith near Sydney's erstwhile second international airport at Badgery's Creek.

Privatisation of urban infrastructure is one arm of government economic management. The other is for governments to continue as suppliers but to increase the levels of costs recovered. In the 1980s preliminary research by the Department of Planning suggested that only a fraction of the costs of providing physical and community services for new urban areas is: 'recoverable from developers and home buyers. In new growth sectors it is estimated that Government will bear a net cost of $20 000 ($1987) per lot for services ranging from water and sewerage to community and education services.'[15] Urban water supply is a case in point:

> *Traditionally, the people of New South Wales have paid less for their water than it costs to supply. This has contributed to over consumption and forced supply authorities to expand supply systems to cope with higher levels of demand ... Many of the expenses of the water supply authorities are now being incorporated in water and sewerage tariffs, but water prices still don't include a component to reflect damage to the environment caused by excessive use of water.*[16]

Systems of cost-recovery pricing for urban infrastructure may be argued for as a strategy for urban management, including the control of social costs such as air and water pollution. But the problem is one of equity and is inherently politically contentious. One method governments use to soften the impacts is to introduce price increases while simultaneously providing substitutes such as public transport. Yet whatever mechanisms are used to privatise services and infrastructure provision, poorer households inevitably suffer.

The broader question as to whether urban sprawl is actually the result of infrastructure subsidies has been more rigorously investigated by the Australian government's Industry Commission. Contrary to the Department of Planning view, the commission's preliminary estimates:

> *Indicate some under-charging of hydraulic services at the fringe, but their magnitude is insufficient — given data limitations and the consequent margins for error — to conclude that there is significant subsidisation in the broad ... The Commission has [therefore] been unable thus far to make comparable quantitative assessments for other forms of infrastructure. Nevertheless its examination of charging arrangements for roads, public transport and energy services suggests that there is scope for better matching of charges and costs which, if achieved, could reduce incentives to develop the fringe relative to other areas. [Overall, though] the Commission considers that urban fringe development is not heavily subsidised ... if this is accurate, this also suggests that reforms are unlikely, on average, to have a major impact on the (relative) cost of serviced land at the fringe.[17]*

The debate remains a contentious one. What is undoubtedly true is that Sydney since the mid-1970s has spread over ever larger tracts of land causing environment degradation and exacerbating social inequalities in fringe areas.

FLATS AND TOWN HOUSES [18]

A fiery source of conflict between state and local government in Sydney since the mid-1980s has been the state's desire to promote higher residential population densities, mostly for financial reasons. In Sydney, as in other Australian cities, most of the new housing is constructed on the outer edge of the city in raw new suburbs. At the same time, the population has been declining or stable in the inner and middle-ring suburbs for many years, mainly as a result of the ageing of the population (essentially children leave home and move to areas of cheaper housing in the west and south-west) and the fact that those moving in, especially the gentrifiers, are smaller households. It is these shifts which have led to the argument that existing infrastructure must be under-utilised and that if population densities can be increased some of the population growth which would otherwise have gone to the new fringe suburbs can be accommodated. It follows from this that the burden of financing fringe expansion would diminish. This is true even at the outer edge of the city. If population densities are increased there, money is saved, especially for roads, drainage and electricity services.

The argument is mobilised on the terrain of reducing the costs of supplying urban infrastructure for new households, but that is not the only reason for promoting higher residential densities. Social trends since the mid-1970s have markedly changed the types of households wanting housing. In the 1950s and 1960s the stereotypical new household of a married couple with one to three or more children would seek detached housing at the edge of the city. Today these nuclear families are in a minority, with single people, both young and old, single-parents and households of unrelated adults becoming more dominant. The types of dwelling units built by the housing industry from the late 1970s were recognised as being less and less appropriate to household needs but the capacity of industry to be more flexible was inhibited by local government regulation. The imperative for reducing the impacts of urbanisation on air and water quality also implies a role for higher residential densities. This is especially the case with air pollution. High levels of dependence on private cars for journeys to work in the outer city are substantially a response to inadequate public transport. Higher densities will improve the economics of public transport and thus in theory enable people to wean themselves from their cars.

Increasing residential densities amounts to increasing the stock of medium and higher density housing (multistorey flat buildings, town houses, villa units and dual occupancies) and decreasing the size of new housing allotments. As with controls on urban social costs, a combination of pricing, regulation and education is needed to promote higher densities. Most of the effort has gone into regulation in one form or another. This has taken the form of state government policies — binding on local councils, which have the responsibility of approving most developments — to increase multi-unit housing stock. These regulations have been fiercely contested due to inherent differences in state and local interests but have been exacerbated by the forms of regulation and the way they are applied.

The policy problem is that the interests of people living in a particular council area are not clearly served by density increases. Especially in the older parts of the city, density increases means more traffic on local roads which are not built for it and a loss of amenity resulting from poor architecture. There is also a class issue since much of the multi-unit housing is rented, and in suburbs of owner-occupiers anti-tenant discourses are rife. Conflicts have emerged over the re-use of redundant waterfront industrial sites on Sydney Harbour. In Balmain, for example, there was a bitter and protracted struggle over the state government's insistence on housing densities which local residents considered too high. The gentrification of the area from the late 1960s has created levels of political common sense which have made the residents savvy political opponents, while the ivory tower of the state planning agency dissociates itself from their concerns. The pattern is a familiar one throughout the older and more established parts of the city.

The metropolitan planning strategy for Sydney, *Cities for the 21st Century*, puts the argument this way:

> *Construction of a greater stock of multi-unit dwellings will occur in a variety of ways. Redevelopment of existing residential areas will be only one approach. The compact city includes making better use of existing urban land of many types.*

Redevelopment of non-residential land such as redundant industrial sites and lands surplus to other requirements can provide a major source of supply. Four current examples of major redevelopment projects are City West; Rhodes Peninsula on the Parramatta River; Olympic Village; CBD Airport corridor. Each of these redevelopments has generated public debate but City West is arguably the most interesting.[19]

Pyrmont-Ultimo on the western side of Darling Harbour, where there are 300 hectares of largely de-industrialised and neglected inner city land, has constituted another key contested site. The area is designated to house a residential population of 25 000 and a working population of 75 000. Under the Keating federal Labor government's *Building Better Cities Program*, $117 million was set aside for infrastructure. The site is managed by the state government's City West Development Corporation, which was set up to manage government-owned land, and fund and promote the revitalisation and redevelopment of the locality. The site's uniqueness derives from its proximity to Sydney's CBD and it has been promoted as yet another opportunity to project Sydney's image in the global marketplace. Local residents have campaigned over several years to fight the development. Conflict has mainly centred over the need for public housing, especially in relation to the small residual working-class and welfare-dependent population, although some gentrification dates back years. Combined with battles over the wresting of planning power from local government by the state, the locality — like the adjacent Darling Harbour before it — has been a key site of inner city urban politics since the mid-1980s.

BIG BANGS AND BUCKS

Major urban infrastructure carving out space in the existing built fabric of a city invariably gives rise to problems and political resistances. In Sydney, urban motorways, Port Botany (commissioned in the late 1970s on the north shore of Botany Bay), and the third runway (commissioned in 1994 at Kingsford Smith Airport) have been particularly contentious. Economic restructuring and technological change lie behind the construction of Port Botany and the third runway at Kingsford Smith Airport, while the privatisation of urban infrastructure is illustrated in motorway building and the threatened further expansion of capacity at the Airport. Widespread community concern about the deterioration of urban environmental quality underpins political resistance to new motorways, and airport and port expansion, reflecting tensions between jobs and convenience on the one hand and the environment on the other, a dilemma heightened in significance by the pressures of change and the fragile state of the Australian economy.

To a large degree negative impacts on the physical and social environment are unavoidable if infrastructure is built in the established city rather than on greenfields sites on the edge, and even then there are likely to be problems. Political considerations weighed against financial calculations come into play, with state and federal politicians balancing potential electoral losses against likely gains resulting from decisions to build infrastructure. To some extent poor strategic land-use planning can be implicated in the scale of conflicts which have arisen as at Port Botany and Kingsford Smith Airport. What is ironic is that far greater environmental assessment was carried out for the airport expansion than for Port Botany in the late 1960s, yet the airport expansion has produced greater conflict. Motorways are more complicated because the growth of car ownership and trucking since the 1950s has obviously meant disruption of the built environment. But decisions could have been made much earlier when potential disruptions would have been so much less. To the contrary, freeway construction is taking place in major road reservations set aside in the late 1940s by the *County of Cumberland Scheme*, Sydney's first metropolitan planning strategy. In a climate of shifting attitudes to the negative impacts of motor cars and increased property values in inner city areas marked for demolition, the implementation of freeways has become both managerially and politically more complex.

Port Botany was commissioned in the late 1970s and is now the major container port in Sydney. The port also has bulk liquids terminals, including a liquid petroleum gas (LPG) 'farm', and other facilities. It sharply illustrates the concrete outcomes of economic restructuring and technological change in Australia since the early 1970s. Changes in the handling of sea freight, especially the shift to containerisation, accompanied by ever larger ships made cargo-handling facilities in Port Jackson increasingly redundant from the early 1960s, leaving empty waterfront industrial locations for factories and warehouses as sites for other struggles over their re-use in places like Glebe and the Balmain Peninsula. The way in which the port's potential impacts on the land were completely ignored in the planning stages in the 1960s is an unimaginable scenario today. When the Maritime Services Board, a statutory authority of the New South Wales government, decided in the 1960s to construct Port Botany there were no formal procedures in place for environmental impact assessment nor, relatedly, for the consideration of the land-based impacts of the development. Legislation with the powers of the New South Wales *Environmental Planning and Assessment Act 1980*, which now provides such procedures, was not in place. Nor did the State Planning Authority, or its successor, the Planning and Environment Commission, have sufficient weight in the state bureaucracy to counter the power of entrenched infrastructure agencies such as the Maritime Services Board, and local residents were quiescent.

In Sydney it was not until the early 1970s that there was major community action against inappropriate and poor development. Mainly middle-class residents banded together to fight for the conservation of The Rocks area and Kellys Bush in Hunters Hill. Gaining the support of the left-wing Builders Labourers' Federation, Green Bans were imposed on development, prohibiting building labourers to work on designated sites.[20] For a short time property developers were stymied in their tracks. The battle was intense in the case of Victoria Street in Kings Cross where violent battles broke out between local residents, bully-boy eviction teams and the local police.

As construction of Port Botany proceeded in the 1970s local political resistance grew to the point were it became a key issue in the state elections of 1976, leading to the election of the Wran Labor government. Neville Wran had promised inquiries and regional plans which proceeded in the late 1970s. But the horse had already bolted from the stable, leaving room only for political posturing. Among the raft of impacts resulting from Port Botany's commissioning the most significant derived from the large numbers of container trucks distributing freight from the port across Sydney and to other parts of New South Wales. One way to alleviate this problem was to shift containers by train to a freight-handling facility at Chullora in Sydney's west, but the idea was successfully resisted by the Transport Workers' Union who wished to keep jobs for its truck-driving members. Another proposal to ease the movement of containers by trucks in large numbers was a freeway to Sydney's south-west. Again, massive resistance to its routing through the Wolli Creek bushland has meant that this link is not yet completed, although a key element, the M4, is now in place. The storage of hazardous substances at the port, especially the LPG tanks, has further contributed to the hazards of the area, which include chemical plants and petrochemical storage right next to residential areas. Planning for the location and transport of toxic and hazardous materials has really only evolved in Sydney since the mid-1980s and is working against the inertia of existing land uses allowed at a time when most of the public was oblivious.

The third runway at Kingsford Smith Airport has been another planning disaster. In the mid-1980s the federal government, which controls the airport through the Federal Airports Corporation, decided to build a third runway rather than to fast-track development of an international airport in Sydney's south-west at Badgery's Creek, the site designated in the mid-1980s. The decision was made in the face of rapid growth of aircraft movements as Sydney was becoming more and more affected by globalisation. Greater capacity was argued to be essential, although the government recognised that the commissioning of a new runway at the airport would impose major noise problems on a large number of people. By the effective closure of the east–west runway relieving an almost equal amount of noise, federal and state governments representing business interests used political muscle to force its construction. Airport expansion was favoured over a fast-tracked Badgery's Creek which would have had to be heavily subsidised for many years by tax-payers.

Campaigners against the third runway argued for Badgery's Creek as the logical alternative. Staging sit-ins at the airport, disruptions at political meetings and colourful demonstrations, the issue has been kept on the public agenda while the runway has caused major noise disruption for households from Hunters Hill to Enmore. Tom Ballantyne from the *Sydney Morning Herald*, commenting on the decision — announced in the 1995 Budget — by the Australian government to fast-track Badgery's Creek in response to the massive protests against aircraft noise, questioned the Badgery's Creek solution.[21] The key problem is that most of the major airlines using the

Airport say that they would not use Badgery's Creek because of its inaccessibility to central Sydney. Badgery's Creek proponents argue that the Federal Airports Corporation can force use of Badgery's Creek, while others consider there is a risk that airlines would then reduce services to Sydney altogether, threatening Sydney's and Australia's economic welfare. Press coverage of a 'Secret $500 million plan for Sydney Airport' [22] added fuel to speculation that then Minister Brereton's promise of $600million to fast-track Badgery's Creek was simply political: a very expensive vote-buying exercise that did not work. The irony is that millions of dollars were spent evaluating alternatives and doing the EIS for the third runway at Kingsford Smith Airport, although many would argue that the EIS was merely an endorsement for a decision that had already been made. Compared with the Port Botany decision of twenty years earlier the airport has been in the limelight. But, not surprisingly, the outcome has been much the same. With the Howard government's election in 1996 the whole issue of airport capacity is up in the air again.

SELLING SYDNEY RE-VISITED

Government to abandon Eastern Creek
The State Government will abandon its involvement in the Eastern Creek raceway this week with little hope of recouping the $134 million spent on the project that the former Coalition Government said would risk no more than $2 million in public funds. [23]

New South Wales taken for a ride
The time has come for the State Government to stop pouring good money after bad to 'save' the Eastern Creek raceway. In June there was a threat by the Grand Prix organisers to abandon the circuit if the Government did not provide nearly $700 000 to resurface the raceway track. The disintegration of the track can stand as a metaphor for the sorry saga of the Eastern Creek project itself, which has provided an object lesson why governments should be extremely cautious about trying to pick entrepreneurial winners. [24]

City marketing means, among other things, the reconstruction — literally and metaphorically — of places like Darling Harbour and The Rocks on the edge of the CBD, the latter a typically postmodern glossed simulacrum of the nineteenth-century working-class inner city. It also means the attraction of hallmark tourist events such as the 2000 Olympics, Mardi Gras and international sporting events. These sorts of projects are typically riven with conflict to varying degrees, with social impacts and opportunity costs the key.

The Eastern Creek motor sport facility in western Sydney is a classic case. It was fast-tracked with heavy subsidy by the New South Wales Government so as to attract the Australian Motor Cycle Grand Prix away from Victoria in 1990. The enterprise has been a minor financial disaster for New South Wales with millions of dollars wasted. In an article headlined, 'Goodbye, good riddance Grand Prix', the *Sydney Morning Herald* motoring writer, Alan Kennedy, chronicled the Grand Prix's impending return to Victoria from which it was pirated by New South Wales when Victoria disallowed cigarette advertising. Kennedy said that:

[t]he track has cost [NSW] tax payers $140 million in the past five years. Staging the bike race has not been the huge boost to the New South Wales economy that was promised … The international and interstate visitors — which the Greiner government promised would pour into Eastern Creek — never came.[25]

The following month David Humphries described the $135m raceway as a 'scandalous waste'.[26] After the Labor Party won power in New South Wales in early 1995, the minister for sport and recreation, Gabrielle Harrison, told Parliament:

… that the raceway and its involvement in the motor cycle grand prix was 'perhaps the most scandalous waste of taxpayers money in the history of New South Wales' … Eastern Creek was a dud ride from day one, a financial fiasco the former State government should have steered clear of. Now the Grand Prix is off to Victoria and New South Wales tax payers shouldn't mind a bit.[27]

Whether Victoria will necessarily benefit from recapturing the Grand Prix, and also the Formula One Grand Prix from Adelaide, is an open question. Certainly Victoria, as part of heightened inter-state competition for mobile investment and consumption flows, is hell bent on competing with New South Wales and elsewhere. As John Huxley satirically put it, in an article entitled 'Victoria finds that too much sport is barely enough':

It is not true that the Victorian Premier, Jeff Kennett, plans to snatch the marathon Iditarod dog-sled race, the Paris-Dakar car rally and the Tour de France. For one thing Melbourne's weather is too appalling. But, yes, there are unmistakable signs that the city's celebrated passion for game-playing has now turned into full-blown sporting megalomania.[28]

Given the approaching millennium, the Sydney 2000 Olympics serves as an apposite and contemporary final case. In *Metropolis Now* Fensham asks: 'when the juggernaut of international capital in terms of investment, sponsorship and viewing rights has halted, will Sydney appear as a complex urban formation or simply as a seaside playground?'.[29] The major facilities at Homebush Bay, in Sydney's central west, are built on the site of Sydney's former state-owned abattoir, partly on swamp and on land owned by the Australian defence forces. Hardly a charming history from which post-modernist architects and urban designers might quote! But what is the Olympic legacy likely to

Olympic Games site, Homebush Bay, August 1995.

be? Critics point to the losses incurred by all Olympic host cities, except Los Angeles, since the mid-1970s. The extent to which the taxpayers of New South Wales will finish up paying a significant part of the bill through higher taxes and charges for government services is a real concern. Here, of course, there is little agreement: 'The case for an Olympic kick start: the Olympics could cost New South Wales taxpayers dear'. Ross Gittins argues that the benefits could outweigh 'even a losing games'[30] while Max Walsh, another *Sydney Morning Herald* journalist, foresees financial disaster for New South Wales in an article titled: 'Risible arithmetic on Olympics bid'.[31] Supporting Walsh, Sam North reported a 'Games bill [of] $2bn in worst case [scenario]'.[32]

On the financial side there are considerable uncertainties on both the expenditure and revenue sides of the balance sheet. Television rights are the major source of income but Australia's global time zone is not optimal for North American and European viewers, which might reduce the value of rights, especially given the losses incurred by media corporations in recent Olympics. Locally there are battles over whether to situate the broadcasting facilities at Homebush or Pyrmont. If it is Homebush, as seems likely, how useful will the facilities be after the Olympics are over?

On the expenditure side there are considerable uncertainties about the New South Wales government's capacity to attract private sector investment at the levels going into the 1996 Atlanta Games, partly because of the small size of Australia's economy. But, as in the important case of the Athlete's Village at Homebush Bay, it also has to do with the investment potential. The plan is for the village to be built by private investors and to be sold off after the Olympic Games for private housing. But there are many large sites of housing development coming on stream up to the year 2000 in Sydney, notably the disused industrial sites near Sydney Harbour and Botany Bay. This creates considerable uncertainty about the potential saleability of village housing. Designing housing for athletes which matches subsequent housing demand and needs represents a potential disjuncture: who gains from this?

Also affecting the viability of the Olympic Games are infrastructure constraints in Sydney. The city's capacity to accommodate visitors is in doubt in the mid-1990s: 'Room shortage risks restricting tourism gains'.[33] Although there is still time for hotel developers to fix this deficit, their willingness to do so depends on their expectations of occupancy rates after the games. The expansion of Kingsford Smith and fast-tracking of Badgery's Creek airports are also inextricably linked to the Olympics. Other transport initiatives for the games infrastructure are road and rail access to the Olympic sites, but these are at hand and, like all the Olympics infrastructure, will produce benefits long after the Olympics are over.

Apart from the financial viability of the games from the point of view of New South Wales taxpayers there are also serious social impacts to consider, the most important of which is housing accessibility. In 'Housing losers and winners in Games study', Matthew Moore discusses the possible impacts of Olympics demand on rental prices.[34] Growth in tourism to Sydney in the 1980s has already been linked to the conversion of boarding houses to backpacker hostels, with loss of low-income housing stock the result. This trend is likely to continue, with possible evictions of private rental tenants by landlords wishing to make a killing on inflated rents during the Olympics swelling the ranks of the homeless. Concern about this possibility led the deputy prime minister, Brian Howe, in the Keating Labor government, to 'flag rent control to offset boom in Olympic city'.[35] While western Sydney's largest hospital, Westmead, will devote sixty beds for the athletes, local residents continue to face long waits for publicly funded elective surgery.

It may be that the Olympic city of Sydney will glitter and bring more tourists and investment in future years. But who will gain and who will lose from the glossy advertisements? It seems worryingly likely, with so little public accountability and involvement in the planning stages, that the Olympics will add one more nail to the coffin of growing inequalities and spatial divisions. Though the new River Cats on the Parramatta River may gentrify the suburbs en route, it is not clear that they will alleviate the major transport problems of western Sydney.

SYDNEY AFTER THE MILLENNIUM

Sydney 2000: what are the likely scenarios post the millennium? Will Sydney's surfaces always sparkle? Will tensions be smoothed over with discourses and illusions of equality and consensus? Will differences be homogenised and erased, fought over or celebrated and enhanced? Will the rich get richer living in ever more privileged parts of the city while the poor get poorer and more embedded in localities where services diminish and the environment deteriorates? Will the fragments of the city splinter into ossified spaces where the boundaries are ever harder to cross? Will Aboriginal people be recompensed for centuries of violence? Will minorities find power in the spaces of the city? There are no obvious answers, no pat solutions, no inevitable paths. There are only stories to tell weaving many diverse narratives. But beneath the complacent and cheerful surface of successful Sydney there are cracks and fissures which are too easy to ignore from the 6-metre catamarans sliding on the harbour past the gleaming sails of the Opera House. Sydney city of surfaces.

Notes

1   *Chain Reaction*, no. 46, 1986, p.18.

2   NSW EPA 1993, *NSW State of the Environment 1993*, Sydney.

3   NSW Department of Urban Affairs and Planning 1996, *State of the Region. Sydney*, p. 50.

4   This is a paraphrased summary from NSW EPA, op. cit.

5   Total Environment Centre 1992, *Newsletter*, vol. 11, pp. 4–5.

6   *Sydney Morning Herald*, 22 May 1995.

7   ibid., 24 May 1995.

8   ibid., 22 May 1995.

9   ibid.

10 *Australian*, 23 May 1995.

11 *Sydney Morning Herald*, 21 October 1995.

12 ibid., 18 December 1995.

13 Commonwealth Industry Commission 1993, *Taxation and Financial Policy Impacts on Urban Settlement*. Draft Report, vol. 1, Canberra.

14 *Sydney Morning Herald*, 7 and 11 October 1996.

15 NSW Department of Planning 1988, *Metropolitan Strategy. Sydney*, p. 11.

16 NSW EPA 1994, *State of the Environment. Sydney*, p. 4.

17 ibid., note 10.

18 An excellent comprehensive analysis was published by Pat Troy 1996, *The Perils of Urban Consolidation*, Sydney. Troy convincingly challenges many of the assumptions on which the policy is based. In particular, he argues that the policy will exacerbate contemporary trends to social polarisation.

19 NSW Department of Urban Affairs and Planning 1995, *Cities for the 21st Century*, Sydney, p. 80.

20 See Jack Mundy 1981, *Green Bans and Beyond*, Angus & Robertson, Sydney.

21 *Sydney Morning Herald*, 30 April 1994.

22 ibid., 8 June 1995.

23 ibid., 18 September 1995.

24 ibid., 19 September 1995.
25 ibid., 6 May 1995.
26 ibid., 8 June 1995.
27 ibid.
28 ibid., 15 July 1994.
29 R. Fensham 1994, 'Prime time hyperspace: the Olympic city as spectacle', ch. 12 in K. Gibson & S. Watson (eds), *Metropolis Now: Planning and the Urban in Contemporary Australia*, Pluto Press, Sydney, ch. 12, p. 181.
30 *Sydney Morning Herald*, 7 July 1995.
31 ibid., 21 December 1992.
32 ibid., 4 May 1994.
33 *Australian*, 9 November 1994.
34 *Sydney Morning Herald*, 9 October 1994.
35 *Australian*, 5 October 1994.

ABBREVIATIONS

AAFI	Australians Against Further Immigration
ACON	AIDS Council of New South Wales
CBD	Central business district
EIS	Environmental impact statement
EPA	Environmental Protection Agency
FPBS	Finance, property and business services
HQs	Headquarters
OBUs	Offshore banking units
RHQs	Regional headquarters
TNCs	Transnational corporations

INDEX

① <u>Few theoretical refs</u> — "new" book.

② Easily readable, almost journalistic.

③ Set up vs. 'Marvellous Melbourne'

④ In 1950's, dev. at too big a rate [sarcastic]
to keep up infrastructure.

⑤ Use of slang (native)
Highly personalised.

⑥ Impact of immigrants — multicultural
focus.
The contrasts inherent in seemingly
arbitrary differences.

⑦ Particular attention → choice of
quotes + e.g.s e.g. poet or novello.

⑧ Seems to imply that, as far as Sydney's
governing body is concerned, anything
goes [culturally] as long as it fits in
with an undefined Anglo-Celtic template

⑨ With a few exceptions, reads like one
long travel brochure and, having said
that, is therefore profoundly interest
if you have a deep interest. Unfortunate
if you do not the $24.95 (£10.00
may be money unwisely spent.

⑩ Promotes importance of homosexual
community; both as great of tension
within Sydney and as a selling point.